DANCING
TILL
DAWN

DANCING★ TILL★ DAWN☆

A Century of Exhibition Ballroom Dance

JULIE MALNIG

NEW YORK UNIVERSITY PRESS
New York and London

NEW YORK UNIVERSITY PRESS
New York and London

DANCING TILL DAWN: A Century of Exhibition Ballroom Dance, by Julie Malnig,
was originally published in hard cover as No. 25 in the series, Contributions to
the Study of Music and Dance (Greenwood Press, Westport, CT, 1992). Copy-
right © 1992 by Julie Malnig. This edition by arrangement with Greenwood
Publishing Group, Inc. All rights reserved.

Library of Congress Cataloging-in-Publication Data
Nalnig, Julie.
    Dancing till dawn : a century of exhibition ballroom dance / Julie
Malnig.
        p. cm.
    Originally published: New York : Greenwood Press, 1992, in series:
Contributions to the study of music and dance ; no. 25.
    Includes bibliographical references and index.
    ISBN 0-8147-5528-3 (pbk. : acid-free paper)
    1. Ballroom dancing—History. 2. Musical theater—History.
3. Musical films—History. I. Title.
[GV1746.M28 1995]
793.3'3—dc20   94-45361
                        CIP

New York University Press books are printed on acid-free paper,
and their binding materials are chosen for strength and durability.

Manufactured in the United States of America

10   9   8   7   6   5   4   3   2   1

For my parents, Laura and Lawrence Malnig,
who inspired my love of the theatre

Contents

Photo essay follows page 68.

Preface

Dancing Till Dawn: A Century of Exhibition Ballroom Dance explores the rich history of a popular dance form whose roots extend back to the first decade of the twentieth century. This dynamic, romantic, and highly expressive genre features male-female teams performing theatricalized versions of contemporary ballroom dance. To date no full-length study has been written concerning the history of exhibition ballroom dancers and their enormous range of dance styles. *Dancing Till Dawn* attempts to fill this gap by examining the development of exhibition ballroom dance as a *profession,* and by exploring the relationship of the teams to the theatrical venues in which they flourished—the cabaret, vaudeville, the musical theatre, film, and eventually television. Additionally, the book considers the dance teams as theatrical personalities, many of whom garnered enormous critical and popular success throughout their careers.

The focus of the work is on exhibition ballroom dance's heyday during the 1910s. Styles and patterns of dance developed then would influence successive generations of exhibition ballroom dancers. The early chapters of the book are organized around the work of several of the most popular and frequently reviewed teams of the day. These teams have been chosen for two reasons: they illustrate the different career paths through which performers became exhibition ballroom dancers, and these teams are examples of the differing styles of exhibition performance established in the early decades of this century, namely the adagio, eccentric, comic, and romantic modes. Subsequent chapters explore the reemergence of exhibition ballroom dance in later decades and the evolution of different styles and methods of performance.

The research for this book is based almost exclusively on newspaper clippings and articles from approximately 1890 through 1960 preserved in library clipping, production, and personality files, and in performer scrapbooks. Many of these newspaper and magazine articles, particularly those from the teens and early twenties, can be identified only by periodical, date, scrapbook number, and collection. Despite the frequent lack of authorship and the incompleteness of many of the citations, these materials nonetheless provided an invaluable source of information on the careers of the teams and on the ways in which they were promoted and popularized.

Other major sources are scripts and librettos, vaudeville and musical theatre programs, dance periodicals and manuals, and photographs. Musical resources consist of dance music used by various teams, as well as sheet music from musical shows. Particularly valuable sources of information are the dance instructions and illustrations printed in newspaper and magazine articles, as well as in sheet music.[1]

The majority of clipping and scrapbook sources are from the Robinson Locke Collection located at the Billy Rose Theatre Collection of The New York Public Library. Other clipping materials were gleaned from files and scrapbooks of The Dance Collection, The New York Public Library; The Theatre Collection, The Museum of The City of New York; The Theatre Collection, The Philadelphia Free Library; and The Shubert Archive. The New York Public Library Dance Collection is the major source for dance magazines and rare dance manuals. The Shubert Archive also provides cabaret contracts and press materials of ballroom dance-agents Elizabeth Marbury and Jeanette Gilder. I am very grateful to the curators and staffs of these institutions for all their assistance.

For many of the iconographic materials, I consulted the photographic files and White Studio Key Sheets of The Billy Rose Theatre Collection, as well as photograph files from The Theatre Collection, Harvard College. The main sources for sheet music are the Bella Landauer Collection of The New York Historical Society and the Special Collection of The Music Division of The New York Public Library. The Rodgers and Hammerstein Archives of Recorded Sound at Lincoln Center provided me with recordings of many ragtime dance songs. Other branches of The New York Public Library that I consulted were the Newspaper Annex, the Forty-second Street Research Branch, and the Schomburg Collection.

Additional libraries and collections consulted include: The New York Society Library; The Archives for the Performing Arts in San Francisco; The Louisville [Kentucky] Historical Society; and The Chicago

Historical Society. The Joseph Urban Papers located at The Butler Library, Columbia University, were helpful in reconstructing the layout and design of the *Ziegfeld Frolics* cabaret productions. The Motion Picture, Broadcasting, and Recorded Sound Division of The Library of Congress also assisted in attempts to locate ballroom dance films.

For agreeing to be interviewed I am grateful to the following individuals: Lola Andre (of the former adagio team of Lola and Andre), Richard Stuart (a former novelty dancer), the late Doris Vinton of the New York Chapter of the Ziegfeld Club, adagio dancer Francois Szony, ballroom dancers Tony and Anne Brienza, and Jennifer Ford, a member of American Ballroom Theatre. I am particularly indebted to Yvonne Marceau and Pierre Dulaine, the Artistic Directors of American Ballroom Theatre, who gave generously of their time, and who shared many ideas with me concerning the role and potential of contemporary ballroom dance.

Special thanks to Amy Revere McCauley (former dance partner to Clifton Webb) for her interviews and her gracious hospitality. I would also like to thank Barbara Kreutz (Irene Castle's daughter) for her lengthy and thoughtful correspondence. For help in tracking down filmed sources of ballroom dance I am obliged to the late Jay Leyda, formerly Professor of Cinema Studies at New York University, and Ernest Smith, who kindly volunteered time to show me excerpts from his film collection. Credit is due Stephen Vallillo, who provided suitable reproductions of the original photographs that appear in this book.

I would also like to acknowledge the valuable assistance of James C. G. Conniff, Edwin S. Robbins, Bob Grossblatt, and the staff of The Feminist Press at The City University of New York. Anita Malnig read several versions of the manuscript and provided expert editorial and critical advice. For her insights and for introducing me to the world of popular dance, I am indebted to my friend and colleague, Barbara Cohen-Stratyner. I would also like to thank Mary Blair, my editor at Greenwood, for her constant enthusiasm for this project. Professor Brooks McNamara of the Department of Performance Studies, New York University, generously shared his expertise throughout the course of this study. Finally, to Richard Roth I owe my deepest gratitude for his patience and optimism, and unswerving support.

NOTE

1. See Julie Malnig, "Researching Exhibition Ballroom Dance: Exploring Nontraditional Sources," *Performing Arts Resources*, Vol. 14 (New York: The Theatre Library Association, 1989), pp. 115–126.

DANCING
TILL
DAWN

----------- *Chapter 1* -----------

The Origins and Rise of Exhibition Ballroom Dance

It was in the early years of the twentieth century that exhibition ballroom dance became one of the most popular forms of theatrical performance in the United States. Ballroom dancers sparked the public imagination and helped establish a style that is still with us today. During the 1910s and 1920s, exhibition ballroom teams became role models and teachers, instructing a dance-mad public in contemporary ballroom forms. The teams would become stars in the popular entertainment of their day, such as the cabaret, vaudeville, and the musical theatre. The rise of exhibition ballroom dance as a theatrical dance form can best be understood by first exploring its social dance ancestry, the varied musical and theatrical forces contributing to its development, and the social changes of its day.

Exhibition ballroom dance emerged in large part as a result of sweeping changes in social dance practice. "Ballroom" or "social" dance (the terms are interchangeable) refers to those dances the public performed for recreation. While nineteenth-century ballroom dancers conformed to group movements, dancing couples of the twentieth century expressed more individuality. The structure of many of the newer social dances, such as the Turkey Trot and the Grizzly Bear in about 1908, allowed couples to improvise steps and be virtually oblivious to the movements of those around them. Exhibition ballroom dancers were professional teams that transformed current social dances into stylized, theatrical presentations. The best of them invented new dances as well.

In fact, their virtuosic presentations of contemporary ballroom dance forms brought couple dancing to new heights of popularity.

A VARIETY OF FORCES

Exhibition ballroom dance emerged from the "social dance revolution" of the early twentieth century. During this time, the formal nineteenth-century ballroom dances in the United States (and in England) evolved into freer, less restrictive forms. Gone was the foot-apart ballet position once espoused by the nineteenth-century dance teacher. Musical developments such as ragtime also influenced this new movement vocabulary. Among the most significant changes in ballroom dance was the context in which it was performed. It gradually moved out of the rarefied atmosphere of exclusive clubs and private homes into more public establishments, such as restaurants and hotels, where people of all classes and backgrounds could perform.

This social dance revolution was clearly a manifestation of larger cultural and technological developments taking place in the United States. Industrialization, for example, led to an increased urban population and brought together people of varied economic backgrounds. With increased leisure and greater spending power than their nineteenth-century counterparts, the middle class was attracted to a host of new mass entertainments, such as vaudeville, motion pictures, and the cabaret.[1] The early twentieth century also witnessed a changing concept of morality, and technological advances such as the automobile and the telephone contributed to an increased intimacy between the sexes.[2] Changes in the status of women, too, affected the growth of social dancing. New labor-saving devices and the psychological freedoms won by the women's suffrage movement gave many more women the time and inclination to pursue business and leisure activities outside the home, such as the afternoon tea dance, a popular activity between 1910 and 1915.[3]

NINETEENTH-CENTURY BACKGROUND

The typical nineteenth-century ball was a highly organized social event. The best documented ones were the lavish affairs given by the upper class, held either in the drawing rooms of private homes, at clubs, or in what were then known as Assembly Rooms, facilities that contained a ballroom, perhaps a billiard room, tea room, and various lounges.[4]

A standard program for a mid-nineteenth-century ball consisted of a mazurka, polka, waltz, and a cotillion.[5] This sequence of dances was usually decided in advance by the hostess and listed on dancing cards given to all the guests. The steps of the dances were performed in a fixed order, and were based on the five ballet positions, characterized by out-turned feet and pointed toes. The physical stance of the social dancers themselves was prescribed and proper. Allan Dodworth, a noted nineteenth-century dance teacher, described the following requirements in a section called "Attitude" in his book *Dancing and Its Relation to Social Life:*

> The upper part of the body should be slightly inclined forward, the hips backward—the forward inclination just enough to cause a tendency in the heels to rise from the floor; the head erect, legs straight, arms hanging by the sides, elbows very slightly turned outward so that the arms will present gently curved lines to the front.[6]

Clearly, these prescriptions were more concerned with creating uniform standards of movement than comfort on the dance floor.

Nineteenth-century ballroom dances reflected a cordial, restrained relationship between the sexes. In the waltz, for example, considered risqué when first introduced in the eighteenth century, the male placed his right arm around his partner's back and extended his left arm out to the side to clasp the woman's hand. With her left hand, the female partner either held the fold of her dress or placed it gently on her partner's shoulder, always mindful of maintaining the required foot-apart distance.

One of the most popular features of the nineteenth-century ball was the cotillion, a group dance involving the continuous interchange of several couples. Normally, it was last in the sequence, sometimes continuing for several hours. Both dance and parlor game, the cotillion served, in part, as a way for men and women to socialize within a well-defined context. It consisted of a series of "figures" or directed movements within which participants performed polka or waltz steps, among others. Up until about 1895, most of these dance patterns were standard in ballrooms throughout Europe and America. Presiding over the cotillion was an esteemed social figure known as the dance master, a leader referred to as "le conducteur" or the "major domo," who called out the order of dances and specified steps, often from manuals or scripts.[7] In some cases the dance masters invented their own dance patterns, which often involved props or favors, such as flowers, pieces of tinsel, or silk scarves.[8]

The following description of "All Hands Round," from *The Director,* a late nineteenth-century dance periodical, was the standard opening figure that served as a means of introducing couples to each other:

I start from five to ten couples, according to the size of the ballroom. Each man takes out a woman and each woman a man, thus doubling the number on the floor. The couples form a large circle in the center of the room, and at my signal they go through 'all hands round,' until each couple is re-united. This gives each man a chance once at least during the evening to clasp each woman's hand, and is a pleasant method of informal greeting. At the same time a wealth of sentiment can be put into the manner in which each hand is taken or pressed, or a world of coldness can be shown by the mere touch of the finger tips.[9]

Some cotillion configurations were even more overtly flirtatious. In one dance sequence called "The False Invitation" the female continually pursued a designated male partner, only to reject him once he consented to dance with her.[10]

THE INFLUENCE OF MUSICAL STYLES

Changing musical styles greatly affected the formal style of nineteenth-century social dance. Naturally, music determines, to a large extent, the overall style and shape of ballroom dance. Born to the strains of John Philip Sousa's "Washington Post March" was the two-step. This lively, rollicking dance consisted of a double-quick march with a slight hop or skip in each step and couples adopted a hip-to-hip position with the man's arms around his female partner's waist. Yet the two-step itself was an outgrowth of the nineteenth-century galop, a social dance characterized by several changes of steps with hopping movements.[11] Significant in the development of the two-step was its signaling of looser, more physically expressive social dancing. As a result of the side-by-side position, dancers began to eschew the ballet foot placement characteristic of nineteenth-century ballroom dance and instead used the flat of the foot. One dance instructor, George T. Dodworth (the son of Allan Dodworth), voiced objection to the two-step in a letter to *The Director:*

The movements of the Two-Step are so easy and simple that a novice with a little knowledge of dancing and more assurance, can pick it up and get around with very little practice, and being satisfied with getting around, style and refinement of motion are out of the question. I do not doubt for a moment but that the awkward and vulgar side position came from self-taught college boys, who, being extremely clumsy with turned in toes and bent knees when dancing with a partner were really obliged to take the side position in order to get their feet and knees out of the way.[12]

Dance teachers feared, of course, that the two-step threatened the classic face-to-face, foot-apart positioning, the backbone of the dances that they had taught for years.

Another musical style influencing a changed look in ballroom dancing was the slower-tempoed waltz, which led to the emergence of a dance known as the "Boston." Dancing to sentimental ballads, such as Charles K. Harris's 'After the Ball,' dancers could interpret the music in a way not possible with the fast-tempoed Viennese Waltz. In the Boston, a full turn consisted of six steps and occupied four bars of music, instead of the two for the Viennese Waltz. Another characteristic of this dance was its forward and backward movement, which promoted a more natural, walk-like step, a feature of many twentieth-century social dances.[13]

An outgrowth of the Boston was a step known as the Boston Dip, a quick, sinking movement made in unison by both partners. A late nineteenth-century dance periodical described the dip as "simply an exaggeration of the glide more like a chassé, each glide being accompanied by a considerable bend of the knees, causing the whole body to sink or dip at constantly recurring intervals. It has now almost entirely lost favor by reasons of its ungraceful appearance."[14] Although this commentator (presumably a dance teacher) may have longed for the dip's quick demise, it continued to be performed and actually became a standard movement of exhibition ballroom teams of the early twentieth century.

Perhaps, however, it was ragtime music that had the most dramatic effect on social dancing. It became prominent in the 1890s through the pioneering efforts of black composers such as Ben Harney, James Weldon Johnson, and Scott Joplin. Ragtime, although written for piano, maintained a close connection with dance. Performers who sang early forms of ragtime songs in minstrel and variety shows, for example, invariably danced to the music as well.[15] Ragtime was (and is) both a musical genre and a rhythmic technique. Early piano ragtime consisted of three separate musical strains, each one played and then repeated, often with embellishments.

The musical quality known as ragtime is the effect produced from a metrically accented (marchlike) bass accompaniment set against a syncopated treble melody. Generally, the accent falls on the second and fourth beats of a measure of music, instead of the first and third beats, which is characteristic of a nonsyncopated melody, thus creating an irregular rhythm.[16] The effect of ragtime on dance can be seen in the hesitation waltz, a popular waltz variation of the teens. In this dance, the performer literally hesitates or pauses on counts two and three in a two-measure musical grouping. "Rag" referred to the process of syncopating a nonragtime musical composition; any music can be "ragged," from Mendelssohn's 'Wedding March' to 'The Star Spangled Banner.'

Ragtime music spawned a variety of ballroom dance forms. One of its earliest was the Cakewalk, popular from the 1890s through approximately 1905. Early ragtime sheet music featuring the Cakewalk sometimes indicated that it could be performed either to two-step or march music. Originally performed by black slaves mocking the customs of their white owners, the Cakewalk was a group dance in which couples moved arm in arm in circular fashion performing a strutting step. The Cakewalk remained primarily an exhibition dance, however; white high society frequently hired professional black performers to present it as a novelty at their society balls.[17]

"RAG DANCING"

Between 1906 and 1908 so-called "rag dancing" became a wildly popular phenomenon in the United States, producing dances with animated names, such as the Grizzly Bear, the Turkey Trot, and the Chicken Reel. The rag dances were essentially fast two-steps or one-steps performed to syncopated rhythms. In the Turkey Trot, for example, couples generally began the dance face to face. As the man moved forward on his left foot, the woman stepped back on her right, both taking a step to each beat. The quick, syncopated rhythm was irresistible as couples literally swayed and rocked back and forth with each step. The pumping motion of the couples' arms supposedly earned the dance its name. Unlike the standard waltz, in which the feet make a pattern on the dance floor, couples simply stepped and moved in a straight line or a circle around the floor.

Furthermore, the rag dances were distinguished by their close body holds; generally the man's right arm was securely gripped around his partner's waist while her entire left arm rested on his arms. A newspaper reporter from Connecticut's The New Bedford Sun Standard described the Turkey Trot as follows:

> Starting as if in the good old-fashioned Two-Step, the dancers suddenly let go hands, the man slipping behind his fair companion, there is a little step and a hop something like a turkey might be expected to do, then a fresh grip around the waist of the young lady, the man snuggles up ever so closely behind her and they hop, skip and jump and half run along.[18]

Many of the older, formal social dance standards were falling away as couples responded naturally to the rhythm of the music, improvising movements, and unabashedly embracing one another.

The origins of the rag dances are obscure, but their development conforms to the evolutionary pattern of other social dances. Most of the dances were performed socially in clubs and dance halls in major cities, San Francisco, Chicago, and Memphis being the most frequently cited, where they were picked up by professional performers as stage dances.[19] The stage versions, in turn, were adapted by the public and dance teachers in simplified form for ballroom use. Many of the rag dances proliferated on the stages of black clubs and theatres, where they were eventually seen and transformed by white performers. Although many of the early individual rag dances quickly passed out of the white, social dance repertoire, they introduced to social dance a heightened awareness of the body and became the basis for many of the dances that exhibition teams would make popular by the mid-teens.

Rag dancing remained popular largely due to the music. Ford Dabney, W. C. Handy, and James Reese Europe, among other black musicians, wrote music specifically for the ballroom dance format, and their compositions helped propel several white ballroom teams into the limelight. Ford Dabney served as the musical director of the Ziegfeld Follies Roof Garden orchestra, while W. C. Handy is credited with composing a major fox trot tune: the Memphis Blues. James Reese Europe was the celebrated bandleader and composer for the popular ballroom team of Irene and Vernon Castle and inspired several of their dances, such as the Castle Walk and Castle House Rag.[20]

By 1910 the press had coined the term "dance craze" to refer to the widespread, enthusiastic public response to these and other rhythmically exciting social dances. Indeed, a distinctly new group of ballroom dances was becoming popular in the United States, reflecting the fusion of syncopated rags with the traditional European-based social dances. The hesitation waltz, for example, popular around 1910, incorporated syncopation into a basic three-step waltz. Latin styles, too, took hold. Variations on the Brazilian and Argentine tangos, for instance, found favor in this country as ballroom style generally began loosening up.

THE FLOWERING OF THE CABARET

Another powerful influence on the development of early twentieth-century social dance was the rise of cabaret society. Born out of the prospering New York City restaurant industry, the cabaret represented one of the first attempts in the United States to take ballroom dance out of private homes and meeting places (characteristic of the nineteenth century) into more public settings. It was a unique institution

that drew women and men of different classes and economic backgrounds under the same roof.[21] In addition to its role as a social meeting place, the cabaret served as a prominent entertainment arena and
helped popularize exhibition ballroom teams.

As early as the 1890s, New York City experienced a rapid growth in
its nightlife establishments. Fashionable Fifth Avenue restaurant-hotels,
such as the Waldorf and Sherry's, began catering to the new monied
classes born of urban industrialism. As New York City became a mecca
for trade, bankers and businessmen congregated at restaurants and hotels to socialize and conduct business. In order to retain their social
position, traditionally prominent families, such as the Astors and Vanderbilts, were forced to mix with these new industrialists. As cultural
historians observe, both "old" and "new" money used public hotels and
restaurants as arenas in which to compete and display their status.[22] To
encourage the upper classes to attend their establishments, owners added
atmospheric decor and gourmet cuisine.[23]

The expansion of nightlife in the Times Square area soon followed,
due in large part to the development of the Broadway theatre. During
the first two decades of the twentieth century the number of metropol-
itan-area theatre productions mushroomed, and the hotel and restaurant business accommodated the burgeoning tourist trade.[24] Restaurateurs quickly discovered that they could attract patrons before, during,
and after theatre performances. The Café des Beaux Arts (at Sixth
Avenue and Forty-sixth Street), and Rector's (at Broadway and Forty-
sixth Street), for instance, catered to theatrical and out-of-town clien-
tele by creating dining rooms with lavish decor, rivaling the opulence
of their Fifth Avenue counterparts.

By 1910 restaurant and hotel owners had capitalized on the growing
dance craze by installing dance floors and offering live entertainment.
George Rector, the owner of the famous restaurant bearing his name,
recalls installing his first dance floor: "All they wanted to do was dance,
and we accommodated them with a dance floor that measured thirty
feet by twenty. The entire 1,500 all tried to dance on this postage stamp
at the same time."[25] The Broadway restaurants were the trendsetters
in this regard, while their more exclusive Fifth Avenue counterparts
cautiously followed. (Lewis Erenberg, in *Steppin' Out: New York Nightlife
and the Transformation of American Culture* offers the fullest analysis of
the development of this phenomenon.) By the early teens the term
"cabaret" became the generic designation for establishments including
hotels, restaurants, and roof-garden theatres that offered a combination of dinner, drinks, and dancing.

The design of the cabaret itself affected contemporary ballroom dance
style. The small, packed dance floors forced dancers to move more naturally, if only to keep from bumping into one another.[26] The balletic

turn-out position was abandoned in favor of straight, pointed feet, and couples, of course, danced closer together than ever before. Increasingly, the movement style depended on a natural, coordinated movement of the body. Perhaps what the cabaret environment most emphatically underscored was the changing *context* of social dance. It came to replace the nineteenth-century ballroom with its emphasis on group movement and sequential ordering of dances. Now, couples might remain partners for an entire evening, instead of following the nineteenth-century dance custom in which men and women constantly changed partners. No dance master was calling out steps and figures; dancers could improvise spontaneously with the music.

It was not only in the cabarets that the dance craze flourished. Between 1900 and 1910 New York City saw the proliferation of club dances and charity balls sponsored by ethnic groups and fraternal societies, which imitated the pattern of dance developing in the more affluent cabarets.[27] Like their midtown counterparts, these dance halls served liquor and provided a continuous supply of music. According to social reformer Rheta Childe Dorr, the dances lasted about five minutes, followed by a ten-to-twenty-minute interval for socializing. A popular dance performed in the clubs in 1910 was the Half Time Waltz (presumably a variation of the hesitation waltz), which Dorr described as containing "a swaying and contorting of the hips, most indecent in its suggestion."[28]

In urban dance halls and social clubs across the country, young men and women performed the latest dances. In more formal circles, too, the influence of contemporary ballroom dance became obvious—often to the consternation of parents and chaperones. A headline in the society section of *The New York Sun*, for example, announced: "TURKEY TROT SEEN AT A PLAZA DANCE. Southern Society Didn't Want It and Was Somewhat Shocked. THREE COUPLES DANCED IT."[29] The article explained how turkey trotters "invaded" the grand ballroom of the Plaza Hotel, the setting for the annual Southern Society Ball. The culprits were three young couples who persisted in performing the dance off in a corner of the ballroom to the strains of the two-step. One of the patronesses of the event complained to the manager who, in an effort to maintain order, allowed the couples to continue. Clearly this article demonstrates that even within the confines of the more ordered, traditional group dance settings couples were beginning to express a sense of individuality and spontaneity.

Many social reformers and moral conservatives objected to the newer social dances because of close body holds. Said one commentator about the cabaret, "The evil influence is inevitable. The very air of these places is heavy with unleashed passions."[30] The Roman Catholic Church held symposiums debating the morality of the dances, and magazines exposed the controversy by publishing articles with such titles as "Is Modern Dancing Indecent?" and "Where Is Your Daughter This Afternoon?"[31] The United Neighborhood Guild in Brooklyn considered it a misdemeanor to dance the Turkey Trot, Bunny Hug, or "similar shoulder rocking, feet-dragging freak dances."[32] Generally, court action was not taken, but these measures served as warnings to club owners to supervise their dance establishments more carefully. While these moral pronouncements may have eased some reformers' consciences, it did little to quell the public's desire for dancing.

THE EMERGENCE OF EXHIBITION BALLROOM TEAMS

The first major form of entertainment featured in the cabaret was exhibition ballroom dance teams, beginning in the 1910–1911 season. Cabaret owners correctly assessed that these professionals would appeal to their dance-enthusiastic customers. In the cabarets the teams performed two or three sets an evening, after which patrons tried the latest steps themselves. One of the earliest cabaret dancers was Maurice Mouvet (1888–1927) who, beginning in 1910, gave late-night performances of his renowned Apache dance at the Café de L'Opera (also known as Louis Martin's) at Broadway and Forty-second Street.[33]

The exhibition ballroom dancers both influenced and were influenced by the social dance revolution of the teens. Drawing on the already existing social dances as raw material, they made popular their own theatricalized versions and promoted new social dance practices as well. They symbolized and reinforced the concept of the individual dance couple performing apart from the group and invented dances that, although modified throughout the decades, are still performed today.

During the teens and twenties the basic set of dances consisted of one-steps, Argentine tangos, Maxixes (also known as Brazilian tangos), hesitation waltzes, and fox trots.[34] The ballroom teams produced hundreds of variations on them, with names such as the Skating Waltz, the Aeroplane Waltz, the Military Glide, the Buena Vista Tango, and the Cinq-a-Sept. While the public had difficulty copying many of these dances, in many cases they adapted the simpler steps and poses for their social dance versions.

By the early teens, dozens of professional ballroom teams were booked as guest entertainers at cabarets and dance halls, and the best of them performed at private parties and social events. To expand their trade, cabaret owners established the afternoon tea dance (or thé dansant, as it was officially known), at which teams entertained and taught ballroom dances to the public. At the same time, exhibition ballroom teams from vaudeville and the musical theatre were becoming cabaret stars.

Exhibition ballroom dance soon became a recognized profession. By combining cabaret appearances with teaching, for example, a team could earn a substantial salary.[35] In addition to professional ballroom dancers, semi-professionals and amateurs proliferated. Many dance teachers, for example, who had recently added contemporary ballroom dances to their curriculum, were themselves giving performances at cabarets or at local community dances. Also entering the ranks of exhibition ballroom dancers were young "society women," who taught private classes to members of their social set (for a fee) and performed at society functions. Some of these dancers eventually gained enough proficiency to win themselves engagements at the higher-paying cabarets.[36]

The best of the teams became national idols; they were in the vanguard of current styles of dress, etiquette, and exercise methods. Manufacturers frequently hired the dancers to endorse their products in fashion magazines. The female dancers, in particular, promoted freer, movement-oriented styles of clothing. By 1913, in fact, designers advertised a dress called the "tango-visite," consisting of a transparent bodice and mid-calf-length layered skirt—a contrast to the tight-waisted, long flowing Gibson Gown fashionable a few years earlier.[37] Another outfit made popular by the female exhibition ballroom dancers consisted of trousers (equivalent to modern-day culottes) worn with a loose-fitting tunic overshirt.[38]

The popular press of the period promoted ballroom teams as well. New York–area daily newspapers and the press syndicates consistently published articles, usually as part of a publicity campaign for an upcoming vaudeville or cabaret engagement. Of course, managers and press agents frequently arranged for these articles in order to publicize their clients, but the press was eager to carry their stories since the teams represented a growing phenomenon. Many of the stories with illustrations and instructions became affordable dance manuals for consumers. Other publications promoting the teams were general interest magazines such as *Scribner's* and *Harper's Weekly,* women's magazines such as *Ladies Home Journal, Vogue,* and *Vanity Fair,* and theatre magazines, which always viewed the teams as theatrical personalities.

One of the most highly publicized and emulated teams was that of Irene and Vernon Castle. Although the exhibition ballroom phenomenon actually had begun before the Castles rose to prominence between 1912 and 1913, they became well known through a combination of talent and shrewd press agentry. By the mid-teens, the Castles had published one of the first texts on contemporary ballroom dance *(Modern Dancing),* operated their own dancing school, Castle House, owned their own cabaret, and even starred in a film biography entitled *The Whirl of Life.*[39]

The mastermind behind the Castles' successful marketing campaign was Elizabeth Marbury, a literary agent and New York socialite. Marbury sensed the financial and cultural potential of the dance craze and sought to establish Irene and Vernon Castle as its premier exemplars.[40] By promoting the team as models of elegance and social grace, Marbury made them appealing to high society. In her introduction to *Modern Dancing*, for example, Marbury commended the Castles in this way: "In Europe as well as in America it has been universally conceded that as teachers they are unequalled. Refinement is the keynote of their method; under their direction Castle House became the modern school of modern dancing, and through its influence the spirit of beauty and of art is allied to the legitimate physical need of healthy exercise and of honest enjoyment."[41] With this endorsement, many of New York City's prominent society women, among them Astors and Vanderbilts, embraced the Castles (and other exhibition teams after them) and frequently presented them at their society balls.[42] Most exhibition teams, in fact, were known as "society dancers," referring to their association with the upper classes. As a result of Elizabeth Marbury's franchising of the Castle name, the couple had a large following among the middle classes as well. By the mid-teens, they had copyrighted merchandise ranging from Castle Corsets to Castle Dance Records, and the press publicized them as "aristocrats of dance."

Most of the popular exhibition ballroom teams of this period had developed similar images of grace and refinement and upper-class sensibility, in part to dispel the negative criticism from some quarters about "modern" ballroom style. The adverse reaction of some to the cabaret and fears about young, unescorted women, alerted professional dancers to the need for defending their profession. Appealing to the sense of freedom and independence many American women sought during these years, Joan Sawyer (herself a suffragist) told the *Los Angeles Examiner,* "It seems evident that the spread of the dancing habit has done much for women; not alone in the acquirement of added grace—for dancing is the best form of exercise, both for the body and the mind."[43]

Dance teachers of the time helped also to foster the persona of grace and cultivation. Ironically, their reasons for doing so stemmed from their own initial ambivalence towards the exhibition ballroom teams. These dancers, after all, represented a changed order of social dance, characterized by greater movement awareness and a less structured format of steps. The dance teachers had been traditionally trained in nineteenth-century social dance conventions that equated ballroom dance with etiquette and social breeding.[44] They looked askance at many of the newer dances. For example, dance teacher Leslie F. Clendenen, in his 1914 book *Dance Mad*, illustrated what he considered "improper" dance movements. The positions, of course, were almost identical to those routinely exhibited by the professional teams.[45]

By 1910 dance teachers found themselves in a professional bind. The dances they had been teaching, such as the cotillion, no longer fulfilled the same social function they once had. Most dance pupils now wanted only to learn the latest one-steps and tangos that the exhibition teams were making popular. Realizing, finally, that the so-called dance craze was more than a passing fad, the dance teachers ultimately embraced the teams. They did this by equating the teams as inheritors of the moral and cultural values associated with social dance of the previous century.

G. Hepburn Wilson, for example, a dance teacher and editor of *Modern Dance Magazine* (a dance periodical of the teens), promoted these values by establishing an organization called the "Inner Circle," consisting of teachers and professional dancers whose aims were to advance social dancing and guide its development.[46] Its members, including prominent exhibition dancers Maurice Mouvet and the Dolly Sisters, frequently graced the pages of his magazine, discussing the "refining" influences of the new dances or demonstrating their latest steps and how to adapt them to the ballroom. The lofty, elitist tone of the group intended to convey the idea that the contemporary ballroom dances were part of a cultured, even aristocratic tradition. To develop this concept further, *Modern Dance Magazine* often published propagandistic articles such as "Modern Dancing is Not Vulgar," "The New Idea in Dance," and "Dance as a Factor in Social Evolution."[47]

Prominent dance teachers Margaret and Troy West-Kinney also set up exhibition teams as examples of social breeding and good manners. Their ploy was to hire the team of John Murray Anderson and Genevieve Lyon to serve as advisors for their 1914 dance manual, *Social Dances of Today*.[48] In the foreword to their book, the West-Kinneys describe Anderson as a model of civility, and as "the teacher of many of those authoritative in New York social matters. His reputation has been attained not chiefly on the stage or in restaurants, but in the homes of leaders of good taste."[49] In discussing the teams' dancing, the authors use the same language that formerly described the more traditional ballroom dances, stating, for example, that their work "is notable for consistent dignity of movement and posture."[50] To illustrate further their affinity for older ballroom dance traditions, Anderson and Lyon are shown demonstrating steps from eighteenth- and nineteenth-century dances such as the gavotte and the waltz minuet. This notion of the exhibition ballroom teams as models of elegance and social stature was, perhaps, never quite as pronounced as it was during this early period in the twentieth century when the dancers were attempting to win widespread acceptance and popularity.

Social dance forms are usually quickly absorbed into the popular theatre of their day, and exhibition ballroom teams soon became featured performers in vaudeville and the musical theatre. For audiences, the appeal of ballroom dance was immediate because of its familiarity—many had already performed simplified versions of these same dances in the cabaret. The teams adapted social dances to the stage in unique ways and continually created new dances that were in turn popularized as social dances. Perhaps one of the most important developments during the 1910s was that a new class of performer was born. Dancers who had an aptitude for ballroom work discovered they could parlay their talent into a career.

NOTES

1. On the growth of the late nineteenth- and early twentieth-century industrialist society, see Frederick Lewis Allen, *The Big Change: America Transforms Itself, 1900–1950* (New York: Harper and Row, 1952), pp. 109–114; Howard Mumford Jones, *The Age of Energy: Varieties of American Experience, 1865–1915* (New York: The Viking Press, 1975), pp. 145–158; Arthur Meier Schlesinger, *The Rise of the City* (New York: Macmillan and Co., 1933), pp. 431–432. On expanding leisure activities see Allen, *The Big Change,* p. 119; Foster Rhea Dulles, *A History of Recreation: America Learns to Play* (New York: Appleton-Century-Crofts, 1965), pp. 119, 288–294; Mark Sullivan, *Our Times, The United States 1900–1924;* vol. 4 (New York: Charles Scribner's & Sons, 1932), p. 55.

2. James R. McGovern offers an interesting analysis of the relationship between the automobile and dating patterns in "The American Woman's Pre–World War I Freedom in Manners and Morals," *The Journal of American History,* September 1968, p. 319.

3. On women's expanding role during this time see ibid., pp. 315–333; Schlesinger, *The Rise of Modern America: 1865–1951,* pp. 141–144, 204; Robert H. Wiebe, *The Search for Order: 1877–1920* (New York: Hill and Wang, 1967), p. 127.

4. For an analysis of the dance habits of nineteenth-century Americans see Linda Sue Bandy, "Dance as a Dramatic Device in Nineteenth Century English Melodrama" (MFA thesis, York University, Toronto, Ontario, 1980), pp. 37–44.

5. A. H. Franks, *Social Dance: A Short History* (London: Routledge and Kegan Paul, 1963), p. 147.

6. Allan Dodworth, *Dancing and Its Relation to Education and Social Life* (New York: Harper & Brothers, 1885), p. 24.

7. Bandy, "Dance as a Dramatic Device," p. 41.

8. Barbara Naomi Cohen, "The Dance Direction of Ned Wayburn: Selected Topics in Musical Staging" (Ph.D. dissertation, New York University, 1980), p. 27.

9. "Leading Cotillions," *New York Herald,* Sunday, 16 January 1908, cited in *The Director: Dancing, Deportment, Etiquette, Aesthetics, Physical Training,* ed. Melvin Ballou Gilbert (Maine: Melvin Ballou Gilbert, 1898; reprint ed., Brooklyn, NY: Dance Horizons), p. 80.

10. Dodworth, *Dancing and Its Relation to Social Life*, p. 171.

11. Franks, *Social Dance*, pp. 147–148.

12. Gilbert, *The Director*, p. 112.

13. For a discussion of the development of the Boston in the United States and England see Franks, *Social Dance*, p. 164, and Frances Rust, *Dance in Society* (London: Routledge and Kegan Paul, 1959), pp. 81–82.

14. *The Two Step Magazine*, November 1897, p. 265, The Dance Collection, New York Public Library. All further references to The Dance Collection will be denoted by the abbreviation DC-NYPL.

15. Edward Berlin, *Ragtime: A Musical and Cultural History* (Berkeley and Los Angeles: University of California Press, 1980), p. 13. Many of the early ragtime songs were known, rather unfortunately, as "coon songs." See Berlin, pp. 33–38.

16. For further discussion of ragtime music see Berlin, *Ragtime: A Musical and Cultural History;* Eileen Southern, *The Music of Black Americans: A History* (New York: W. W. Norton and Co., 1971); Trebor Jay Tichenor, *Ragtime Rarities* (New York: Dover Publications, 1975).

17. Marshall and Jean Stearns, *Jazz Dance: The Story of American Vernacular Dance* (New York: Schirmer Books, 1968), pp. 122–123.

18. "The Turkey Trot, Grizzly Bear and Other Naughty Diversions," *The New Bedford Sunday Standard*, 4 February 1912, p. 24.

19. Marshall and Jean Stearns suggest that many of the rag dances developed in dance clubs and honky-tonks in western and southern cities in the early 1900s, and then migrated east onto vaudeville and cabaret stages. They trace one dance, the Texas Tommy, to a black club in San Francisco (*Jazz Dance*, pp. 95–96). For a discussion of the migration of rag dances from the western to eastern parts of the United States see H. E. Cooper, "Rag on the Barbary Coast," *The Dance Magazine*, December 1927, pp. 31–60; Brenda Dixon Stowell, "Dancing in the Dark: The Life and Times of Margot Webb in Aframerican Vaudeville of the Swing Era" (Ph.D. dissertation, New York University, 1981), pp. 380–382.

20. Eileen Southern, *The Music of Black Americans*, pp. 350–352; "Steppin' on the Gas: Rags to Jazz 1913–1927," by Lawrence Gushee, New World Records, NW 269.

21. Lewis Erenberg, *Steppin' Out: New York Nightlife and the Transformation of American Culture 1890–1930* (Westport, CT: Greenwood Press, 1981), p. 113.

22. Ibid., pp. 33–40.

23. For further discussion of the activities of the late nineteenth-century upper classes see Dulles, *America Learns to Play*, pp. 230–231; Allen, *The Big Change*, p. 28; Lloyd Morris, *Incredible New York* (New York: Random House, 1951), pp. 234–246. One writer from 1908 commented on the breakdown of the upper classes in New York City: "It is true that aristocracy just at this moment is in a state of disruption on account of many existing feuds, all of which have their foundation in financial matters, in the conduct of railways and of manipulation of shares." "The Promenade," *Dress and Vanity Fair*, February 1907, p. 3.

24. Erenberg, *Steppin' Out*, pp. 40–41. Also see Stephen Burge Johnson, "The Roof Gardens of Broadway Theatres, 1883–1941" (Ph. D. dissertation, New

York University, 1983), Chapter 8, p. 1. This dissertation has been published as *The Roof Gardens of Broadway Theatres, 1883–1942* (Ann Arbor, MI: UMI Press, 1985).

25. George Rector, *The Girl from Rector's* (New York: Doubleday, Page and Co., 1927), p. 204.

26. Albert and Josephine Butler, *The Encyclopedia of Social Dance* (New York: Albert and Josephine Butler, 1975). Typescript in DC-NYPL, p. 337.

27. For a description of dance halls in the teens and twenties see "Dance Halls," *The Survey*, 3 June 1911, p. 385; Rheta Childe Dorr, *What Eight Million Women Want* (New York: Small, Maynard and Co., 1910; reprint ed., New York: Kraus Co., 1971), pp. 199–200; Russell Nye, "Saturday Night at the Paradise Ballroom, or Dance Halls in the Twenties," *Journal of Popular Culture* 7 (Summer, 1973): 14–22.

28. Dorr, *What Eight Million Women Want*, pp. 208, 210.

29. *New York Sun*, 14 January 1912.

30. Ethel Watts Mumford, "Where is Your Daughter This Afternoon?" *Harper's Weekly*, 17 January 1914, p. 28.

31. For further discussion on the church debate see Ellis Loxley, "The Turkey Trot and Tango in America, 1900–1920," *Educational Dance* (December 1930): 8. Articles cited are by William Inglis, *Harper's Weekly*, 17 May 1913, and Ethel Watts Mumford, *Harper's Weekly*, 17 January 1914.

32. "Brooklyn in Throes of Turkey Trot Craze," *The New York Sun*, 21 January 1912.

33. For more information on Maurice Mouvet see Chapter 2.

34. See Appendix A for further description of these dances.

35. The average ballroom dance team could earn between $75 and $100 at a cabaret (*Variety*, 17 October 1913). For dance lessons, performers usually charged from $10 to $20 an hour (Harrydele Hallmark, "If You Dance You Must Pay the Piper," *Vogue*, 15 January 1914, pp. 24–25, 104).

36. For information on debutantes becoming ballroom dancers see Irene Castle, as told to Bob and Wanda Duncan, *Castles in the Air* (New York: Doubleday and Co., 1958), p. 118, and "Miss Willard Has New Dance for Newport," undated *New York Herald* newspaper clipping ca. 1913 (Irene and Vernon Castle scrapbook, vol. 21, 499), Billy Rose Theatre Collection, The New York Public Library). All further references to The Billy Rose Theatre Collection will be denoted by the abbreviation BRTC.

37. "The Dance Craze in Paris Creates New Types of Gowns," *Dress and Vanity Fair*, November 1913, pp. 59–60.

38. Exhibition ballroom dancer Joan Sawyer often wore this type of outfit. See *The New York Dramatic Mirror*, 29 July 1914, p. 17.

39. For further discussion of these projects see Irene Castle, *Castles in the Air*, pp. 88–89, 107–112.

40. During her long and varied career Elizabeth Marbury managed several performers who eventually rose to stardom. Elizabeth Marbury, *My Crystal Ball* (New York: Boni and Liveright Publishers, 1933), pp. 242, 249.

41. Irene and Vernon Castle, *Modern Dancing* (New York: The World Syndicate Co., 1914), pp. 19–20.

42. "Women of Society to Open Dancing Academy," *The New York Herald*, 6

December, 1913; Elizabeth Marbury, "Real Tango Akin to Minuet," unidentified clipping (Irene and Vernon Castle scrapbook, vol. 21, 499, BRTC); Erenberg, *Steppin' Out*, pp. 160–161.

43. Otheman Stevens, "Healthfully Stimulating, Says She, and Curtails Temptation," *The Los Angeles Examiner*, 11 September 1915.

44. Rosetta O'Neill, "The Dodworth Family and Ballroom Dancing in New York," *Dance Index*, April 1943, pp. 54–56.

45. Leslie F. Clendenen, *Dance Mad or The Dances of the Day* (St. Louis: Arcade Print Co., 1914).

46. "Maurice and Duryea Cooperating," *The Modern Dance Magazine*, December–January 1917, p. 39.

47. *The Modern Dance Magazine*, December–January 1917, pp. 23, 24; April–May 1917, p. 9.

48. From 1919–1928 John Murray Anderson produced and directed the renowned *Greenwich Village Follies*, which were considered one of the most elegant and sophisticated revue series of the twenties. See Cecil Smith and Glenn Litton, *Musical Comedy in America* (New York: Theatre Arts Books, 1981), p. 130.

49. Troy and Margaret West Kinney, *Social Dancing of Today* (New York: Frederick A. Stokes Co., 1914), p. 7.

50. Ibid., p. 8.

Dancing Deities: Career Paths
of the Early Innovators

From 1910 through 1917 exhibition ballroom dance moved from amateur status to professional. Spurred on by the public's love of social dancing, producers and dance directors added novel exhibition ballroom numbers to their musical theatre productions. Booking agents and personal managers got in the act as well: they paired exhibition ballroom teams to satisfy the public's desire for more novelty in vaudeville routines; cabaret owners, not to be outdone, sought out teams to enliven their clubs. Thus, the flow of professional ballroom dancers among the cabaret, vaudeville, and the musical theatre created a healthy climate in which the genre itself began to flourish. As teams picked up ideas from each other, new dances and increasingly innovative routines graced the floors. Also, with opportunities available in these theatrical venues, many dancers, formerly specialists in ballet or eccentric dance, turned to exhibition ballroom work to broaden their range.

Clearly, for many performers, exhibition ballroom dance represented a promising professional opportunity. For some, it was a steppingstone toward soloist work in the musical theatre or a career as a film dancer. For others, the addition of spirited, often spectacular, exhibition ballroom routines to their repertoire helped revive a lagging popularity. Of course, for hundreds of performers, exhibition ballroom dance was their sole—and profitable—career. At the height of the ballroom craze, in the mid-teens, the most popular teams commanded astounding fees for the day: up to $500–$700 a week for a cabaret engagement. This was usually combined with a vaudeville or musical theatre engagement from which they could easily earn $1,000 a week! Exhibition ballroom was becoming a booming business.

What was the reason for this success? A group of innovative teams had a lot to do with it. The meteoric rise of teams such as Maurice Mouvet and Florence Walton, Irene and Vernon Castle, Joan Sawyer and her many partners, Mae Murray and Clifton Webb, Adelaide and Hughes, and the Dolly Sisters prompted scores of other performers to jump on the bandwagon. While some teams found glory in the cabaret, others made their mark in the musical theatre or vaudeville. Extensive press coverage helped them all during the years 1910–1915, when news of exhibition ballroom teams dominated the arts and society pages of the major newspapers. Readers who were just learning these new dances themselves yearned to discover the secrets to success of their favorite teams.

MANY PATHS TO FOLLOW

The paths that led the dancers to fame became models for the hundreds of other teams. Although some exhibition ballroom dancers began their careers as actors or singers, most simply started out as dancers. In general three broad categories defined the origins of the teams: professionals with theatrical dance training, those with cabaret experience, and amateurs with only social dance experience, or little professional training.

However, the majority of teams had *some* form of theatrical dance experience. Many young performers had worked as chorus members, juvenile performers, or featured soloists in the musical theatre. Some were seasoned professionals, already established as solo or team dancers. Yet all of these performers had particular reasons for choosing exhibition ballroom work. Chorus dancers, for example, tried to acquire different specialties to distinguish themselves on the chorus line; during the fertile years of the 1910s, they turned to ballroom work, as they might have previously chosen tap, ballet, or acrobatics. Young musical theatre performers specializing in juvenile or soubrette roles often switched to ballroom work as a means of proving their adult status, since ballroom numbers frequently provided adult love interest in a performance. And seasoned dancers incorporated ballroom dance into their repertoire to expand and diversify their range.

The road most traveled went from the chorus line to the exhibition ballroom floor. Young chorus girls dreamed of being spotted by an influential agent or producer—and in many cases, particularly for the most enterprising, this dream came true. During the height of the ballroom dance craze, talent scouts of all kinds haunted dance halls and cabarets, on the lookout for promising young dancers.

Mae Murray (1893–1965), a popular ballroom dancer of the 1910s, and remembered today as a beauty from the silent screen era, was one such plucky chorus girl. Murray appeared in the chorus line of *The Ziegfeld Follies of 1908,* the second of the famous producer's elaborate and fashionable revues. The role, in which she portrayed one of the "Nell Brinkley Bathing Girls," earned her a photograph in the local newspapers, but it was not enough to satisfy her deepest professional aspirations of becoming a soloist. So, in an attempt to capture the attention of prominent producers and choreographers, Murray supposedly went to Europe to learn the "authentic" versions of such dances as the tango and the maxixe. When she returned, with some experience and publicity under her belt, she got the chance to present her ballroom specialties in a romantic operetta, *Her Little Highness* (1913), with partner Wallace McCutcheon. Although one reporter called the show "an almost instant failure," Murray nevertheless displayed her newly acquired ballroom panache.[1]

One famed New York agent who liked her style was William Morris, who had recently opened a popular cabaret, The Jardin de Danse, and was looking to snap up some ballroom dancers. So, during the 1913 season Murray became a featured dancer at Morris's fashionable roof-garden cabaret. By 1914, the Shuberts had hired her away as the hostess-manager of their Folies Marigny, another roof-garden cabaret at the Forty-fourth Street Theatre, where she performed ballroom exhibitions nightly, and at afternoon tea dances.[2]

Murray quickly established herself as a ballroom dancer of skill and grace. Ballroom dance gave her the perfect vehicle for her natural flamboyance; Murray's performances were heralded as much for their dramatic postures and lavish clothing as for their dancing. Eventually she landed a coveted replacement role for Irene Castle in the 1915 Castle vehicle *Watch Your Step.* From there, Murray garnered a featured role in the *Ziegfeld Follies of 1915.*[3] Hollywood and celebrity status awaited her with one of her most memorable roles, playing opposite John Gilbert in the 1925 film version of *The Merry Widow.* Clearly, while Murray enjoyed great success as an exhibition ballroom dancer, it was that work which fueled her later career as a film star.[4]

The chorus continued to provide solid training for many other dancers. Joan Sawyer (1890–?), one of the most popular ballroom dancers of her time, began her career in such productions as *The Vanderbilt Cup* in 1907 ("a glorified vaudeville affair"), and the 1911 replacement cast of *The Pink Lady,* composer Ivan Caryll's long-running musical comedy.[5] In that same year she landed a brief and fortuitous engagement with professional cabaret dancer Maurice Mouvet at the Café de L'Opera (also known as Louis Martin's), a renowned restaurant-cabaret at Broadway and Forty-second Street.[6]

Sawyer's unique style, tenacity, and shrewd approach to management propelled her to the status of one of the first women identified as the leading member of a ballroom team. She operated a successful cabaret, The Persian Garden (at the Winter Garden Building at Broadway and Fiftieth Street), and taught and performed ballroom dance there during 1914 and 1915.[7] Unlike Murray, for whom ballroom dancing was a steppingstone to the silent screen, Sawyer stayed with ballroom dance and eventually became known for her inventive vaudeville acts, which incorporated pantomime and ballroom work within dramatic narratives.

Another common career route was from juvenile actor (or soubrette) to ballroom dancer. A juvenile performing in exhibition ballroom numbers signaled that he had "come of age" on stage. Clifton Webb (1891–1966), for example, is largely remembered as a film actor. Webb spent most of his early career as a musical comedy dancer, after receiving training as an opera singer. He appeared with a professional opera company for several seasons, then landed a role as a juvenile in a forgettable 1913 comic opera, *The Purple Road.*[8] His role of the young bridegroom included a notable comic singing and dancing turn, but it wasn't until the professional cabaret engagement that followed that critics began to take note.

In 1913, while Webb was out dancing socially at the popular Jardin De Danse cabaret after one of his performances, celebrated ballroom dancer Bonnie Glass spotted him and after a brief "audition" in which they danced a couple of numbers together, she proposed a partnership.[9] Webb, of course, had had little or no training as a ballroom dancer, but he jumped at the offer to perhaps gain greater exposure and to develop a new line of expertise. It took just a few performances for Webb and Glass to become an admired ballroom couple both on the fashionable after-hours club circuit and in vaudeville. One critic from the period called Webb's foray into exhibition ballroom work "a sheer fluke," but in fact many professional ballroom teams began careers in this informal manner.[10] He learned the basics of ballroom dance from his partner, then relied on his native talents for the rest.

For the entire 1913–1914 season, Webb was the ballroom dance man of the week, his slim physique and suave manner typifying the classic ballroom dancer. As he hoped, Webb's successful partnership with Glass brought offers from several other professional exhibition ballroom dancers; the already popular Mae Murray sought him out at the end of his union with Glass, and their ballroom team had a long-lasting vaudeville run on the Keith circuit.[11] Other partners included Gloria Goodwin and Mary Hay, with whom Webb developed a unique eccentric-comic ballroom duo.

After Webb was established as a glamorous ballroom dancer, contracts from Broadway producers followed. He became a featured dancer in the first of a series of stylish revues by Ned Wayburn, *Town Topics of 1915,* and garnered praise for work in the Elizabeth Marbury–produced musical, *Love O'Mike* (1917). With dance partner Ada Mae Weeks, Webb scored a hit in the popular musical *Listen Lester* (1917). It was his featured number, a sprightly waltz dance, that critics assured "will be heard in the dance halls for a long time to come."[12] Critics marveled at Webb's versatility; in these shows and others that followed he demonstrated his penchant for both straight exhibition ballroom and comic-eccentric dances. Webb, in fact, often resisted the label of ballroom dancer, since his dancing covered such a broad range, but clearly his ballroom prowess brought him the recognition he needed to further his career.[13]

MUSICAL COMEDY AS THE STARTING POINT

Some of the most successful exhibition ballroom dancers started their careers as featured soloists in musical comedies. Florence Walton (1891–1981), who eventually became half of the renowned team of Maurice and Walton, made her stage debut in the chorus of the musical comedy *The Girl Behind the Counter* (1907), a "light-headed medley of song, dance and frolic" produced by the burlesque impresario Lew Fields. Soon after, Walton was promoted to specialty dancer and featured in a Spanish dance sequence in Ziegfeld's 1908 musical, *Miss Innocence.* Other featured character dance roles soon followed, such as a Parisian Two-Step performed at the "Al Fresco Ball" in Ivan Caryll's musical *The Pink Lady* (1911).[14] While Walton was in rehearsal for a Ziegfeld production of a Viennese-based musical, *The Rose Maid* (1912), the expedient producer selected her to team up with ballroom specialist Maurice Mouvet, who needed a replacement partner.[15] Obviously her prominence as a solo dancer increased the likelihood of her being spotted by an influential scout. While it is not certain that Walton had hopes of becoming an exhibition ballroom dancer, she clearly did not turn down an opportunity to perform with renowned Mouvet. As it turned out, not only did Maurice and Walton become one of America's best-known exhibition teams, they married in 1911 and remained a ballroom dance partnership until 1920, when they divorced.

Another foremost exhibition ballroom dancer of his day was Vernon Castle, who began his career as a featured musical theatre soloist. Though his specialty was comedic dance, he was a highly versatile and talented performer, adept in several styles of popular dance. In productions such as Lew Fields' *About Town* (1907), *In Old Dutch* (1909), and *The Midnight Sons* (1909), Castle displayed a penchant for highly physical comedy such as the "gentlemanly drunk" who tries to maintain his composure while bumping into furniture and sliding down staircases.[16] His dance numbers included a Merry Widow Waltz burlesque with specialty dancer Lotte Faust in the 1907 production of *The Girl Behind the Counter* (Florence Walton's debut production). Castle's unique acrobatic-eccentric dance style prompted one reviewer to describe him as "an attenuated youth with voluble legs."[17] Of course, the skills associated with eccentric dance—timing, balance, and precision—would serve him well on the ballroom floor.

Vernon Castle got his first opportunity to experiment with ballroom dance while he was unemployed. In 1911 he and his wife Irene were performing in Paris in a show called *Enfin un Revue*, a melange of variety acts featuring Vernon's well-known barbershop scene from *The Henpecks*, in which Castle, as a magician, dodges the slapdash habits of the barber.[18] It closed unexpectedly and the couple found themselves down on their luck. So they began performing impromptu renditions of American social dances at the popular Café de Paris, even though neither of them had ever performed the latest ballroom dances, which were just beginning to become the rage in the United States. They had simply read newspaper accounts and apparently seen some photographs that Irene's mother had sent her.[19]

These improvised ballroom renditions delighted the Parisians so that the Castles were soon performing nightly on the Café de Paris's tiny dance floor, which Irene Castle said resembled "dancing in the aisle of a pullman car."[20] For Vernon, however, this was a fortuitous opportunity; he was able to prove his versatility as a performer and expand his range beyond the comic-dance roles with which he had become associated.

SEASONED DANCERS

Another group of ballroom dancers were those professionals who had spent years in another specialty, then discovered exhibition ballroom dance. These artists turned to ballroom work to revitalize careers or to diversify themselves artistically. One example was the American vaudeville-ballet dancer, Adelaide (born Mary Dickey, ca. 1884–1960). Her career longevity—she performed actively from about 1905 to 1930—was the envy of many popular theatre performers. When only a little past her infancy, Adelaide became an acrobatic dancer billed as "La Petite Adelaide." The four-foot five-inch dancer went on to become a ballet specialist and was featured in several musical productions including *Babes and the Baron* (1904) and *The Orchid* (1907). One of her best-known routines from this period was her doll act in which the dancer, mimicking the mechanical movements of a doll, emerged from a wrapped gift box and performed a spirited toe dance. In fact, for a 1907 Hippodrome production she performed the doll dance en point on horse-back.[21]

Adelaide's success certainly came in part from her inventiveness and ability to vary her routines to keep up with current theatrical styles. In 1910, for example, she teamed up with a male partner, J. J. (Johnny) Hughes in what may be viewed as an attempt to expand her repertoire and avoid being typecast in juvenile roles. At first their numbers consisted of Adelaide's ballet dances, with Hughes serving as assistant, but when the newer ballroom styles came into vogue she wove them into their act. The unique routines Adelaide and Hughes eventually developed for vaudeville and the musical theatre were descriptive story dances incorporating ballet, ballroom dancing, and pantomime. The act usually concluded with a "star turn" by Adelaide, consisting of a virtuosic toe dance. Trying to encapsulate their style, one reviewer described their work as "operatic, ballet and stage dancing, dashed through with the paprika of the Cakewalk and the Tango."[22]

Adelaide and Hughes gained equal acclaim on the cabaret circuit. During the 1914 season they performed at the Jardin de Danse and at other fashionable cabarets, offering evening shows and afternoon tea dansants. They also taught ballroom classes to New York City socialites at various mid-town clubs and their Brooklyn dance school, "Bensonhurst-by-the-Sea"—an allusion, no doubt, to Irene and Vernon Castle's popular dance school, Castles by the Sea.[23] For Adelaide, including exhibition ballroom dance into her routines clearly helped her maintain the popularity she had established as a child performer; as a team Adelaide and Hughes continued to be vaudeville headliners through the mid-twenties.

Another seasoned team whose long-lasting career included diverse popular dance styles was the Dolly Sisters, Roszika (1892–1970) and Yancsi (1892–1941). Immortalized in the 1945 film, *The Dolly Sisters,* with June Haver and Betty Grable, the famous duo became known for their extravagant costumes and theatrical personalities. The Dolly Sisters were unique in that they were a single-sex exhibition ballroom team. The basis of their act—known in theatre parlance as a tandem act—revolved around their identities as twins. Dressed in identical clothing, using mirror and shadow techniques, they imitated each other's movements.[24]

The Dolly Sisters originated this style of dance as child performers in Hungarian and German music halls at the turn of the century and made their American debut in a pony ballet in *The Maid and the Millionaire* (1907), an operetta at the Madison Square Roof Garden.[25] The sisters entered vaudeville largely because of the regulations of the Gerry Society (for the protection of children), which forced them to either retire or move out of New York City. So, for two years they performed on the Orpheum vaudeville circuit in the Midwest, until they came of age, when they opened at a Keith house in New York City in 1909.[26] Until 1910 or so their youthful routines incorporated then-popular clog dances and French and Spanish folk dances, but by the mid-teens they drew increasingly on contemporary ballroom forms to create a stylish, tandem-exhibition, ballroom style.

In a carefully calculated move to enhance their careers, during the 1912–1914 season the Dolly Sisters each paired themselves with male partners; Roszika (or Rosy) with specialty dancer Martin Brown, who had recently appeared with them in the 1913 musical *The Merry Countess*, and Yancsi (or Jenny) with comic-eccentric dancer Harry Fox.[27] Although critics bemoaned the apparent loss of the popular female team, each of their respective partnerships won critical praise on the vaudeville circuit.[28]

The Roszika Dolly–Martin Brown combination, created in the erotic-romantic ballroom style, was especially popular. Audiences and critics alike enjoyed their Spanish numbers and as respected dance critic Caroline Caffin remarked, their dances "infused a diablerie, a fire and passion, something reserved for our cooler natures."[29] Jenny Dolly and Harry Fox (who eventually married) worked more in a light-hearted, romantic flirtation vein, combining song and banter. The two teams, who often appeared on the same vaudeville bill, were set up as rivals to create audience interest.

The Dolly Sisters' alliance with male partners was temporary yet successful, for when they reunited as a tandem-exhibition team in 1914 they were even more popular than before. From the mid-teens through the 1920s, the team appeared regularly in both vaudeville and musical theatre productions, most notably the Ziegfeld Follies and the Shubert Winter Garden shows. Their ability to combine ballroom work into their already novel tandem routines gave their act a distinctiveness that contributed to their longstanding success.

CABARET BACKGROUND

Many dancers started out in the cabaret and retained the identity of cabaret dancers throughout their careers. Some of these dancers had actually been performing as semi-professionals in saloons and rathskellers as early as 1906. When the cabaret boom of the 1910s hit, with exhibition dancing as a major feature, these dancers made swift transitions onto the cabaret circuit. Typically they learned their trade informally, having served as apprentices to other performers. Some began as "demonstration dancers," teaching patrons how to dance, and hoping for a break to perform professionally at the club.

One of the best-known, influential cabaret specialists during the years

1908–1918 was Maurice Mouvet, who was in many respects ahead of his time. As early as 1906, Mouvet (usually referred to as "Maurice") won acclaim in Parisian cabarets performing a professional repertoire of variations on nineteenth-century waltzes, mazurkas, exhibition cake-walks, and jigs.[30] Several accounts of Maurice's life claim that he started out as a page, then worked his way up as a performer.[31]

Perhaps Maurice's greatest renown came through his performances of the Apache Dance (pronounced a-posh), which he introduced at the Café de Paris, in France, around 1907. The colorful, suggestive Apache was originally a social dance born in the dives of Paris. Performed as a slow waltz, it depicted the jealous relationship between a young thug and his girlfriend. It never became a ballroom dance (that is, it was never performed extensively by the public), but it was very popular with audiences from about 1908 to 1912.

In 1910, as the social dance craze was taking hold in the United States, Maurice introduced his ballroom specialties to an eager New York City public. With his French partner, Madeleine D'Arville, he performed his waltzes and mazurkas, but also added to his routine the American so-cial dances currently the rage, such as the Turkey Trot and the Grizzly Bear. Maurice and D'Arville were a smash hit, and as one of the earliest exhibition ballroom teams they led the way for this type of entertain-ment in American restaurants and cabarets. After a brief engagement with D'Arville in the Casino Theatre musical, *Peggy* (1910), Maurice met Florence Walton, and the couple went on to become one of the most successful exhibition ballroom teams of their day.[32]

Another popular cabaret-based exhibition ballroom performer of the 1910s was John Jarrott (1893–1966). Though not as well-known as Maurice Mouvet, Jarrott was an extremely talented performer and sought-after partner by many professional women dancers. His "ap-prenticeship" was perhaps the most unusual of them all. After working with a heavyweight boxer in a theatricalized fight-act, Jarrott worked as a dancer in Chicago clubs owned by "horseman" August Reiley, from about 1908 to 1910.[33] At one such club, the Ray Jones Café, he and Louise Greuning introduced the Turkey Trot and the Grizzly Bear. He went on to perform with a variety of female dancers, including Mae Murray, Ivy Sawyer, Louise Alexander, and Joan Sawyer, with whom he gained the most renown.[34] Jarrott's classic good looks, sturdy build, and honed ballroom form (and, no doubt, his colorful past) made him an enviable partner.

The renowned tangoist and movie idol Rudolph Valentino also got his start in New York City's cabaret world. At Maxim's cabaret on West Thirty-eighth Street he worked as a demonstration dancer, teaching social dancing and serving as a partner to unescorted women.[35] As Val-entino gained greater confidence and skill, he soon came to the atten-

tion of the prominent women exhibition dancers of the day. With Bonnie Glass, a former musical comedy soloist turned ballroom dancer, he
had his first successful partnership. Accounts differ as to how they met,
but Glass, searching about for a new partner after her year-long stint
with Clifton Webb, saw Valentino at one of his club engagements and
suggested they dance together professionally. Billed as "Bonnie Glass
and Rudolpho," during the 1915–1916 season they performed at Glass's
Montmartre Café and toured on the Keith vaudeville circuit, headlining at the Palace.[36]

Also during 1916, Valentino performed for a brief time in vaudeville
with celebrated exhibition dancer Joan Sawyer. They too performed
on the Keith circuit, visiting most major eastern cities. Frequent partner changes like this were common among exhibition ballroom dancers,
who were forever in quest of the perfect "match." Once Valentino's
partnership with Sawyer came to an end, in the late teens, he headed
west, first sharing a cabaret act with a sister-brother ballroom team,
Fanchon and Marco, and then was eventually snared by the movie industry. One of his first, small, film roles was in *A Rogue's Romance* (1919),
in which he performed an exhibition Apache dance. The film that led
him to stardom, however, was *The Four Horsemen of the Apocalypse* (1921),
and his celebrated tango with Alice Terry. By the time Valentino starred
in *The Sheik* (1921) he had become a nationwide idol, epitomizing the
idea of the romantic hero.

THE AMATEUR ROUTE

Some exhibition ballroom dancers who became prominent during the
teens began as virtual amateurs, with little or no prior dance training.
Dance competitions, one of the many new popular amusements that
sprung up then, were one means to professional status. At fashionable
cabarets, restaurants and hotels, and social clubs, enthusiastic dancers
competed for best one-step, waltz, or tango category. The contests offered amateurs a means of honing their ballroom skills and, if they
won, were a vehicle to break into the business. As sometimes happened,
a theatrical manager or producer might spot a particularly talented amateur in the competition and offer an engagement at a club, or perhaps
even a professional contract.

Amateur performers frequently were drawn into the profession by a
spouse. Usually one of the team members was a dancer with professional training who taught his or her mate the rudiments of ballroom
form. Irene Castle, in fact, began this way. Before teaming up with her
husband, Irene had little professional experience, although she aspired
toward a career in the theatre and had studied theatrical dance technique with noted dance teacher Rosetta O'Neill, a protégé of the fa-

mous Dodworth family of dance teachers. It was Vernon Castle, then her fiancé, who had helped her get her first role in the Lew Fields production, *The Summer Widowers* (1910).[37] As Irene Castle remembered, "I was supposed to be devoting my time to establishing a foothold in the theater, an occupation which consisted of sitting through fifty performances of *The Summer Widowers* as Vernon's guest."[38] When an actress in a minor role suddenly dropped out of the musical production, Fields cast Irene in the part.

While Irene Castle was not destined for an acting career (Lew Fields cast only Vernon, not her, in his next musical production, *The Henpecks*), she and Vernon would soon make dancing history. It was as a ballroom dancer with Vernon at a small club in Paris that Irene obtained her first truly professional experience.[39] Their partnership was a team effort, with Vernon choreographing their numbers and Irene serving as artistic advisor. As Irene Castle's daughter has remarked, "he (Vernon) developed the dances primarily, she was interested in how they would dress, how effective the setting would be in which they would perform—that sort of thing."[40]

Conversely, a husband might be drawn into a professional ballroom partnership through his wife's career. One such example was the team "Mr. and Mrs. Douglas Crane," considered by some reviewers as the west coast equivalent of Irene and Vernon Castle, who toured in New York City during the teens. Mrs. Crane, the former Ivy Payne, began her career as a featured solo dancer in musical comedy, most notably as one of the Egyptian dancers in a 1911 production of *Kismet*.[41] Sometime between 1911 and 1914 she married Douglas Crane, purportedly a portrait artist by trade, and the two formed a team.

While marrying into a team was a convenient way to get started professionally, it did not guarantee success. Rather, the appropriate pairing of the partners was crucial to the team's popularity. Much of the art of exhibition work stems from the dancers' ability to combine each other's qualities to create a sense of oneness. The best teams became so because of their ease and fluidity of movement, their gracefulness, and that elusive quality known as "personality."

TEAM-PAIRING

For the most part, dancers paired themselves into teams, either through a personal or romantic alliance, as in the case of the Castles, or after having performed together in a musical theatre production, similar to Roszika Dolly and Martin Brown from *The Merry Countess*. In some instances, an exhibition ballroom dancer with an established reputation might contract a lesser-known partner with a compatible style. This was true for several women exhibition ballroom dancers who, by

virtue of their headliner status, could attract and hire their own partners. Many of these women served as hostesses and managers of fashionable midtown cabarets. Depending on the man's popularity with audiences, he might remain a partner for as little as two engagements, or
for as long as two to three months.

Joan Sawyer, for instance, as manager of the Persian Garden Room
(at the Winter Garden building) had the power to hire and fire all of
her own male partners (and she had several during her career).[42] In
fact, Sawyer ingeniously turned this business practice into an artistic
and promotional device: to differentiate herself from other ballroom
dancers, she employed two male partners for one engagement—one to
accompany her in tangos, another for waltzes and one-steps. While at
the Persian Garden (1914–1915) Sawyer performed with as many as
six different male partners, several of whom went on to become prominent ballroom dancers themselves, such as Quentin Tod, Wallace
McCutcheon, and Carlos Sebastian.

Other women dancers contracting their own partners included Bonnie Glass and Mae Murray. During her years in vaudeville, from 1914
through 1916, Glass had a string of male partners, from an ex-jockey
named Harry Davis to Clifton Webb. In 1915 she managed the Café
Montmartre (at Broadway and Forty-first Street), and hired and performed with Rudolph Valentino. In their cabaret as well as vaudeville
acts, Glass controlled the act; she designed their dance numbers and
always received first billing.[43] Murray ran the Folies Marigny cabaret
(at Broadway and Forty-fourth Street) in 1914, where she received a
percentage of the profits and wielded considerable control over her
choice of partners.[44]

Many novice dancers, eager to break into the business, formed their
own duos, such as Percy Oakes and Pamela De Lour, an exhibition
team popular in the mid-to-late teens. Though not of the stature of
such ballroom dancers as Maurice and Walton, Oakes and De Lour are
examples of the many hundreds of popular but less publicized ballroom teams that toured the vaudeville circuits across the country. Oakes
started out as a chorus boy at the La Salle Theatre in Chicago and then
sought work as a juvenile to improve his status.[45] Soon after, during an
interview with a booking agent, he learned that Irene and Vernon Castle had cancelled their proposed appearance at Rector's cabaret in Chicago. By convincing the agent he was part of a dance team, he won an
audition. Quickly, Oakes put together an exhibition ballroom act with
his girlfriend Pamela De Lour, whose only prior dance experience was
Saturday night social dancing with Oakes at the local dance hall. They
rehearsed constantly for two days, during which time they developed
an acrobatic-ballroom dance number with a breathtaking overhead spin.
It secured them the job. Oakes and De Lour (by now husband and

wife) played in Chicago clubs for nearly two years, until vaudeville im-presario Martin Beck spotted them and offered them a coveted Or-pheum circuit contract.[46]

If dancers did not form the team themselves, often industry profes-sionals, from personal managers and booking agents to producers, would make the match. Such a person was Elizabeth Marbury. With an eye for talent and a keen business sense, Marbury became Irene and Ver-non Castle's manager just as they were taking New York by storm and was largely responsible for their enormous popularity. She also man-aged the team of Maurice and Walton for a brief period in 1915, after the Castles left her management over a financial dispute.[47]

An interesting Marbury find, and a good example of her profes-sional matchmaking efforts, was Helen Clarke and Quentin Tod. Mar-bury discovered seventeen-year-old amateur dancer Helen Clarke at her Strand Roof Garden Theatre, at Broadway and Forty-seventh Street, which she had established in 1913 with socialite Anna Morgan. Mar-bury chose Clarke as the winner of one of the many dance competitions held there and immediately offered her a five-year contract to appear in a succession of musicals that she was producing at the Princess The-atre on Thirty-ninth Street.[48]

For the first of the Princess shows, *Nobody Home* (1915), Marbury paired Clarke with San Francisco-bred professional exhibition ballroom dancer Quentin Tod, already familiar to New York audiences through his brief association with Joan Sawyer in 1914. Originally trained in acting and classical ballet, he eventually moved into musical-comedy dancing and became skilled as an exhibition ballroom dancer.[49]

To showcase the couple and publicize the show, Marbury had Clarke and Tod perform at the Strand Roof Garden for several nights before the opening of *Nobody Home*. Clarke and Tod received highly enthu-siastic notices, some of which compared them to Irene and Vernon Castle, and as was typical of successful musical theatre ballroom teams, Clarke and Tod's partnership endured beyond the closing perfor-mance. They appeared nightly at the Biltmore Hotel cabaret for sev-eral weeks, and in 1917 they appeared in another Marbury musical, *Love O'Mike,* also featuring Clifton Webb.[50]

Famed producer Florenz Ziegfeld also created several important teams during the teens. He discovered the maverick performer Jack Clifford when he realized he needed another ballroom dance team for an up-coming production, *The Winsome Widow* (1912). Reportedly a former prize-fighter and jockey, Clifford had been working for several months as a demonstration dancer at Shanley's restaurant on Broadway (be-tween Forty-first and Forty-second Streets). Ziegfeld approached Clif-ford after a performance at the club and immediately offered him a contract.[51] Clifford released his current partner, Hazel Murray, and teamed up with Ziegfeld protégé Irene Weston. The couple performed several popular exhibition ballroom dances and scored a hit with an acrobatic whirlwind waltz that Clifford choreographed.[52]

Although Clifford left Weston soon after *The Winsome Widow*'s run, his featured appearance there helped secure his reputation as a ballroom dancer. He continued performing with other partners, and made newspaper headlines when he formed a partnership in 1914 with former chorus girl Evelyn Nesbit, just emerging from a ten-year seclusion after the Harry Thaw–Stanford White scandal. Since her comeback was major entertainment-page gossip, they were showered with enormous preshow publicity. A *Variety* commentator noted ironically that "The name 'Thaw' has brought money to others besides the lawyers."[53] Clifford and Nesbit played to packed houses for nearly two years in a highly successful vaudeville ballroom act. For one of their engagements, at New York City's Victoria Theatre, Nesbit herself earned close to $3,000.[54] It seems likely Nesbit's managers (Comstock & Gest) gambled that her return as a "society" dancer might go far in restoring her credibility as a performer after her scandalous past, and, of course, a ballroom act was an excellent vehicle to showcase her talent. Clifford did not earn nearly that amount, even though he was responsible for teaching her his exhibition ballroom specialties. Nevertheless, the publicity was a boon to his career.

Personal managers and booking agents, too, had their hand in the creation (and promotion) of exhibition ballroom teams. William Morris was one such agent. Of course, his own club, the popular Jardin de Danse cabaret at the New York Theatre, was a big motivator. In fact, during the height of the ballroom craze, Morris engaged seven ballroom dancers "of the 'classy type,' " such as Joan Sawyer, Mae Murray, Billie Allen, Carlos Sebastian, and Enrico Muris, who alternated evenings at his cabaret.[55] Morris teamed up Sawyer with Sebastian, for example, who had begun his career as a singer in the Paris Opera Comique; the team went on to great popularity in vaudeville, as well.[56]

Finally, choreographers (or dance directors as they were called in the teens and twenties) had an influential hand in creating ballroom teams. From 1911 through 1915, Broadway shows regularly featured teams in their productions. Dance directors might pair solo dancers in ballroom routines, for one number or for the duration of the show. If the team was a hit, they generally then moved into vaudeville and the cabarets, usually with an expanded act, as in the case of Rosy Dolly and Martin Brown.

Ned Wayburn, the prolific dance director and teacher, formed several teams that became quite famous, among them Harry Pilcer and glamorous musical comedy star Gaby Deslys, Clifton Webb and Mary Hay, and Fred and Adele Astaire.[57] In the 1911 production of *Vera*

Violetta Wayburn initially assigned Pilcer to help him coach Gaby Deslys and then choreographed an exhibition ballroom number for them— the Gaby Glide—which became a hit dance of the 1911–1912 season. After the close of the show, Pilcer and Deslys brought their successful dance act to several Parisian clubs, then returned to New York where the Shuberts featured them in their Winter Garden musical *The Honeymoon Express* (1913).[58]

Wayburn also groomed the highly successful brother-sister team of the Astaires, Fred (1899–1987) and Adele (1897–1981). After early ballet training, the Astaires appeared as a child act in vaudeville from 1906 through 1908. During a two-year reprieve from performing, the young dancers rejuvenated their act by studying at the Ned Wayburn Institute of Dancing where they took classes in ballet and tap as well as ballroom. The pair purchased from Wayburn a vaudeville act that they performed on the Keith-Orpheum circuit in the Midwest from about 1910 until some two years later when they were old enough to perform in New York City. Their eccentric act combined, in a unique way, elements of ballet, tap, and whirlwind dancing, interspersed with exhibition ballroom work.

Wayburn also elicited from the dancers their natural sense of showmanship and personality. The Astaires continued in vaudeville from approximately 1912 through 1916, and then made their transition to Broadway musicals, appearing in such productions as *The Passing Show of 1918*, *Apple Blossoms* (1919), and the Gershwins' *Lady Be Good* (1925).[59] Fred Astaire, of course, would become a star of the next generation of ballroom dancers in the 1930s and 1940s, blazing a path difficult for others to follow. For now, he was learning his craft from the dancing of Vernon Castle, and others, who would have an immense influence on his later style.

NOTES

1. Mary Morgan, "The Secrets of Mae Murray's Success," *Photoplay*, 1 January 1922, p. 112. Wallace McCutcheon, originally a lead dancer in *The Slim Princess* and *The Pink Lady* (1911), was a prominent exhibition ballroom dancer of the teens. He performed frequently with Joan Sawyer and former chorus girl Vera Maxwell (1892–1950). McCutcheon also became a producer for Kalem Films, a silent film company of the teens.

2. *Variety*, 24 April 1914, p. 18. For further discussion of the Folies Marigny see Stephen Burge Johnson, "The Roof Gardens of Broadway Theatres," Chapter 8, pp. 15–16.

3. Carol Lee, "A Bit of Fluff from Folly Land," unidentified article (May Murray scrapbook, Robinson Locke Collection, ser. 2, vol. 281, BRTC).

4. Exhibition ballroom dancing was a departure point for many types of professional dancers, not only those in the popular theatre. For example, Ted

Shawn, the so-called "father" of American modern dance, used exhibition ballroom dance as a steppingstone toward his eventual career as a concert dancer with Ruth St. Denis. From 1912 through 1914, Shawn and his partner Norma Gould performed at tango teas at hotels in the Los Angeles area. See Elizabeth Kendall, *Where She Danced* (New York: Alfred A. Knopf, Inc., 1979), pp. 106–107; Jane Sherman, *Denishawn: The Enduring Influence* (Boston: G. K. Hall, 1983), p. 7.

5. "She's the Spirit of the Dance," *The New York Dramatic Mirror*, 29 July 1914.

6. Ibid.

7. Sawyer's Persian Garden was part of a dance establishment owned by the Shubert brothers called the *Palais de Danse*, in the Winter Garden Building. The Persian Garden occupied the third floor; the second floor housed a larger cabaret and restaurant known as the Parisian Room, which the team of Maurice and Walton managed in 1915.

8. Program, *The Purple Road*, 7 June 1913, BRTC.

9. "Webb Began Dance Career by Sheer Fluke," Unidentified newspaper clipping, ca. 1913 (Clifton Webb File, Theatre Collection, The Philadelphia Free Library); unidentified newspaper clippings (Clifton Webb File, Harvard Theatre Collection, Harvard College).

10. Ibid.

11. *The New York Clipper*, 21 March, 28 March, 5 April, 1914.

12. "Listen Lester," unidentified newspaper clipping (Clifton Webb scrapbook, BRTC).

13. See Chapter 6 for discussion of some of Webb's eccentric dancing roles.

14. Program, the New Amsterdam Theatre, 13 March 1911, BRTC.

15. Maurice Mouvet, *Maurice's Art of Dancing* (New York: Schirmer Books, 1914), pp. 51–55.

16. Unidentified newspaper clippings (Irene and Vernon Castle scrapbook, no. 21,499, BRTC).

17. Sime, "The Midnight Sons," undated *Variety* article (Irene and Vernon Castle scrapbook, no. 21,499, BRTC).

18. Unidentified newspaper clippings (Irene and Vernon Castle scrapbook, 21,499, BRTC); Irene Castle, *Castles in the Air*, pp. 42–47, 53–54.

19. Elroy Foote, "The Story of the Castles," *Theatre Magazine*, March 1915.

20. Castle, *Castles in the Air*, p. 57.

21. Ralph H. Craig, "La Petite Adelaide," unidentified magazine article (Adelaide and Hughes clipping file, BRTC). For descriptions of Adelaide's doll act see "In the Theatres," *The Syracuse Post*, 28 September 1906 (Adelaide and Hughes scrapbook, no. 4423, BRTC).

22. "Adelaide and Hughes Do Not Like to Be Misrepresented," *The New York American*, 24 August 1912 (Adelaide and Hughes scrapbook, no. 4423, BRTC).

23. Untitled newspaper article, *The Ohio State Journal*, 16 February 1916 (Adelaide and Hughes scrapbook, no. 4423, BRTC).

24. Other popular sister tandem acts from the period were the Fairbanks Twins (Madeleine and Marion) and the Cameron Sisters, who performed in several Ned Wayburn shows. Tandem work was not limited to siblings, however. Between 1912 and 1913 Carter De Haven and the comic Fred Nice teamed

up in a rube tandem act. Another male tandem team was that of George Moon and Daniel Morris (an English comic), who performed largely in musical comedies of the teens. Morris was, in fact, almost a head taller than Moon, but their act was still of the tandem mode because of its precision and parallel movements.

25. "The Dolly Sisters at the Star," *Cleveland Plain Dealer*, 9 February 1908 (Dolly Sisters scrapbook, Robinson Locke Collection, no. 371, BRTC). Pony ballets, teams of six to eight precision dancers, appeared in most musical comedies during the period 1900 to 1911. The "ponies" were the shortest of the chorus dancers.

26. *The Biographical Dictionary of Dance*, s.v. "The Dolly Sisters," by Barbara Cohen-Stratyner.

27. *The New York Herald*, 14 November 1912.

28. See Chapter 4 for more on the Dolly–Brown vaudeville act.

29. Caroline Caffin, untitled newspaper clipping (Dolly Sisters scrapbook, ser. 3, no. 371, BRTC), p. 53.

30. Mouvet, *Maurice's Art of Dancing*, p. 50.

31. "Mons. Maurice Says," *The New York Review*, 31 October 1914; "Maurice Mouvet, Dancer, Is Dead in Switzerland," *The Herald Tribune*, 19 May 1927.

32. Ibid.; "Doctored *Peggy* Is Offered Here," *The New York Telegraph*, 8 December 1911 (*Peggy* Clipping File, BRTC).

33. *The Biographical Dictionary of Dance*, s.v. "John Jarrott."

34. See Robinson Locke clipping file on Jarrott, BRTC.

35. Untitled, undated article, ed. by James R. Quirk, in *Photoplay* (Robinson Locke Scrapbook, BRTC).

36. *The New York Dramatic Mirror*, 8 January 1916; "Palace Offers Lively Bill," *Journal of Commerce*, 12 January 1916.

37. Program, *The Summer Widowers*, 5 December 1910.

38. Castle, *Castles in the Air*, p. 37.

39. See newspaper clippings (Irene and Vernon Castle scrapbook, 21,499, BRTC).

40. Barbara Kreutz, personal correspondence, 14 February 1985.

41. *The Milwaukee News*, 4 October 1914 (Mr. and Mrs. Douglas Crane scrapbook, Robinson Locke Collection, ser. 3, vol. 433, BRTC).

42. *Palais de Danse*, Contracts, Groups I-IV, II, 88, The Shubert Archive. Sawyer became manager of the Persian Garden with the help of her press agent, Jeanette Gilder, who was the editor of *The Century* magazine and the aunt of critic Rosamund Gilder. Jeanette Gilder discovered Sawyer during her engagement at the *Jardin de Danse*. See "Two Feminists and Dance Managers," *Vanity Fair*, August 1914, p. 70.

43. "Bonnie Glass Goes to Europe," unidentified newspaper article, ca. 1914 (Bonnie Glass clipping file, BRTC); "Bonnie Glass is Doubling in 'Vode' and Cabaret," *The New York Review*, 6 March 1915. "Palace Offers Lively Bill," *Journal of Commerce*, 12 January 1916 (Bonnie Glass clipping file, BRTC).

44. *Variety*, 24 April 1914, p. 18.

45. "Percy Oakes" in Bill Smith, *The Vaudevillians* (New York: Macmillan Publishing Company, 1976), p. 204.

46. Ibid., pp. 206–207.

47. See Marbury, *My Crystal Ball.*

48. "Clarke and Tod, A Dancing Team of Intelligence as Well as Grace," *The New York Star,* 24 June 1917 (Helen Clarke scrapbook, Robinson Locke Collection, no. 312, BRTC).

49. *The New York World,* 29 April 1917; *The New York Times,* 15 April 1917 (Helen Clarke scrapbook, Robinson Locke Collection, ser. 2, vol. 312, BRTC).

50. "Is the Castle Reign Over?" Newspaper clipping ca. 1915 (Quentin Tod clipping file, BRTC).

51. "Ziegfeld 'Discovers' Another Dancer at B'way Restaurant," *The New York Telegraph,* 23 March 1912 (Jack Clifford scrapbook, Robinson Locke Collection, no. 334, BRTC).

52. "1912 Dances on B'way," *Stage Pictorial,* July 1912.

53. *Variety,* 5 September, 1913.

54. Ibid. For more on Clifford and Nesbit, see Jack Clifford clipping files (Robinson Locke Collection, ser. 3, nos. 334, 360, BRTC).

55. "Chicago Makes High Bid for 'Society Dancer,' " *Variety,* ca. 1913.

56. Ibid. *The New York Clipper,* 28 June 1913.

57. See Cohen, "The Dance Direction of Ned Wayburn," Introduction; and Ned Wayburn, *The Art of Stage Dancing* (New York: The Ned Wayburn Studio of Dancing, Inc., 1925, 1927), pp. 144–145.

58. "Gaby Deslys Comes to Winter Garden," *New York Sun,* 7 February 1913 (*The Honeymoon Express* Clipping File, MWEZ, no. 21,053, BRTC).

59. See Stearns and Stearns, *Jazz Dance,* pp. 221–225; Morton Eustis, "Fred Astaire, the Actor-Dancer Attacks His Part," *Theatre Arts,* May 1937, pp. 371–386; "*Apple Blossoms* Proves a Delight," *The World,* 8 October 1919; "*Apple Blossoms,*" *The New York Evening Post,* 9 October 1919 (NBL Collection, BRTC).

_____ *Chapter 3* _____

Cabaret Dancing

The cabarets of the teens made stars of the ballroom teams who danced
there. The public flocked to cabarets to see theatricalized versions of
contemporary social dances. A unique pattern developed: on the heels
of the ballroom teams' performances, couples crowded the dance floor
to imitate them. As a result, ballroom dancers became entertainers and
"teachers" for their dance-loving fans. The teams developed a close
rapport with their audiences, and drew them into activities ranging from
dance contests and costume balls to dance lessons.

But just what were these cabarets? Restaurants, hotel dining rooms,
and roof-garden theatres were the most typical sites. The similarity of
all these venues was that they featured food, drink, and floor shows—
all at the same time. The initial inspiration for this came primarily from
Paris, which in the 1890s encouraged the development of the cabaret
as meeting places for artists and intellectuals. Singers and dancers typically performed on small platforms and mingled with the audience
during breaks.[1]

An American precursor of the cabaret was the so-called "joint," usually an underground rathskeller popular in the late nineteenth and early
twentieth century.[2] Usually attended by men only, joints were frequently nestled in red-light districts. They served food and liquor and
featured simple entertainment, such as pianists and vocalists. Gradually
the idea of combining modest entertainment and refreshment moved
up to the more fashionable New York City restaurants. Around 1906
respected restaurants such as the Café des Beaux Arts (West Fortieth

Street and Sixth Avenue) introduced professional vaudeville performers.[3] This trend continued into the teens as the Broadway area restaurateurs jumped on the bandwagon.

One of the first formal experiments with the cabaret was the Folies
Bérgère Theatre on Forty-ninth Street in New York City. Established
in 1911, the club featured an expanding stage over the orchestra pit
with small, glass-topped tables for the patrons. The entertainment consisted of two revue-format shows, one from 8 p.m. to 11 p.m., and the
other from 11 p.m. to 1 a.m., for the after-theatre crowds. Although
this early enterprise was a financial failure, the concept of presenting
entertainment in a contained and intimate environment began to catch
on.[4]

Soon after the Folies Bérgère venture, many more restaurateurs began experimenting with the cabaret idea. Some owners interspersed an
occasional musical number during dinner, while others added separate
rooms and charged an admission fee for the performances.[5] However,
it was around 1912, when hotels and restaurants began installing dance
floors and featuring glamorous ballroom teams, that the cabaret really
took hold. All of the major midtown restaurants, such as Bustanoby's,
Shanley's, the Café des Beaux Arts, Rector's, and Reisenweber's, opened
their doors for social dancing.

The dancers helped popularize two basic types of cabarets. So-called
"restaurant cabarets" offered dinner as well as a full-length floor show,
with variety performers and exhibition ballroom teams. There were
generally two shows, one at 8 p.m. and the other at 11 p.m., with intervals in between given over to social dancing. At the "dancing cabarets,"
which were oriented more toward drinking and dancing, exhibition
ballroom teams were the main entertainment and performed until two
or three in the morning.[6] The general pattern of dance, however, was
identical in both places—as patrons dined or drank, the ballroom dancers
appeared on the dance floor, after which the spectators followed suit.

The dance floors in the restaurant and hotel cabarets were small and
unobtrusive at first, but as cabarets became more financially viable many
owners enlarged them, placing them in the center of the room. Murray's Roman Garden, at West Forty-second Street, for instance, in-
stalled a novel, revolving dance floor measuring thirty by fifty feet.[7]
Arranged around the dance floor, usually in a horseshoe shape, were
small tables for the patrons. A live band always accompanied the dancers
directly on or just to the side of the dance floor.

At the roof gardens, originally designed as summer theatres on the
roofs of playhouses, owners created dance floors by removing the seats
from the orchestra section, which was then made level. After about
1915, some of the roof-garden clubs made greater use of their stages
in order to present more elaborate revue-format entertainment; how-

ever, the floor remained the primary place to dance for both the professionals and the public.[8]

HOW THEY DANCED

A new dance style was emerging, one that fostered greater individuality and freedom of expression, and the teams' intimate and exuberant couple dances were an open invitation to patrons to experiment with these dances themselves. Through their stylish interpretations of one-steps, hesitation waltzes, and tangos the teams suggested new movement possibilities. Couples could "linger" with their partner for a sequences of dances, inventing their own personalized movements. The teams embodied the idea of a single dance couple performing as a separate entity, instead of the concept of "group dancing" characteristic of nineteenth-century social dance.

A great part of the appeal of cabaret dancing was its feel of intimacy and romance. Couples were dancing close to each other and close to neighboring couples. The atmosphere of the cabaret, too, fostered this intimacy. At the Jardin de Danse, a roof-garden cabaret on top of the New York Theatre, hundreds of small white lights illuminated the dance floor. The Folies Marigny cabaret, on the Forty-fourth Street Theatre roof, was filled from floor to ceiling with palms and wisteria.[9] Dimly lit chandeliers, subtly colored draperies, and plush carpets adorned most of the cabarets so that the sight of a single exhibition ballroom couple created a sensuous image for audiences.

PERFORMERS AS HOSTS

In addition to their roles as performers, the teams served as hosts and hostesses, providing atmosphere and spirit, and encouraging guests to participate in dance activities. This, too, created a more intimate involvement with the audience, departing even more from nineteenth-century strictures. Dancers led costume balls and special themes at the clubs. Bonnie Glass, for instance, arranged a "Mephisto Ball" at the Café Montmartre in which patrons were to wear "some suggestion of red."[10] One team held an "Apache Night" at Bustanoby's restaurant-cabaret (on West Thirty-ninth Street) for which the club was decorated like an Apache "den" and the public was asked to dress in Parisian-styled "underworld" outfits. The professional dancers, of course in costume, kicked off the evening's revels by introducing a variety of ballroom numbers that the public eagerly imitated.[11]

The dancer-hosts frequently judged dance contests, healthy outlets for the competition that had developed among social dancers. Joan Sawyer, at her Persian Garden Club in the Winter Garden Building,

led such dance contests and personally awarded trophies to the winners.[12] For an entire week, the Strand Roof Garden (on West Forty-
seventh Street) ran contests to find the best one-step couple from each
of New York's boroughs. Referred to as "Queens Night," "Bronx Night,"
and so on, the competitions led up to an "Interborough Finals" night
at which a professional dance team chose the champions.[13]

Exhibition ballroom teams also presided over afternoon "tea dansants" held in the cabaret. Alternately called "matinee dances" or "tango
teas," these afternoon soirées were really opportunities for men and
women to socialize and learn ballroom dance from professionals. A one-
dollar admission fee entitled guests to fifty cents worth of tea or liquor.
The tea dances became so popular that department stores even held
them as a diversion for their afternoon customers.[14] Of course, the
dancers didn't host merely for the pleasure of it. Hosting a matinee
dance was generally profitable with an average take of 50 percent of
the admission charge, plus 15 to 20 percent of the refreshment sale.[15]

Not everyone approved of the profit and pleasure of the tea dance,
however. As the tea dances increased in popularity, they invited sharp
criticism from social reformers. Although this time was seeing relatively
relaxed mores between the sexes, it was also an era of intense reform
efforts. Women and men lobbied vigorously to eradicate a variety of
social ills created by industrialization, including poverty, poor working
conditions, and prostitution, and the well-being of the new class of young
working women, drawn to the new popular amusements such as cabarets and dance halls, was a top priority.[16] Commentator Ethel Watts
Mumford worried, for example, that the unprecedented numbers of
women drawn to the tea dances might succumb to the wiles of the "tango
pirates"—the popular name then for gigolos. In her January 1914 article "Where Is Your Daughter This Afternoon," Mumford asked, "Just
what is an afternoon tea? Do you picture it, oh, New York Mother, as
a peaceful gathering over a silver pot and a steaming cup?"[17]

In response to such outbursts, cabaret owners began advertising their
dansants as opportunities to learn "graceful" and "refined" ballroom
dance from the finest exhibition ballroom teams. They also emphasized
the health benefits to be gained from this afternoon exercise. Irene
Castle herself, in a 1914 article entitled "What is a *Thé Dansant?*", noted
that this new amusement is "taking the place of the old-fashioned afternoon tea."[18]

In fact, Irene and Vernon Castle as well as other prominent teams
made an all-out effort to ease this clash. For example, at Castle House,
their dance school, the team sponsored events similar to the subscription dances of the late nineteenth century, in which only invited guests
could attend. They sent invitations asking guests to become members
of the "Castle Tango Club." The fee for the dance series, which in-

cluded tea and the opportunity to dance with Vernon Castle, cost fifteen dollars—a large sum for that time.[19] By creating a hint of exclusivity, the Castles seemingly hoped to preserve some of the more traditional values associated with ballroom dancing.

THE TEAMS AND THEIR DANCES

The potential financial reward of the cabaret actually lured all classes of teams; the amateur dancer, the dance teacher wanting to break into the field, and the professionals. Arthur Murray and Oscar Duryea (a one-time president of the Dance Masters Association) were two prominent teachers who doubled as performers. The most popular and frequently reviewed cabaret teams, however, tended to be those with some prior professional dance experience, such as Maurice and Florence Walton, Irene and Vernon Castle, Joan Sawyer, Clifton Webb and Mae Murray, and the Dolly Sisters. Many of these dancers were fresh from musical theatre or vaudeville engagements publicized in local newspapers so that audiences knew of many of them.

Average teams earned between $60 and $125 a week, depending on their ability and popularity, while the best of the "class" teams earned up to $500 for week-long cabaret engagements.[20] The higher-paid teams certainly felt justified in claiming these salaries. For one thing, their clothing expenses were exhorbitant since female dancers were expected to make from three to six costume changes weekly. Also, cabaret dancing was extremely demanding. Typically the dancers made two appearances nightly. With constantly changing audiences, teams had to vary their routines and cater to the differing moods of each crowd.

Sometimes the crowd's mood demanded an on-the-spot creation. Irene and Vernon Castle, for example, supposedly "invented" their renowned Castle Walk during an engagement in 1912 at Louis Martin's fashionable cabaret in New York City. While doing the basic one-step, a series of smooth walking steps taken to each beat of the music, the Castles simply hopped up on each beat. Thus the Castle Walk; novel yet easy to perform. It caught on instantly with the public.[21]

Exhibition ballroom dancers used numerous techniques to sustain audience interest. Some used costume to highlight the dance's theme. In one of her specialty numbers called the "Tipperary Trot," ballroom dancer Bonnie Glass sported a pleated skirt resembling a Scottish kilt and tartan cap and scarf.[22] Trickier dancing often accompanied these themes as well. Others actively cultivated various personas. A popular team image was the American woman paired with a European (or at least "European looking") male partner. The highly popular ballroom dancer Maurice Mouvet, of the team of Maurice and Walton, was actually born in Brooklyn, but was described by the press alternately as

French, Belgian, or Swiss.[23] His European "air," cultivated by his extensive performances in Western Europe, coupled with the dark-haired, sultry-looking Walton produced a magnetic, mysterious team image.

CABARET FAVORITES

Maurice and Florence Walton adapted well to the rigors of cabaret life and became two of the cabaret's earliest stars. In 1911 at Louis Martin's, the popular Broadway restaurant-cabaret, they introduced their exhibition tangos, turkey trots, and Apache dance to the burgeoning cabaret public. Their Apache dance, in particular, established Maurice and Walton as dancers of imagination and verve. Performed for late-night patrons only, this highly physical "Dance of the Underworld" began in a slow waltz and concluded in a death-defying spin, in which Walton clutched her arms around her partner's neck and whirled around him like "a floating sash."[24]

From 1911 through 1914 Maurice and Walton, with the Castles, set the standards by which other teams were measured. Recognizing Maurice and Walton's vast popularity, the Shuberts hired them in 1914 as managers of their restaurant-cabaret, The Parisian Room, located in their Palais de Danse roof garden. Aptly, management renamed the restaurant "Chez Maurice." One of the more stylish after-hours clubs along Broadway, Chez Maurice brimmed with potted palms and glistening chandeliers, and featured murals designed by Leon Bakst.[25] It held up to 400 diners, with a dance floor in the center of the room. Maurice and Walton performed there nightly from 11 p.m. to 2 a.m., and supervised all of the room's entertainments and dance contests.[26]

Maurice and Walton generally opened their act with their standard favorites, perhaps the Maurice Tango, then a hesitation waltz and one-step plus a new specialty dance, followed by an encore. One specialty dance that caught on with the public was the Canter Waltz, basically a combination of the lame duck step of the waltz and a long gliding step.[27] (In the lame duck step, introduced by Vernon Castle, the man starts forward on his left foot and performs a half-sliding dip and limps slightly for two counts.)

During their stint at Chez Maurice, Maurice and Walton introduced intriguing ballroom numbers based on European folk dances, such as the French Pericon, which was "one of the most beautiful drawing-room dances we have ever done," according to Florence Walton, and their own variation of the Portuguese Lulu Fado.[28] While these impressive exhibition dances demonstrated Maurice and Walton's versatility, they were not the ones that eventually caught on with the public. Most probably Maurice and Walton brought these dances, more traditional in style, into their repertoire to assuage moralists' objections about modern cabaret dancing. Whatever they performed, however, critics and public alike were enthusiastic. Even after their contract with the Shuberts expired in 1915, Maurice and Walton continued to perform at other fashionable clubs and in vaudeville.

The team that constantly crossed paths with Maurice and Walton were Irene and Vernon Castle, who made their New York City debut at Louis Martin's cabaret in 1912. The rivalry seemed only to increase the team's popularity. When *The New York Times* reported on their earlier success in France and their brush with European nobility the public was primed for the Castles' return to the United States.[29] At Louis Martin's, the Castles dazzled New Yorkers as they did the Parisians. At midnight a drum roll sounded and spotlights signaled the public to clear the dance floor. The Castles rose from a table in the audience and seemingly glided to the dance floor. The idea was for the audience to identify with the performers and this habit of rising from their midst soon caught on with other exhibition ballroom dancers.[30] Typically the Castles opened their act with the Castle Walk—their signature dance—and followed it with a one-step, an Argentine tango, and a Brazilian maxixe, and concluded with a specialty number.[31]

THE "QUEEN" OF EXHIBITION BALLROOM DANCING

Joan Sawyer made her name in the cabaret. Labeled by the press as the "queen" of exhibition ballroom dance, Sawyer continually developed new and intriguing dance acts. After her brief engagement with Maurice Mouvet at the Louis Martin's cabaret in 1911, Sawyer received offers to appear at several other fashionable New York City cabarets. In 1913 theatrical agent William Morris put her under contract and featured her (along with several other ballroom teams) at his Jardin de Danse cabaret at the New York Theatre.[32] This was Sawyer's first extended engagement and one for which she eventually received top billing. After her success at the Jardin de Danse, other club owners and managers showered her with tantalizing offers.

For example, while still performing at Morris's club in 1913, she received an offer from the manager of Rector's cabaret in Chicago who wanted to "borrow" her for an appearance. He offered her $1,200 for a week-long engagement, the highest amount she had commanded yet. Morris consented to the arrangement, but only under the condition that Rector's pay the Jardin de Danse a bonus of $1,000 weekly during Sawyer's absence.[33]

Sawyer moved quickly up the exhibition ballroom dance ladder. In January of 1914, the Shuberts contracted her as general manager and hostess of their dance club, The Persian Garden, in the Winter Garden Building above The Perisian Room restaurant-cabaret (where Maurice and Walton would perform a few months later). Sawyer's rigorous performance schedule included evening appearances between 11 p.m. and 1 a.m. (except on Sundays) and weekday performances at the tea dances. She also supervised all dance activities, including contests and dance lessons.[34]

Accompanied by her Persian Garden Orchestra, Sawyer presented basic tangos, maxixes, and one-steps flavored with innovative numbers, such as her Aeroplane Waltz, a picturesque dance choreographed to represent the movements of an airplane. The dance was basically a hesitation waltz, consisting of distinctive sways and glides during the "hesitating" sequences. The names of the steps reflected the dance: "preparing the aeroplane," "leaving the hangar," and "spiral flight."[35]

The Aeroplane Waltz is an interesting example of how ballroom teams borrowed and combined steps and movement phrases from each other to create entirely new ones. For example, it began in a tango pose and incorporated a criss-cross step similar to the scissors (also of the tango) and the lame duck step, characteristic of the Castles' basic waltz. The Aeroplane Waltz was such a huge success that Sawyer copyrighted instructions that were published widely in syndicated newspapers and in sheet music. Many dance teachers liked the Aeroplane Waltz and taught versions of it to their students. Other professional teams adapted it as well.

Like other ballroom dancers managing clubs, Sawyer worked on a percentage basis, earning a weekly 25 percent profit on the club's intake. Her contract differed from others in its stipulation that if the gross weekly receipts from the cabaret fell below $2,500 for two or three consecutive weeks, she had the power to terminate the contract. Indeed, when Maurice and Walton began their engagement at The Parisian Room, one flight down, in the fall of 1914, the attendance rate at Sawyer's club dropped considerably. This would seem to explain her decision not to renew her contract at the end of the season.[36]

OTHER NOTABLE TEAMS

As the "hostessing" idea caught on in the cabarets, the ever-enterprising Shuberts extended their base of operation. At their roof-garden club The Folies Marigny, set atop the Forty-fourth Street theatre, they hired the attractive and personable Mae Murray as mistress of ceremonies. Murray was fresh from an extended engagement at William Morris's Jardin de Danse. The Folies Marigny (which later became Castles in the Air) was a popular evening spot, boasting a dance floor that held up to ninety couples. Murray, who by now had made a name as a ballroom dancer in the popular clubs, had considerable drawing power. Like Sawyer, she invented many of her own dances. Murray performed

there nightly during the spring of 1914, with a variety of male partners.[37]

One of her most popular and physically attractive partners at the
Folies Marigny was Clifton Webb. Webb's partnership with Bonnie Glass
had dissolved so Murray quickly snatched him up for her act. His dark
features and cool demeanor set the perfect counterpoint to Murray's
blonde, sylph-like aura. Part of Mae Murray's appeal lay in her arresting physical appearance; she traditionally danced with a long scarf tied
around her neck (Murray was credited with starting the scarf fad among
women ballroom dancers) and struck artistic-looking poses. The May
1914 program from the club describes an elegantly staged cabaret show
choreographed by Jack Mason, with Murray and Webb as the star performers.[38]

The floor show began when the house lights dimmed and white spotlights were thrown onto the four corners of the dance floor. For the
opening number four female dancers entered, performing to a tango
rhythm. Through song they invited four men (planted in the balcony)ment
to accompany them in the dance. All eight couples then whirled through
the spirited ensemble number. Several variety acts followed, including
ragtime singer Harry Carroll, and a comedian. The finale was the ballroom routine of Murray and Webb. They opened with a Brazilian
maxixe, followed by the "Barcarole Waltz," Murray's version of the hesitation waltz, and closed with a number called the Cinquante-Cin-
quante, a variation of the Castles' Half and Half. For an encore they
performed the Pavlova Gavotte, a dance inspired by the Russian balle-
rina, and adopted widely by exhibition ballroom teams.[39]

The colorful Dolly Sisters were also favorites on the New York cabaret scene. After a two-year span in which each of the twin sisters performed with a male partner, they reunited as a tandem-ballroom team
and joined William Morris' roster of prominent ballroom dancers at his
Jardin de Danse cabaret. For their fall 1914 engagement they teamed
up with noted musical comedy performer Carlos Sebastian, who accompanied them in unusual ballroom duos and trios.

For each of their four numbers the dancers wore costumes and incorporated the footwork and positions of contemporary ballroom dance.
In their first dance, the Dolly Waltz, the team appeared in airy, Gre-
cian-like frocks, and executed this unique waltz in a side-by-side position, mirroring each other's kicks, pirouettes, and gliding steps.[40] Following the opener, Carlos Sebastian and Jenny Dolly entered, clothed
in what were described as "Castillian" costumes, and performed the
"Papalatsa," which appeared to be a variation on the maxixe.

Sebastian reappeared with Roszika Dolly for their third number, the
"Arhumba" (also known as the Havana Rhumba). Roszika created a
captivating picture in her fringed, bare-back dress and "abbreviated

stockings." It appears that this rumba bore little resemblance to the rumba popularized in the early 1930s, which contained distinctive, rhythmic hip movements performed to a moderate tempo, and a box-step sequence. The Havana Rhumba also included a basic box-step, but it contained slides to the left and to the right and a periodic foot stomping (reminiscent of folk dance movements.)[41] The final number in the Dolly Sisters' act was a novel trio dance named the High School Gallop. For this quick one-step, the twin sisters donned pony masks with ears while Sebastian, dressed as a riding master, "coaxed" the Dolly Sisters around the stage. The "trotting" steps characteristic of this dance could have been performed to any basic one-step or rag rhythm.[42]

KEEPING UP INTEREST

By 1915, many cabaret owners began devising new forms of entertainment to vary their programs and thus boost their trade. Although the exhibition ballroom teams were still very popular, some cabarets were reportedly losing money because of the high salaries demanded by the exhibition ballroom dance teams.[43] To remedy the situation, theatrical producer Florenz Ziegfeld pioneered a form of entertainment that quickly took root in the cabaret community—the midnight revue.[44] At his roof-garden cabaret, The Danse de Follies, set atop the New Amsterdam Theatre at Broadway and Forty-second street, Ziegfeld mounted the highly successful *Ziegfeld Midnight Frolic*. This more expansive form of cabaret entertainment—which ran year-round from 1915 through 1921—helped draw more crowds and presented new opportunities for ballroom dancers.

Ziegfeld's renovations at the Danse de Follies preserved the cabaret's sense of intimacy. Ziegfeld enlarged the already existing dance floor and lowered the former stage to floor level, increasing the performance area. Clusters of small tables bounded the dance floor on three sides, so that the public would remain close to the teams as they performed. The fourth side contained a large curtain by the designer Joseph Urban, which filled the high, square proscenium arch.[45] At either side of the dance floor were steps leading to a balcony, also crowded with tables. A unique feature of this cabaret was its glass walkway, located directly under the balcony and used as a performance area. The balcony and accompanying walkway were of a horseshoe shape and paralleled the layout of the tables that surrounded the dance floor.

The revue itself consisted of a series of variety acts grouped together into a lavishly designed fifty-minute show. Although Ziegfeld's emphasis was on the presentation of more elaborate musical and chorus numbers (many of them imported from *The Ziegfeld Follies*, one flight below), exhibition ballroom dancers still formed an important part of the evening's entertainment. In fact, Ziegfeld and his dance directors devised some clever and innovative uses of ballroom forms. For instance, often one ballroom dance form provided the dominant motif or "theme" of the show. The February 1915 edition of the *Frolics* highlighted the tango. An early number, called "My Tango Girl," consisted of lead singer Muriel Hudson attended by a bevy of appropriately clothed "tango girls." Other numbers featured tightrope walker Bird Millman, who performed her dancing act, "Tango in the Air," and solo tangoist Isabella Rodriguez, who danced along the glass walkway.[46] Other well-known ballroom dancers, such as the Dolly Sisters, graced the stage of *The Midnight Frolics* with their unusual and arresting ballroom dance variations.

The ballroom numbers in the show still stimulated dancing among the patrons. Before and after the show, and at twenty-minute intervals, social dancers swarmed to the large dance floor. An orchestra, seated on either side of the proscenium ara, supplied a steady accompaniment for the latest one-steps, tangos, and fox-trots. Ziegfeld himself tried to promote audience involvement directly with the show. The program for the *Frolics* of 1915 cited the intermission as an actual part of the show, billing it as "cast—the patrons; scene—the dancing floor of the Danse de Follies."[47]

The cabaret remained a highly popular entertainment establishment throughout the teens, but Prohibition was destined to ruin its existence. As early as 1917 many clubs had banned serving liquor past one a.m. By January 16, 1920—when Prohibition became official—most cabarets had already closed or were attempting last-ditch efforts to salvage their businesses. Some clubs presented leading orchestras or elaborate vaudeville acts as a ruse to draw in customers. But as one *Variety* commentator remarked concerning the current cabaret atmosphere, "The patron is 'nicked' heavy for couvert, the food and the thrill are lacking and patronage slack."[48] Without the liquor income, cabaret owners could not profitably operate their dance floors, many of which were quite large. Neither could they afford the salaries of the top exhibition ballroom teams. Thus, without the cabaret, ballroom teams lost a major venue for professional work. Exhibition ballroom teams continued to perform in the nightclubs of the twenties, but they no longer enjoyed the same prominence as they once did in the cabaret of the teens.

NOTES

1. I. B. Pulaski, "Origin of the Cabaret," *Variety*, 20 December 1912, p. 51.

2. Julius Keller, *Inns and Outs* (New York: G. P. Putnam's Sons, 1939), pp. 154–155.

3. Lewis A. Erenberg, *Steppin' Out: New York Nightlife and the Transformation of American Culture*, pp. 75–76.

4. Ibid., pp. 115–116.

5. Ibid., pp. 75–77, 114–119.

6. "The Dance Craze," *Variety*, 25 December 1914, p. 8; *Variety*, 2 March 1913, p. 17.

7. *Variety*, 11 April 1913.

8. See Stephen Burge Johnson, "The Roof Gardens of Broadway Theatres," for a full discussion of roof-garden entertainment.

9. *Variety*, 26 December 1913.

10. Unidentified newspaper clipping (Bonnie Glass clipping file, BRTC).

11. "A Night with the Apaches of Paris Underworld," *The New York Review*, 18 January 1913.

12. *The New York Review*, 2 March 1914, p. 6.

13. Program, Strand Theatre, ca. 1913 (Adelaide and Hughes clipping file, BRTC).

14. "Department Store Tango Now Going on at Gimbels," *Variety*, 3 March 1914, p. 6. For more on the *thé dansant* see *Variety*, 17 March 1914, p. 201; Harrydele Hallmark, "If You Dance You Must Pay the Piper," *Vogue*, January 15, 1914.

15. *Palais de Danse*, Contracts, Groups I-IV, II, 88, The Shubert Archive.

16. For further discussion of United States progressive era history and the concern about new entertainment forms and women see Glenda Riley, *Inventing the American Woman: A Perspective on Women's History 1865 to the Present* (Arlington Heights, IL: Harlan Davidson, Inc.); Sara M. Evans, *Born for Liberty: A History of Women in America* (New York: The Free Press, Macmillan).

17. Ethel Watts Mumford, "Where is Your Daughter This Afternoon?" *Harper's Weekly*, 17 January 1914, p. 28.

18. Irene Castle, "What is a *Thé Dansant*?", *The Delineator*, May 1914, p. 10. To calm some of these criticisms one restaurant-cabaret, Shanley's, initiated a campaign to bring traditional folk dancing to the club. They hired the well-known dance teacher Louis Chalif to teach contra-dancing in an effort to "supplant the present popular evolutions." See "Contra Dances Innovation at Shanley's," *The New York Review*, 12 April 1913, p. 14.

19. Invitation (Irene and Vernon Castle folder no. 1, folio II, Theatre Collection, The Museum of the City of New York).

20. *Variety*, 17 October 1913.

21. Mrs. Vernon Castle, *My Husband* (New York: Charles Scribner & Sons, 1919; reprint ed., New York: Da Capo Press, 1979), p. 54.

22. "Bonnie Glass A Pretty and Popular Dancer at Cabarets," *Metropolitan* magazine, March 1916 (Bonnie Glass scrapbook, NAFR + ser. 2, BRTC).

23. "Mons. Maurice Says," *The New York Review*, 31 October 1914; "Maurice Mouvet, Dancer, Is Dead In Switzerland," *The Herald Tribune*, 19 May 1927; Mouvet, *Maurice's Art of Dancing*. Also see Erenberg, *Steppin' Out*, for discussion of Mouvet, p. 165.

24. Keller, *Inns and Outs* (New York: G. P. Putnam's Sons, 1930) p. 168. The Apache was very similar to the whirlwind (see Appendix B), except that the whirlwind was not a characterizational dance like the Apache.

25. The *Palais de Danse* was, in fact, not an actual roof-garden theatre. It was located above and to the side of the Winter Garden Theatre and did not contain a proscenium stage as did classic roof gardens. For further descriptions of the Palais de Danse and of Chez Maurice specifically, see *The New York Review*, 12 April 1913, p. 4; *Variety*, 21 March 1913, p. 17; *The New York Dramatic News*, 24 October 1914.

26. *Palais de Danse*, Contracts, Group I-IV, II, 88, The Shubert Archive.

27. *The Dancing Times*, April 1915, pp. 235–236.

29. For a filmed rendition of the Lulu Fado see *Theatrical and social Dancing: 1909–1936*, DC-NYPL.

29. See "Mr. and Mrs. Castle Blythe Make Great Hit in Unexpurgated Dances," *The New York Times*, 10 July 1912 (Irene and Vernon Castle scrapbook, 21,499, p. 85, BRTC).

30. Castle, *Castles in the Air*, pp. 66–67; Erenberg, *Steppin' Out*, p. 126.

31. Program, Rector's Cabaret (Chicago), ca. 1913 (Irene and Vernon Castle scrapbook, 21,499, p. 85, BRTC).

32. "Chicago Makes High Bid for Society Dancer," *Variety*, ca. 1913 (Irene and Vernon Castle scrapbook, 21,499, p. 85 (BRTC).

33. Ibid.

34. *Palais de Danse*, Contracts (Groups I-IV, II, 88, The Shubert Archive).

35. "Pivot Steps and Glides Chief Motions in Aeroplane Waltz, says Joan Sawyer," unidentified newspaper clipping (Joan Sawyer clipping file, BRTC). For sheet music cover featuring Sawyer in the Aeroplane Waltz and accompanying instructions see Ragtime Sheet Music Collection (1914), The Shubert Archive. Also see The Bella Landauer Sheet Music Collection, Box 4, Waltz (folder 23), The New York Historical Society.

36. See *Palais de Dance* contract, and *Variety*, 31 December 1914, p. 23.

37. *Variety*, 24 April 1914, p. 18; *The New York Clipper*, 16 May 1914, p. 7.

38. *The New York Review*, 9 May 1914.

39. *The New York Clipper*, 21, 28, March 1914; *Variety*, 1 May 1914; *The New York Dramatic Mirror*, 6, 8, May 1914, pp. 16, 19.

40. "The Dolly Waltz and How to Dance It," undated clipping in the *The Buffalo Enquirer* (The Dolly Sisters scrapbook, Robinson Locke Collection, ser. 2, vol. 127, BRTC).

41. "Cuba Contributes to the Rhumba," *The Newark Star-Eagle*, 25 October 1915; *Variety*, 29 May 1914; *The New York Tribune*, 5 May 1914 (The Dolly Sisters scrapbook, Robinson Locke Collection, ser. 2, vol. 127, BRTC).

42. Variety, 15 May 1914; *The New York Dramatic Mirror*, 3 June 1914.

43. Johnson, *The Roof Gardens of Broadway Theatres*, Chapter 8, p. 18.

44. "Cabaret Girly Revues Spreading Over New York," *Variety*, 26 March 1915, p. 5.

45. Johnson, *The Roof Gardens of Broadway Theatres*, Chapter 8, p. 22.

46. *Variety*, 20 February 1915, p. 13.

47. 1915 programs for *Ziegfeld Midnight Frolics* (Ziegfeld Midnight Frolics program file, BRTC).

48. "Chicago Raids to Close Most All City Cabarets," *The New York Clipper*, 1 December 1920, p. 7; "The Cabaret," *Variety*, 30 December 1921, p. 3.

Chapter 4

Taking the Palace by Storm: Exhibition Ballroom Dance in Vaudeville of the Teens and Twenties

Novelty is the thing with the modern dancers. Anything unusual is considered the only dancing step in the right direction just now. The terpsichorean stars who possess ideas and imagination are the ones who will survive and win the maximum of applause.

New York Dramatic Mirror, July 29, 1914

This entertainment critic accurately summed up the state of ballroom (or so-called "modern") dance in vaudeville during the 1910s. From approximately 1911–1916 exhibition ballroom dance numbers saturated vaudeville. In addition to renditions by the standard exhibition ballroom teams, many other kinds of vaudeville teams, including song and dance couples, comedy duos, and singing acts, devised ingenious ways to incorporate ballroom work into their routines. The great numbers of teams performing exhibition ballroom dance and the resulting competition that ensued forced teams to come up with new and intriguing acts. Indeed, some of the most novel and innovative numbers originated in vaudeville.

The proliferation of exhibition ballroom teams coincided with vaudeville's heyday. Like the cabaret, dance hall, phonograph, and moving pictures, vaudeville was part of a new wave of leisure activities popular with audiences in an increasingly urban, industrialized America. By now an entirely "respectable" entertainment (no longer associated with the moral indecencies of its predecessor, the all-male concert saloon),

vaudeville drew unprecedented numbers of men, women, and children
into its audiences. To appeal to this increasingly mixed-sex, middle-
class audience, vaudeville gradually moved away from acts dealing with
overt sexuality to those focusing more on the concerns of romance,
courtship, and marriage. Exhibition ballroom acts were part of this trend
toward the "domestication" of vaudeville acts, offering vivid yet "gen-
teel" images of romance appealing to both sexes.[1]

The enthusiasm for ballroom dancers swelled quickly, in part because vaudeville's reach extended to hundreds of cities and towns across
the country. As an industry, vaudeville of the teens consisted of several
national circuits that owned theatres and controlled their bookings. Two
of the largest were the Keith-Albee chain, which operated theatres in
the east, and the Orpheum circuit, which controlled theatres west of
Chicago. In addition to these and other circuits there were hundreds
of small, independent theatres presenting variety entertainment across
the country. Theatres were generally distinguished as either "small-time,"
those located in small towns and neighborhoods offering four to five
shows a day, and "big-time," found in major cities, featuring two shows
a day with name performers.[2]

At the big-time vaudeville houses during the teens, audiences could
often see half a dozen star performers in a single evening. To provide
the best possible entertainers, vaudeville managers poured large sums
of money into acts employing top names from the legitimate and musical theatre. In order to satisfy an audience now educated in the conventions and traditions of vaudeville, managers continually sought out
novel acts and entertainers. Stars imported from the musical theatre,
for example, impressed female vaudeville spectators with their smart,
stylish clothing. Exhibition ballroom dancers, with their elegant and up-
to-date outfits, their star status, and their intimate couple dances, represented the epitome of glamour and romance.

For the predominantly middle-class audience to which the big-time
catered, exhibition ballroom teams had an immediate appeal. Audiences had become familiar with many of the exhibition teams from the
cabaret and dance halls, and had practiced many of the new social dances
themselves. Others were familiar with the teams because their dances
were recognizable through advertising in mass-subscription magazines
and newspapers. The exhibition teams were particularly popular because of their image as exemplars of grace and their hint of high society. Through them, audiences could express vicarious social aspirations.

Vaudeville houses catered to the burgeoning dance craze in several
ways. A frequent practice during the teens and twenties was to trans-
form lobbies or other public spaces in theatres into makeshift ballrooms
for social dancing by patrons during intermissions. In 1915, for ex-

ample, managers of New York's Century Theatre provided social dancing in the Vanderbilt Room on its mezzanine floor.[3] Star exhibition ballroom teams were often placed in the spot on the bill just before intermission. Thus, "lobby dancing" offered audiences an outlet after being inspired by the professional dancers.

Ballroom dance "lessons" conducted by teams were another innovation in audience attraction. These were usually conducted after matinee performances. During her 1914 tour, specialty dancer Gertrude Hoffmann gave an "afternoon tea" on the stage of Cleveland's Colonial Theatre, demonstrating the tango with her partner, Lee Chapin. The local newspaper explained that "They will show just how the Tango should be danced and let each person form his or her opinion."[4] During the performance of the team of Vera Maxwell and Wallace Mc-Cutcheon, popular during the 1913–1914 season, the couple invited members of the audience onto the stage to dance with them.[5] Clearly these ploys were designed to foster publicity for the team, but in a larger sense they directly fed the public's appetite for social dancing as well. This audience involvement was a part of vaudeville's unique ability to draw audiences into the energy and excitement of the entertainment.

By the 1911–1912 season, vaudeville bills at the major New York houses featured at least one or two exhibition ballroom teams, generally referred to as "ballroom dancers," "modern dancers," or "society dancers," depending on the billing practice of the particular house. The measure of their star status was reflected in their coveted placement on the vaudeville bill. At the peak of their popularity, the teams usually received prominent billing in the number-five spot on a nine-act bill, just before intermission. Although not quite as enviable as the fourth or seventh spots (the next-to-closing act) the fifth was a favored position since it was the climax of the first act. Typically, when two ballroom teams appeared on the same bill, one team appeared before and the other immediately following intermission. Thus, at critical points in the bill, ballroom teams served to rouse and then sustain audience enthusiasm.[6]

It was not enough, however, for these dance teams simply to transplant a cabaret act or musical theatre number to the vaudeville stage. For vaudeville audiences expecting novelty, excitement, and variety, the cabaret teams had to expand their dance routines into fully formed acts, interpolating singing or dialogue, or comedy. One of the challenges of vaudeville was performing to a heterogeneous crowd, which, for the teams, meant presenting numbers that were varied and appealing to a range of tastes. Many a team was mercilessly censured by critics for an act lacking the necessary bounce and vigor. In addition to originality, a prerequisite for all of the teams was sufficient sense of grace, style, and "class," as the reviewers noted, to win over an audience.[7]

"STEPPERS OF VARIED SCHOOLS"[8]

The Standard Teams

Many ballroom teams began as little-known and struggling vaudeville performers eager to break into the business. Spurred on by enthusiastic booking agents, these novices donned tuxedos and ballroom gowns and polished their ballroom technique. Comedian George Burns actually started out in this way. After several thwarted attempts at establishing himself as a vaudeville comic, Burns turned to ballroom work. Encouraged by the success of such teams as Irene and Vernon Castle, whom he had seen perform, Burns attempted a similar act. Like other newcomers, he perfected his ballroom abilities by dancing at local dance halls and by entering dance contests.

At one contest Burns chose the young Hannah Siegal as his partner. She changed her name to Hermosa José (to reflect their Latin-flavored act), and as Burns and José they won several dance competitions, which led to short engagements in and around New York. As George Burns reminisced years later, "She wore a bright red dress covered with rhinestones. It had only one sleeve. . . . I wore a 'walk up a flight and save $10' full dress suit that was supposed to be black but after one cleaning turned green."[9] Their native abilities won out, however, and the team secured a thirty-six week road tour performing their Spanish-style ballroom act. Burns and José split up as a team after the tour, but for Burns, the brief foray into ballroom dancing was invaluable, since it afforded him important professional experience and exposure.

Of course, the most popular ballroom dancers on the vaudeville circuit were those "name" teams with established reputations in the cabaret or in musical theatre. The best of these teams, including Maurice and Walton, the Castles, and Joan Sawyer and Wallace McCutcheon, starred at the major New York City vaudeville houses, such as the Victoria, the Colonial, the Riverside, and the Palace. These "straight" or "standard" acts as they were known, generally revolved solely around the dances, in contrast to other kinds of ballroom acts in which the dance was an embellishment for song or dialogue.

The basic format of the standard teams was similar: a set of four or five dances, including variations on the tango, maxixe, one-step, and hesitation waltz. Because of the competition among dancers, however, and the nature of vaudeville, which prided itself on the new and unusual, it became imperative for teams to differentiate themselves from one another. Some varied individual steps in the set dances. They might, for example, embellish a basic one-step by incorporating solo breakaway movements, or add ballet steps to their hesitation waltz. Typically, the dancers named these new dances after themselves for promotional purposes, such as the "Dolly Waltz," the "Sascha Rag," and the "Clifford Trot," to name just a few.[10] Many ballroom teams achieved distinction through a particular method of stylization—a lyrical, interpretive mode, for instance, or perhaps an acrobatic mode, characterized by lifts and fast turns. Of course, the most popular of the teams were those that invented unique innovations and possessed that indefinable star quality that transcended the dances.

Irene and Vernon Castle had already achieved success in the cabaret, with their school—Castle House—and through promotion in leading society and fashion magazines. However, the Castles were slow to arrive in vaudeville. Irene Castle herself admitted that she didn't particularly like performing in vaudeville; she hated two shows a day and preferred instead the intimate atmosphere of the cabaret.[11] Despite the fact that the Castles went into vaudeville largely when they were hard up, they became instant Keith headliners, billed as the "World's Greatest Society Dancers." Of their 1914 engagement at the Colonial, one reviewer remarked that "it is relieving to know that the Castles have given the varieties their stamp of approval."[12]

Because of their fame, the Castles did not experience pressure felt by some other teams to continually diversify and expand their repertoire. Normally their standard act consisted of three or four dances and an encore. In their January 1914 engagement at the Palace, for example, the team performed (in sequence) their Tango Argentine, Maxixe Brésilienne, and Castle Walk.[13] In many ways, the Castles' act was atypical of standard ballroom acts in that it reflected the self-consciousness of their identity as America's foremost exhibition ballroom team. At performances during their 1914 cross-country tour, Vernon Castle would advance to the footlights and preface the act with advice on how it ought to be performed, should audience members attempt it themselves. Only after this introduction did Irene Castle then enter from the wings for the team's performance.[14]

The Castles' rivals, Maurice and Florence Walton, made more frequent forays into vaudeville, attempting to turn their acts into highly elegant, stylized affairs. Their basic act from the teens is a good example of how ballroom dancers adapted their material to the requirements of vaudeville, by interpolating music, flashy dances, and other bits of novelty. For one, the announcement of their act on the bill prepared the audience for something special: "Maurice and Walton: Sec-

ond Big Week, Back from France on a Short Furlough." After three or
four numbers, including a Syncopated Fox Trot and Maurice's Step
Dance, the team inserted a classy touch, an interlude by violin soloist
"Monsieur Dolin." Their act concluded with a number that they presumably brought back with them from Europe, such as their Chasseurs
Fox Trot, "as danced at the front by Mr. Maurice and Miss Walton for
the French and English soldiers." Maurice and Walton alternately closed
this act with their renowned Apache dance—always a sure crowd-
pleaser.[15]

Ballroom dancer Joan Sawyer, like the Castles and Maurice and Walton, had established her reputation in New York City's cabarets, but
she won particular acclaim in vaudeville. Both an innovator and popu-
larizer, Sawyer knew how to construct an act designed to appeal to a
wide variety of tastes and styles. No doubt her early vaudeville career
as part of a singing act prepared her for the rigors of this entertainment form.[16] Sawyer's vaudeville routines of the teens were unique
amalgams of exhibition ballroom routines, popular vaudeville ballet
numbers, and contemporary interpretive dance.

Her 1914 engagement at the Palace Theatre with the talented partner Jack Jarrott bore the Sawyer stamp of originality. She entered re-
gally with typical dramatic flair, in her long black gown, with a pink
scarf swirled about her neck. After the team's highly acclaimed Aeroplane Waltz and Argentine Maxixe, they launched into a new addition
to the repertoire called the Three-in-One, combining steps from three
popular exhibition ballroom dances—the one-step, hesitation waltz, and
tango. Another new dance, the Congo Tongo, most likely choreographed by Jarrott, was a ragtime one-step incorporating breakaway
movements. At various points Jarrott performed a solo buck-and-wing
movement and then resumed the dance with Sawyer.[17]

During her 1914 summer season at the Palace, Sawyer diversified her
act further by drawing on motifs from currently popular ballet and
vaudeville dance routines. The richly adorned set of heavy, blue velvet
curtains created a striking background for Sawyer who emerged dressed
in a white chiffon gown with a black satin sash. The number that critics
called "artistic and ambitious" was a dance performed with Lewis Slo-
den named "Dance in the Shadows" (or simply "In the Shadows").[18] It
began as spotlights were thrown on the velvet curtains, opening slowly
to reveal the couple in tableau fashion. Amid simulated lightning and
thunder, Sawyer emerged, bound in veils and barefoot as she and her
partner performed what one reviewer described as a "duet scarf dance,"
using ballet steps and tableau poses to create a picture effect. Gradually, as the thunder faded, the dancers moved upstage and disappeared
from view. After a brief musical interlude by the Clef Club Orchestra,

Sawyer returned with another partner, Bennie Dixon, for a polka and tango. The final dance in the act was the varsouvienne, an eighteenth-century ballroom dance performed in period costume, in which "the two seemed to have stepped from an old painting." [19]

Clearly, several of Sawyer's numbers were reminiscent of popular "exotic" dance styles of previous vaudeville seasons, as well as the interpretive dance style of the early modern dance pioneers. With its shedding of the veils and draperies of clothing, "In the Shadows" recalled the wildly popular "Dance of the Seven Veils," also known as the "Salome Dance," introduced in vaudeville by Mlle. Dazie in 1907, then popularized by Gertrude Hoffmann, and others. The undulating, romantic gestures and pictorial effects suggested the dancing of Isadora Duncan.

Reviewers lavished Sawyer with praise for the "beauty" and "artistry" of her acts. In fact, some observers compared her to the great Russian dancer, Anna Pavlova, in her scarf dance, the Autumn Bacchanale. Said the critic of the *New York Dramatic Mirror:* "Not that it [Sawyer's act] reveals great art of dancing, such as is caught in the pagan grace of Anna Pavlova's Bacchanale or the exquisite charm of her gavotte. But Miss Sawyer shows a commendable sense of the best in dancing and, in actual accomplishment of execution, she has achieved something which would be impossible to most of our modern dancers." [20] That "something" was Sawyer's ability to incorporate interpretive gestures and ballet poses within a conventional ballroom dance frame.

A formidable vaudeville rival to Joan Sawyer during the teens was the exhibition ballroom dancer Adelaide. In a publicity campaign designed to enhance both reputations, Joan Sawyer and Adelaide appeared on the same bill at the prestigious Palace Theatre during the summer of 1914. A veteran vaudeville performer, Adelaide, like Sawyer, understood the need for novelty in vaudeville and ingeniously adapted her material to prevailing tastes and styles. When she teamed up with J. J. Hughes in 1910, Adelaide retained the pantomimic features of her original at, but blended popular ballroom steps to create a distinct style.

For their ten record-breaking weeks at the Palace, Adelaide and Hughes developed a varied act that "kept the audience busy applauding." [21] This "song and dance act of the modern type" opened with their song rendition of 'I Like Everything About You But the Boys,' followed by a set of standard exhibition ballroom dances, including the tango and the hesitation waltz. [22] The ballroom numbers, however, were really the frame for the heart of the act, which was a pantomimic harlequinade featuring Adelaide and Hughes as Pierrette and Pierrot. The dancing-dialogue number culminated in a star turn by Adelaide.

"Putting It Over"

The ability to assemble inventive or unusual acts had clearly become a prerequisite for ballroom performers. As early as 1913, vaudeville critics were grumbling about the "hum-drummed 'society dances,'" and the "deluge of 'modern dancing.'"[23] The ballroom dance phenomenon was still at its peak, but many reviewers discerned a definite lack of variety in ballroom acts. Even a celebrated dance team like that of Rosy Dolly and Martin Brown could not escape the ire of dissatisfied critics.

While temporarily separated from her sister, Dolly had teamed up with Brown (1885–1936), her partner from the musical comedy *The Merry Countess* (1912). Their premiere vaudeville act in 1913 recreated a scene from the production in which the couple had performed a series of contemporary ballroom dances. But the critics lambasted them for failing to provide the required "punch" to carry a vaudeville act. They complained that the setting was neither lavish nor stylish enough, and that, apart from the performers' native talents, the act itself lacked surprise.[24]

After a few months of polishing up their act, in the fall of 1914 Dolly and Martin unveiled their latest vaudeville creation, a twenty-eight-minute-long "miniature revue" called *Danceland*. Considered a "gem" by one reviewer, the act consisted of a series of historical and contemporary ballroom dances spiced with the music of popular musical comedy composer Jean Schwartz. *Danceland* was a type of historical review of past and present ballroom styles, employing a narrator in Pierrot costume. The act featured several changes of elegant, elaborate clothing showing "that money had been no object in making this one of the classiest dancing acts in vaudeville."[25] A description of one scene reveals the way in which musical revue techniques were beginning to influence exhibition ballroom acts.

The act opened with a prologue in words and song by actor James Moore, dressed in a Pierrot costume. His first song, 'Old Fashioned Days,' introduced the kinds of ballroom dances seen in the seventeenth and eighteenth centuries. Directly following the song, Dolly and Brown emerged before a flowered backdrop, clothed in crinoline and ruffles, and performed a minuet and a polka. The second historical period of social dancing was introduced by the Pierrot's song, 'Classical Waltzes,' after which the team presented their Waltz Classique. The final sequence focused on the Spanish-derived social dances. Moore's song, 'Tango, I Love You,' provided Dolly and Brown the opportunity to perform their Habanera Hesitation and Galop Brazilian.[26]

The act was a hit, considered by some to be "one of the classiest dancing acts in vaudeville." The same *Variety* critic who criticized their first, unsuccessful vaudeville act quietly praised the dancers for knowing how to "frame their act for vaudeville."[27] The idea was original, the presentation "artistic," and the set and costuming appropriately lush and lavish. Their dancing, of course, possessed Dolly and Brown's usual dramatic flair. Their style was a blend of ballroom and theatrical dance steps embellished with expressive poses and gestures.

The Song and Dance Teams

Perhaps one of the best indicators of the success of exhibition ballroom dance in vaudeville was the adaptation of ballroom work by the standard song and dance teams—for years the backbone of vaudeville entertainment. Always popular vaudeville fare, the song and dance team was infused with new life around the season of 1905–1906, in part due to the influence of trends in musical theatre. The more traditional Viennese operetta importations were being upstaged by the productions of Florenz Ziegfeld and George M. Cohan, replete with their star performers, lavish costumes and sets, and novel song and dance routines.[28] Many of the most popular vaudeville song and dance teams now incorporated similar Broadway-styled material into their acts, along with ragtime tunes and topical humor, all presented in a snappy, fast-paced style.

To incorporate the new ballroom styles into their acts was also a way for teams to demonstrate their contemporaneity. The glamour, elegance, and sophistication associated with ballroom dance rendered it a perfect type of act to fit in with modern vaudeville. Some song and dance teams used ballroom dance as a specialty number to wind up an act or as a dramatic device to comment on the action of a scene. For other teams, performing in what was known as the flirtation mode, ballroom dance became a heightened visual symbol of the couples' romantic interests and allegiances.

A particularly glamorous team, representative of new vaudeville trends, was that of Jack Clifford and Evelyn Nesbit. Their sumptuous act—arriving on the heels of Nesbit's much-publicized divorce from Harry Thaw in 1913—was one of the most lucrative ever to play at Hammerstein's famous vaudeville house. Billed as "Evelyn Nesbit and Jack Clifford in their Original Song and Dances," the team wove exhibition ballroom numbers in between flirtatious songs and extravagant costume changes.

Their vaudeville act during the 1915–1916 season typically opened with the romantic song-duet 'Tumble in Love' (or as one reporter called it, "a duet built about a rustic bench"), followed by a solo song by Nesbit.[29] The act then shifted quickly to full stage, with Nesbit appearing before plush purple curtains, attired in an elegant orange gown with fur trimming. She and Clifford next performed two ballroom specialties, which they called the Evelyn Fox Trot and the Clifford Walk. The act concluded with their signature dance, an acrobatic whirlwind, in which Nesbit swung in mid-air with arms around her partner's neck.[30]

Most critics concurred with the *New York Star* reviewer who called Nesbit and Clifford's act "a great display of talent and wardrobe."[31] By 1917 they had begun to add flirtatious pantomime to their basic format: in a full-stage setting, Clifford mimed a monkey cavorting in a coconut tree while Nesbit sang to him. The act continued with a song-duet, followed by the usual whirlwind finish.[32] The enormous success of the Nesbit-Clifford act can be attributed to their sense of showmanship, as well as their swift timing, elegant sets, and attire. The exhibition ballroom numbers functioned largely as specialties designed to accent the dancers and their talents.

The popular song and dance team of William Rock and Maude Fulton discovered that exhibition ballroom dance could be adapted to their distinctive brand of performance. William Rock began his career as an eccentric comic in vaudeville and the musical theatre, while Maude Fulton started out as a chorus dancer in the Madison Square Roof Garden shows. After performing together in the musical comedy *The Orchid* in 1907, Rock and Fulton teamed up as a duo and performed in vaudeville until 1914.[33] Their distinguishing feature was their "depictions" of characters or scenes from life expressed through song and dance. In their 1908 "Dance of the Devil" number, for instance, Fulton portrayed a young girl seduced by the powers of alcohol. Its "theme" gave Rock and Fulton an opportunity to perform a variety of characterizational dances such as the Apache, the Salome dance, and their own Hypnotic Waltz.[34]

To this repertoire of characters, they soon added depictions of ballroom dancers from different walks of life. In their 1912 repertoire Rock and Fulton closed their act of song and dance medleys with an exhibition ballroom turn in which they demonstrated how contemporary social dances, such as the Turkey Trot, were performed in different parts of the country. For one number they danced the Turkey Trot in a straight, identifiable manner—supposedly as a Bostonian couple might perform it. Immediately following, they illustrated how the same dance might be performed by a pair of Quakers.[35] Presumably the constricted, straight-laced Quaker performing the spirited Turkey Trot created a humorous effect. By grafting specific characterizations onto their ballroom dances the team created entirely unique, often comic, exhibition versions of social dances.

Flirtation Acts

It was in the routines of the *flirtation* song and dance acts of the teens that ballroom dance became most synonymous with romance. The flirtation act, or domestic-flirtation two-act as it was technically called, can be traced back to the courtship sketches of the late nineteenth century that depicted humorous aspects of male-female relationships. These acts usually had happy endings and typically concluded with a sentimental song or perhaps a specialty dance of some sort. However, by the teens, with changing vaudeville audiences and changing styles of comedy, the traditional courtship sketch had gone out of favor. Their slower-paced plots and stereotyped characters did not have as great an appeal for the new vaudeville audience, accustomed as it had become to a faster-paced, telegraphic style of banter. When exhibition ballroom dance became the rage, however, the flirtation teams began using ballroom dances both to express their modernity and to symbolize the idea of love and reconciliation.[36]

A classic flirtation team was the husband-wife duo of Carter De Haven and Flora Parker. De Haven began his career as a vaudeville singer on the Orpheum Circuit, working his way up to song and dance roles in Weber and Fields productions. In 1909 he teamed up with musical comedy ingenue Flora Parker, and until 1919 the couple performed as a song and dance team in vaudeville and the musical theatre. The De Havens' dance acts used "modern" vaudeville methods, incorporating popular musical comedy songs, snappy comic patter, and contemporary dance steps. In ballroom dance they found a pertinent visual metaphor for love and marriage. Typically, after patching up their marital differences, they would express their new-found harmony with a passionate ballroom number.

One of their most popular acts was their 1914–1915 offering entitled *The Masher,* a flirtation act in four scenes. More so than their other acts, *The Masher* contained a semblance of a genuine storyline. The act revolved around a young man's courtship of a budding actress, or as one reviewer neatly summed up the "plot": "The flower of youth [De Haven] takes the beautiful actress to supper . . . he escorts her home, she shuts the door in his face—and he is left to trudge back in a thunderstorm."[37] The act opened with a song by Parker, singing about her stagefright when DeHaven rises from the audience in awe of the young woman, and sings to her of his love. After several scene changes—a stagedoor, a restaurant, and a country bungalow, where the forlorn lover is jilted by the young woman—the lovers are finally reconciled; they concluded the act with a song ('Marriage is a Grab Bag') and an accompanying exhibition ballroom number.[38]

The popularity of flirtation teams such as the De Havens and others prompted many standard ballroom teams to begin presenting their numbers within the romantic-flirtation mode. In these cases, the flirtation seems to have been depicted solely in terms of the dances, without song or dialogue. The team of Carlos Sebastian and Dorothy Bentley (who before entering vaudeville in 1913 were a noted cabaret team) appeared before an opulent scenic drop depicting a Venetian canal while an onstage orchestra played a variety of sentimental melodies. Soon a simulated gondola appeared, moving through a cutout in the drop, transporting Bentley across the length of the stage. As the gondola "docked" the gentlemanly Sebastian helped her to shore, at which point a spotlight was thrown on the couple, and they performed an exhibition waltz—the Valse Artistique. A flirtatious tango followed in which Bentley "glided with a red rose, just out of reach of the pursuing Mr. Sebastian."[39] Although no singing or dialogue took place, the entire motif for the act was flirtation, and each of the ballroom numbers underscored the romantic attachment between the two characters.

Comic-Flirtations Teams

Many comedy teams also, adapted flirtatious-ballroom material into their acts. As was common in vaudeville, once a novelty act took hold, there followed scores of variations on the theme. For many comedy-based teams, ballroom dance numbers served as the highpoint of the scene, framed by a series of comic songs and dialogue. The reigning vaudeville comedy team of the teens was Pat Rooney II and his wife Marion Bent who, like other established teams, discovered ballroom work as a key to career longevity. Son of the famous comedian, Pat Rooney II began his vaudeville training as a child in a song and dance act with his sister Mattie. After Rooney's next partner, Emma Francis, left the act in 1904, Rooney brought his wife Marion into his act and one of the most successful song and dance teams was born.[40]

Rooney and Bent's early acts were distinguished by Rooney's skillful eccentric dancing and his signature ethnic solo dances, such as the Waltz Clog, the Irish Jig, and the Yiddish Hornpipe. Marion Bent was a novice performer who, under Rooney's expert guidance, perfected her dancing ability and her penchant for comedy. By 1909 their act *At the Stand* scored a large success and set a precedent for a type of routine they would eventually perfect. In the routine, performed in a "rapid fire conversational sort of presentation," Rooney portrayed a newsdealer and Bent an actress who makes a purchase at his stand.[41] After exchanging some comic dialogue with Bent, Rooney discovered that she was a performer. To impress her he demonstrated some comic ballet steps. Marion then picked up a songbook—the cue for a song-duet by the couple. Following the song, Rooney concluded the act with his Yiddish Hornpipe dance.[42]

By the early teens, they had updated the act and retitled it *Twenty Minutes with Marion and Pat.* They replaced the newsstand with a drop representing the exterior of a dime store and made the opening dialogue between the couple more overtly flirtatious to appeal to contemporary taste. Marion dropped one of her packages in front of the store, Rooney rushed to her aid, after which they engaged in some snappy banter, and the couple wound up singing a duet. The revamping of their act included the addition of exhibition ballroom numbers, of course. The song duet led into a series of exhibition ballroom dances performed by the couple before a curtain depicting a ballroom interior. "Here they do some of the newfangled steps and fatten their average," noted one wry *Variety* commentator.[43] Certainly the incorporation of ballroom work was Rooney and Bent's attempt, in part, to demonstrate their versatility. At the same time, the endorsement of ballroom work by so acclaimed a team helped to underscore ballroom dance's primary function as one of representing romantic harmony and bliss.

ONE-ACT SKITS, EXTRAVAGANZAS, AND FILMS

During the teens, exhibition ballroom dances permeated all kinds of vaudeville entertainments. A popular vehicle for the presentation of the dances was the one-act comedy sketch. One-act sketches of all kinds— melodramas and tragedies, as well as comedies—had been popular vaudeville items since early in the century. Sometimes they consisted of excerpts from dramatic offerings currently on Broadway, or original skits offering a melodramatic slice of life.[44] The effects of the dance craze that swept the nation in the teens was actually ideal subject matter for the comedy sketches. Through humor and satire these mini-dramas revealed some of the public's anxieties about the "new" social dancing and the changing concepts of morality the dances reflected.

One such act, called *The Tango Teacher,* which toured on the Keith Circuit in 1914, concerned the illicit visits of husbands, wives, mothers, and daughters to the local tango parlor and the resulting complications when all parties are "discovered." The feature of the sketch was the exhibition ballroom routine performed by society dancer Walter Jarvis portraying a dance instructor. After the main characters learned that their spouses and children had all been secretly attending the local dance hall, Jarvis and his partner launched into three specialty dances including the Jarvis Waltz and the Brazilian Maxixe.[45]

During the height of the dance craze, vaudeville houses often sponsored what could be called ballroom dance extravaganzas—entire bills consisting solely of prominent exhibition ballroom dance teams. These productions typically had week-long engagements at major vaudeville houses and, like other acts, toured on the Keith and Orpheum circuits. Part of the attraction of these performances was their participatory aspect—amateur dancers were invited onto the stage for competitions judged by the professional teams.

At the Shubert Theatre in Boston in 1914 dancer Joan Sawyer organized her "Dancing Carnival," as it was billed, boasting the "Greatest Aggregation of Dancers of All Kinds Ever Assembled in One Show."[46] Sawyer was the principal dancer, although she was joined by a variety of performers ranging from whirlwind teams to toe dancers. A highlight of the event was the unveiling of Sawyer's latest creation, the Joanelle, a waltz-minuet backed by a corps de ballet.[47]

Similarly, ballroom dancer Joseph C. Smith managed and performed in an extravaganza called "Congress of the World's Greatest Dancers." The program, from Keith's Boston Theatre in May of 1914, reads like a "Who's Who" with sixteen contemporary ballroom dances featuring a variety of performance styles and repertoires. The exhibition team of Natalie and Martin Ferrari, for instance, presented "a cycle of classic and modern dances," consisting of the one-step, a habanera, and a solo Dance of the Hours from the opera La Gioconda, performed by Ferrari.[48] The final "act" on the bill was a contestant dance in which several amateur couples vied for honors in the one-step, hesitation waltz, tango, and maxixe. Extravaganzas like these foreshadowed a type of show typical of the 1940s, featuring a single prominent exhibition ballroom team in an evening of ballroom dance.[49]

By the 1910s film had claimed a place on the vaudeville bill, and soon cinematic images of ballroom dancers captivated the public imagination. Several exhibition ballroom teams appeared in silent film shorts, either in what were known as "exhibition reels," consisting of three or four consecutive exhibition numbers, or instructional dance films. The films were about fifteen to twenty minutes long and appeared as an item on a standard vaudeville bill. The Castles were one of the first exhibition ballroom teams to have a motion picture short of their dancing shown in vaudeville theatres. In 1914 they made a fifteen-minute film of five of their best-known dances, featured as the fifth act on a standard nine-act vaudeville bill. For the Castles, who basically disliked performing in vaudeville, the film was an ingenious way to have themselves represented in vaudeville while they continued to appear on Broadway and in cabarets.[50]

In 1915, the team of Rosy Dolly and Martin Brown followed suit with an exhibition dance reel for Universal Films, featuring dances previewed in their latest musical theatre appearance. Deemed "of exceptional merit and interest" by the local press, the film featured five specialties—a Crinoline Polka ("an antebellum reminiscence"), the Waltz Classique, the Clown Trot, the Habanera Hesitation, and something called Chopsticks, curiously described as a "Chinese Fantasy."[51]

Instructional dance films in particular were hailed as the latest revolution in vaudeville entertainment since, producers reasoned, for the price of admission audiences could get a free dance lesson. Advertisers' appeals to vaudeville managers minced no words: "Book this feature and you will show the greatest novelty since the invention of the motion pictures. It is something absolutely new and it actually teaches."[52] The Kalem Film Company had particular success with their instructional dance film featuring the team of Joan Sawyer and Wallace Mc-Cutcheon. Called *Motion Picture Dancing Lessons,* the movie begins at a fashionable cabaret where a group of amateur dancers are interrupted periodically by Sawyer and McCutcheon who, as dance teachers, demonstrate the "correct" method of performing the numbers.

In what was considered one of the most innovative sequences, the camera focused just on McCutcheon's feet as he demonstrated a series of dance patterns. Music for the film was generally prerecorded, although some enterprising vaudeville producers might hire live musicians to accompany the dances.[53] The film made an entertaining vaudeville act, while it simultaneously functioned as an important teaching tool: advertisements and reviews of the film appeared in dance periodicals such as the *Dancing Times,* which had a large readership of dance teachers. One can guess that these teachers may have picked up some tips from the movie, or they may have urged their students to view it as a learning tool.

CHANGES IN STYLE

By the late teens and into the early twenties exhibition ballroom dance acts became larger and glossier to rival the increasingly lavish productions being presented in the musical theatre. Many ballroom teams expanded their routines by adding singing, while several of the song-and-dance teams developed their acts into small-scale musical revues. In the 1919–1920 season, vaudeville favorites Pat Rooney and Marion Bent presented a song and dance revue called *Rings of Smoke,* a forty-six-minute production employing fourteen performers. Rooney portrays a young romantic who dreams that he travels around the world in search of true love. At the end of his reverie he discovers true love (Marion Bent) waiting on his own doorstep. The seven scenes in the production all took place in different parts of the world, and afforded Rooney and his dance partners the opportunity to perform characteristic dances such as an Irish jig, a tango, and a ragtime waltz. A highlight of the act was Vincent Lopez and his Kings of Harmony Jazz Band, who apparently "held the audience spellbound" during their jazz renditions.[54]

With the rise of jazz music in the early twenties, dance bands were frequently presented as featured acts on vaudeville bills. The popular ballroom team of Tony and Nina De Marco rose to prominence in the mid-twenties with their seven-member band the Seven Musical Shieks. They were clothed in what one reviewer described as "Arabian robes" and played an assortment of instruments from the ukulele to the bass viol. The act was organized so that their musical numbers neatly framed the De Marcos' dancing—first a series of their trademark tangos and other Spanish-based ballroom dances, and then an elegant waltz rendition with a whirlwind finish.[55] The De Marcos were one of several teams who ushered in the popular ballroom-adagio dance—a smooth, seamless style of exhibition ballroom work characterized by breathtaking leaps and lifts. It was a type of ballroom dance that would reemerge with full force in the late thirties and early forties, during the second heyday of exhibition ballroom dance.

NOTES

1. See Douglas Gilbert, *American Vaudeville: Its Life and Times* (New York: Dover Publications, Inc." 1940), pp. 120–123; Robert W. Snyder, *The Voice of the City: Vaudeville and Popular Culture in New York* (New York: Oxford University Press, 1989), pp. 30–33, 150–152; and Shirley Staples, *Male-Female Comedy Teams in American Vaudeville: 1865–1932* (Ann Arbor, MI: UMI Research Press, 1984), pp. 94, 127, 178.

2. Robert C. Toll, *On With the Show* (New York: Oxford University Press, 1976), p. 273; Alfred L. Bernheim, "The Facts of Vaudeville," *Equity News* 9 (November 1923): 33–40, in Charles W. Stein, *American Vaudeville As Seen By Its Contemporaries* (New York: Alfred A. Knopf, 1984).

3. "Town Topics Proves to Be Biggest of Shows," *The New York Morning Telegraph*, 24 August 1915 (Ned Wayburn scrapbook, MWEZ, 21,063, BRTC). For the occurrence of the same phenomenon in the twenties, see "Dance Salon in [George] White's Theatre," *The [New York] News*, 27 December 1923 (George White scrapbook MWEZ, 22,852, BRTC).

4. "Gertrude Hoffmann Will Give Tango Tea," *Cleveland News*, 20 January 1914 (Evelyn Nesbit scrapbook, MWEZ, 24,271, BRTC).

5. "Audience May Participate," *New York Telegraph*, 13 November 1913 (Vera Maxwell Clipping File, Robinson Locke Collection, BRTC).

6. Maurice and Walton and the Dolly Sisters, for instance, often performed on the same bill. See Program, B. F. Keith's, Week of March 1916 (Theatre Programs of Performances Given in New York City, BRTC).

7. See Sime, "Palace," *Variety*, 14 November 1914, p. 20, for a good example of the kind of language used by vaudeville critics to describe a desirable act.

8. See *The Chicago Herald*, 17 September 1914.

9. George Burns and Cynthia Hobrait Lindsay, *I Love Her, That's Why* (New York: Simon and Shuster, 1955), p. 59.

10. Most of the major teams of the period named dances after themselves, such as the Castle Walk, the Clifford Trot, Maurice's Tango, etc.

11. Castle, *Castles in the Air*, p. 101.

12. *The New York Dramatic Mirror*, 21 October 1914.

13. Program, Palace Theatre, Week of 12 January 1914 (Theatre Program of Performances Given in New York City, BRTC).

14. "The Castles in the Two-a-Day," *The New York Dramatic Mirror*, 21 October 1914, p. 19.

15. Program, Palace Theatre, Week of 6 March 1916 (Theatre Programs of Performances Given in New York City, BRTC); Program, Palace Theatre, ca. 1916, date obscured (Maurice and Florence Walton scrapbook, MWEZ, 461–467, BRTC).

16. "She's the Spirit of the Dance," *The New York Dramatic Mirror*, 29 July 1914, p. 16.

17. *Variety*, 20 February 1914, p. 19; *The New York Dramatic Mirror*, 4 March 1914.

18. *The New York Dramatic Mirror*, 1 July 1914, p. 17; *The New York Clipper*, 27 June 1914, p. 6.

19. *The New York Dramatic Mirror*, 1 July 1914, p. 17.

20. Ibid.

21. *The New York Clipper*, 27 June 1914, p. 6.

22. *The New York Dramatic Mirror*, 1 July 1914, p. 17.

23. Sime, *Variety*, 16 May 1913; unidentified *Variety* clippings, ca. 1913 (The Dolly Sisters scrapbook, ser. 3, no. 371, BRTC).

24. Sime, *Variety*, 16 May 1913.

25. "Jack," unidentified *Variety* clipping, ca. 1914 (Martin Brown scrapbook, MWEZ, 18, 445, BRTC).

26. *The New York Dramatic Mirror*, October 1916, p. 18; Sime, *Variety*, 24 October 1914.

27. *Variety*, 24 October 1914.

28. Cecil Smith and Glenn Litton, *Musical Comedy in America* (New York: Theatre Arts Books, 1950, 1978, 1981), pp. 86–87. Toll, *On With the Show*, pp. 192–193; Staples, *Male-Female Comedy Teams in American Vaudeville*, pp. 130–131.

29. "Dance Still Popular," *The New York Star*, 29 December 1915, p. 15.

30. *The New York Dramatic Mirror*, 30 October 1915.

31. A. Herbst, *New York Star*, 20 January 1915 (Jack Clifford scrapbook, NAFR, ser. 3, 360, BRTC).

32. Wynn, *Variety*, 26 January 1916.

33. Miscellaneous newspaper clippings (William Rock clipping file, Robinson Locke Collection, BRTC).

34. *The New York Telegraph*, 5 June 1908; Miscellaneous newspaper clippings (William Rock clipping file, BRTC); *Variety*, 20 September 1912.

35. Unidentified Minnesota newspaper clipping, 18 November 1912 (William Rock clipping file, BRTC); *Variety*, 20 September 1912. The team also performed this number at the Fifth Avenue Theatre in New York City.

36. Flirtation acts assumed several forms. Some were primarily talk or song acts, while others combined song and dance. For more on the standard two-act material see Brett Page and Milton Berle, "The Two Act As Seen in Typical Vaudeville Skits," in Stein, *American Vaudeville*, pp. 182–183. For information on the modernization of traditional courtship sketches see Staples, *Male-Female Comedy Teams in American Vaudeville*, p. 137.

37. *The Minnesota Journal*, 5 April 1915.

38. *The New York Dramatic Mirror*, 14 October 1914; "The Actor Dances His

Way Through the World," *The Pittsburgh Leader,* 27 November 1914 (Carter De Haven scrapbook, Robinson Locke Collection, ser. 3, vol. 363, BRTC); Undated, unidentified program (Martin Brown scrapbook, MWEZ, 22,532, BRTC).

39. *The New York Dramatic Mirror,* 15 April 1914.

40. See newspaper clippings in Rooney and Bent clipping file, Robinson Locke Collection, BRTC.

41. *The New York Dramatic Mirror,* 25 September 1909.

42. Ibid.

43. *Variety,* 3 April 1914.

44. Gilbert, *American Vaudeville,* pp. 357–365.

45. *The New York Dramatic Mirror,* 22 April 1914, p. 21; Program, B. F. Keith Theatre, 25 May 1914 (Theatre Collection, The Philadelphia Free Library).

46. "The Queen of Modern Dancers, Miss Joan Sawyer," advertisement in unidentified magazine clipping (The Theatre Collection, Harvard College).

47. "Joan Sawyer's Art in Modern Dances," *The Philadelphia Record,* 29 May 1914.

48. Program, *Boston Theatre,* 18 May 1914 (George White scrapbook, MWEZ, 22, 852, BRTC).

49. For example, in the late thirties and early forties the popular team of Veloz and Yolanda gave ballroom dance recitals at Carnegie Hall. The program consisted of an entire evening of their exhibition dances. See Chapter 6.

50. Program, Temple Theatre (Detroit), Week of 26 January 1914 (Irene and Vernon Castle file MGZB, The Dance Collection, NYPL).

51. "They Made the Brown-Dolly Record," *Photoplay,* April 1915 (The Dolly Sister clipping file, The Dance Collection, NYPL); "Universal Film's Martin Brown and Roszika Dolly," unidentified newspaper clipping (Roszika Dolly clipping file, BRTC).

52. "Kalem Klip Sheet," *Kalem Calendar,* 15 October 1913 (Kalem Company scrapbook, MFL—n.c. 249, BRTC).

53. Ibid.

54. "Rings of Smoke," *Variety,* ca. 1923 (Rooney and Bent clipping file, BRTC).

55. *Variety,* 24 January 1924, p. 23.

Plate 1. The Parisian Room restaurant-cabaret at the Shuberts' Palais de Danse, ca. 1914. (Courtesy of the Shubert Archive.)

Plate 2. Newspaper advertisement for an afternoon tea dance by Broadway ballroom dance couple, Anna Wheaton and Donald MacDonald, ca. 1913. (The Billy Rose Theatre Collection Theatre Photos, New York Public Library for the Performing arts, Astor, Lenox and Tilden Foundations.)

Plate 3. Exhibition ballroom dance star Irene Castle displays proto-typical dance dress of the period, of chiffon-like material with layered skirt and loose bodice, ca. 1913. (The Billy Rose Theatre Collection, The New York Public Library for the Performing Arts, Astor, Lenox and Tilden Foundations.)

Plate 4. Irene and Vernon Castle in the Castle Polka from their 1915 star vehicle, *Watch Your Step*. (The Billy Rose Theatre Collection Theatre Photos, The New York Public Library for the Performing Arts, Astor, Lenox and Tilden Foundations.)

Plate 5. Renowned exhibition ballroom dancers Maurice Mouvet and Florence Walton in their Apache dance, initially performed for "late-night audiences only." (Maurice Mouvet, *Maurice's Art of Dancing* (1915), The Dance Collection Dance Photos, The New York Public Library for the Performing Arts, Astor, Lenox and Tilden Foundations.)

Plate 6. Maurice and Walton in a dip position emblematic of their sultry, sensuous exhibition ballroom style, ca. 1913. (International News Service. Courtesy of the Theatre Collection, The Museum of The City of New York.)

Plate 7. An illustration of the kinds of dips and bends the average social dancer should *avoid* in Leslie F. Clendenen's *Dance Mad*. (The Dance Collection Dance Photos, The New York Public Library for the Performing Arts, Astor, Lenox and Tilden Foundations.)

Plate 8. Popular exhibition ballroom dancer Joan Sawyer and partner
unabashedly executing dip position "disapproved of" by dance teachers, ca. 1914. (The Billy Rose Theatre Collection Theatre Photos,
The New York Public Library for the Performing Arts, Astor, Lenox
and Tilden Foundations.)

Plate 9. Joan Sawyer and another of her many partners, Carlos Sebastian, in the heel-step position of the maxixe, ca. 1914. (J. S. Hopkins, *The Tango and Other Up-to-Date Dances* (1914), The Dance Collection, The New York Public Library for the Performing Arts, Astor, Lenox and Tilden Foundations.)

Plate 10. Exhibition ballroom dancer and film idol Rudolph Valentino and his wife (and professional partner), Natacha Rambova, in their Argentine Tango, ca. 1920. (The Dance Collection Dance Photos, The New York Public Library for the Performing Arts, Astor, Lenox and Tilden Foundations.)

Plate 11. The balletic-ballroom team of Adelaide and Hughes in an exhibition waltz from *The Passing Show of 1912*. (The Billy Rose Theatre Collection Theatre Photos, The New York Public Library for the Performing Arts, Astor, Lenox and Tilden Foundations.)

Plate 12. The whirlwind-ballroom team of Jack Clifford and Evelyn Nesbit performing their characteristic acrobatic finale. (The
Billy Rose Theatre Collection Theatre Photos, The New York Public
Library for the Performing Arts, Astor, Lenox and Tilden Foundations.)

Plate 13. Clifton Webb and Mary Hay in a comic-eccentric ballroom number from *Sunny* (1925). (The Billy Rose Theatre Collection Theatre Photos, The New York Public Library for the Performing Arts, Astor, Lenox and Tilden Foundations.)

Plate 14. In their typically lavish and elegant clothing, the Dolly Sisters performed an exhibition one-step for the 1916 musical *His Bridal Night*. (The Billy Rose Theatre Collection Theatre Photos, The New York Public Library for the Performing Arts, Astor, Lenox and Tilden Foundations.)

Plate 15. The popular twenties team of Tony and Nina De Marco in one of their graceful, trademark lifts. (The Billy Rose Theatre Collection Theatre Photos, The New York Public Library for the Performing Arts, Astor, Lenox and Tilden Foundations.)

Plate 16. Amy Revere and Charles Ames capture the sublime grace of exhibition ballroom dance of the thirties. (Courtesy of Amy Revere McCauley.)

Plate 17. The immensely popular team of Veloz and Yolanda at the start of their exhibition waltz. (Veloz and Yolanda, *Tango and Rumba, The Dances of Today and Tomorrow,* HarperCollins Publishers.

Plate 18. Ballroom-adagio dancers Lola and Andre (left) and company in a scene from a Twentieth Century Fox film sent to the American armed forces during World War II, ca. 1940. (Courtesy of Lola Andre.)

Plate 19. Marge and Gower Champion in a story ballet from their early night club act, ca. 1947. They were then known professionally as Gower and Belle. (Courtesy of David Payne-Carter.)

Plate 20. Contemporary ballroom dancers Yvonne Marceau and Pierre Dulaine, founders of American Ballroom Theatre. (Courtesy of Yvonne Marceau and Pierre Dulaine.)

Exhibition Ballroom Dance in Early Musical Theatre

It was not only in vaudeville that exhibition ballroom dance rose to prominence. During the teens and twenties, musical theatre producers eagerly capitalized on the latest social trends, drawing in crowds craving the excitement and novelty of stylized intimacy in dancing. More than a passing fad, however, the incorporation of exhibition ballroom numbers helped rejuvenate early twentieth-century musical theatre, and signaled a new era in musical theatre dance. During the teens and early twenties exhibition ballroom dance was the predominant form of specialty dance featured in Broadway musical theatre productions. Indeed, many of the techniques used to integrate exhibition ballroom dance into productions during this time have endured to the present day.

BACKGROUND

The concept of individual couples performing virtuosic ballroom numbers was not known to musical theatre audiences prior to 1910. In the predominant forms of musical theatre in the late nineteenth century—comic operas, melodramas, and spectacles—ballroom numbers tended to be large, group-dance affairs, mirroring the ways in which social dances were performed by the populace. In the 1887 production of *Erminie*, for example, a very popular stage spectacle of the time, the Act II finale occurred in a lavishly decorated ballroom and featured a gavotte performed by the ensemble.[1] The popular European light operas featuring the melodious harmonies of Lehar, Strauss, and Offenbach typically contained grand ballroom scenes and usually featured some sort of group waltz.

By the turn of the century, changes in popular musical styles gradually affected the look of dance in musical production. The operettas, for instance, began featuring slower, more leisurely, and even sensuous-looking waltzes in contrast to the whirling Viennese dances. Some of these waltz numbers may have actually foreshadowed exhibition ballroom dances such as the hesitation waltz, which became popular in the teens.[2] One musical considered the precursor of a more intimate presentation of ballroom dance was *The Merry Widow*. With a musical score by Franz Lehar, Henry Savage's 1908 production is said to have breathed new life into the operetta, largely because of its intimately styled ballroom numbers.[3]

The Merry Widow also illustrated a trend, which later became widely used, toward using ballroom numbers as structural devices to link together parts of the plot or to serve the narrative in some way. For example, the operetta contained three renditions of the Merry Widow Waltz, each of which underscored the relationship between the protagonists, Sonia, the merry widow (Ethel Jackson), and Prince Danilo, her suitor (Donald Brian). At the conclusion of Act I, a ballroom scene, the couple performed their first waltz rendition after a heated exchange in which Sonia had accused Danilo of pursuing her only for her fortune. In the second act, Sonia and Danilo finally admitted their love for one another and performed the same waltz more seductively, which one reviewer described as possessing "an audacious, wicked swing."[4] In the third and final act the couple performed a dreamy rendition of the waltz symbolizing their union. In essence the Merry Widow Waltz, performed each time in a different mood and tempo, served as a leitmotif tracing the couple's romantic relationship.[5]

THE BEGINNINGS OF EXHIBITION BALLROOM DANCE ON STAGE

It wasn't long before a slew of similar operettas followed with a lilting ballroom waltz as the pinnacle of the production.[6] The dancers performing these exhibition ballroom numbers, though, were not yet called exhibition ballroom dancers. Typically they were principal cast members who also doubled as dancers (as was the case with Ethel Jackson and Donald Brian) and had not been specifically trained as ballroom dancers. It was not until around the season of 1909–1910 that exhibition ballroom dance became fully recognized as a theatrical dance genre. By that time dancers were labeled as exhibition ballroom dancers, and audiences were coming to productions *expecting* to see a specific ballroom number performed by a certain team. The dances had most likely been the subject of countless newspaper and magazine articles. The teams themselves were also known to audiences, since many of them were stars from the cabaret and vaudeville.

At the same time that ballroom dance was enlivening the waltz operas, it added inspiration to a newly emerging form of American popular theatre, the musical revue. Epitomized by the renowned *Ziegfeld Follies*, these glossy, spectacular compendiums of song, dance, and comedy routines found success by drawing on the latest styles of popular song and dance. Early versions of the rag dances, and some of the South American numbers, such as the maxixe, were first seen in the early *Ziegfeld Follies of 1907* and 1908.[7] By the 1910–1911 season *The Follies*, as well as other notable revue series, including the Shuberts' *Passing Show* and the *Greenwich Village Follies*, became vehicles for exhibition ballroom dancers.

A key to the rising status of exhibition ballroom dance in musical theatre was the pioneering work of several important choreographers, such as Ned Wayburn, Julian Mitchell, Edward Royce, and Jack Mason, who used ballroom forms as the basis of their specialty and chorus numbers.[8] Through the work of these professionals, exhibition ballroom dance became a codified musical theatre dance technique. Wayburn, for example, created hundreds of dance variations on the basic one-steps, tangos, and maxixes. He choreographed exhibition dances on stage for specific teams and also coached the stage work of some of the most popular exhibition dancers of their day. Thus, as a result of the training of performers in ballroom work and the development of an exhibition ballroom dance vocabulary, the form grew to become a widely used musical theatre dance genre.

STYLES OF BALLROOM DANCE INTERPOLATIONS

The cabaret fervor at the beginning of the teens was an enormous inspiration for the integration of ballroom teams into musical theatre productions. Producers borrowed many of the big-name dancers from the newly established cabarets, and the entire ballroom dance craze itself quickly became a "theme" for many musical productions. The Shuberts' 1914 Winter Garden revue, *The Whirl of the World*, for example, was subtitled "The Delirious Dance Craze." It featured an abundance of ragtime music specialties and scenes named after the latest social dances themselves, among them the "Rue de Tango" and the "Maxixe Restaurant."[9] Also, an increasing number of plotted shows began structuring their story line around the exploits of a ballroom dancer or dance teacher. This approach created a rationale for the inclusion of the exhibition ballroom numbers that were featured throughout the show. The dance craze—and the zeal with which the public clamored to learn the latest dances—provided a convenient satirical theme for many shows. *The Ziegfeld Follies of 1913* opened with a group of turkey trotters cavorting in New York City's Bryant Park after cabaret closing hours. The show concluded with the same group of avid dancers, who wound up reveling in "A Room in the Satanic Cabaret." [10]

The two major forms of shows, then as now, were musical comedies and revues. By and large, musical comedies (also referred to as musical farces or simply musical shows) contained a trace of narrative, whereas the revues typically functioned as a series of acts connected by some overall theme, idea, or design concept. However, in this early period of musical theatre, the distinction between revues and musicals was not always very clear. Many revues contained segments that were plotted, and many so-called musical comedies were simply collections of song and dance acts woven around the thinnest of plots. One reviewer, commenting on the 1911 production *Over the River* featuring Maurice Mouvet noted, "There is enough vaudeville to prevent any one tiring of the plot, and not enough plot seriously to interrupt the vaudeville." [11] Reviewers of the period, in fact, often used the terms revue and musical comedy interchangeably, thus compounding the confusion.

But whether in plotted revues or in thinly plotted musicals, exhibition ballroom teams were incorporated using basically similar strategies and techniques. The first of these were what can be referred to as "incidental insertions," a phrase that actually encompassed a wide variety of dance numbers. For the most part, these dances bore no intrinsic relationship to the plot or theme of the show; rather, their main purpose was to highlight a featured dance or dance team. At the height of the ballroom craze, musical producers and choreographers were intent on featuring the latest dances, even if at the expense of maintaining continuity of plot or action. In fact, audiences (and critics) came to expect these divertissements, since they were opportunities for star turns from their favorite performers. Exhibition ballroom numbers were sure to enliven a scene and, if nothing else, served as a convenient and entertaining way to segue into another scene.

The use of such an incidental insertion in the 1911 operetta-waltz *The Kiss Waltz* (by Edgar Smith and Matthew Woodward) offers a dramatic instance of the ways in which the soft-tempoed operatic waltzes were being upstaged by American ballroom dances. Although the public's taste for the revue and the American musical comedy was at an all-time high, the comic opera, with its more tightly constructed plots and lyrical melodies, had not died. [12] Many of these productions, however, were more often than not Americanized adaptations of Viennese musicals, whose frothy plots typically involved romance and intrigue among the European nobility. *The Kiss Waltz* brought to life the escapades of the Fuhringer family and their efforts to rise from the nouveau riche into titled aristocracy. All types of romantic complications arose, involving the Fuhringers' daughter Antschi (played by Adele Rowland), the Countess Wildenburg (Elsa Ryan), and her jealous husband (William Pruette). The count believed that his wife had been flirting with the court composer (Guido Spino) so he hired the Baroness von Vernau to steal the affections of the composer. As planned, Spino became infatuated with the baroness and professed his love to her. At the end of Act I, Spino taught her to dance to one of his compositions, 'The Kiss Waltz,' a romantic Viennese concoction.[13]

The fun really began when Spino and the Baroness concluded their dance, and three other principals unexpectedly entered—Adele Rowland, Elsa Ryan, and specialty dancer Martin Brown (who later formed an exhibition team with Rosy Dolly of the Dolly Sisters). They immediately picked up the lulling, three-quarter rhythm of the preceding waltz when the music suddenly lapsed into a brisk syncopated melody; at that point the dancers offered their own "dancing lesson" consisting of the latest one-steps and turkey trots. One reviewer, apparently jolted by this outburst of contemporary ballroom work claimed, "It was with regret that one saw the three [dancers] pass from the charming swing of the Waltz into the comparative riot of the ragtime dance that immediately followed."[14] Said another reviewer, "even the real Viennese Waltz is split in the middle, and Yankee rag and jigsaw tunes are inserted."[15] The dance number, of course, was a wonderful parody of waltz sequences so typical of Viennese operettas, but it served primarily as a way of showcasing the talent of the three performers, and catering to the public's taste for rag tunes. Judging by the numerous encores, which left the three dancers "dishevelled, limp and breathless,"[16] the audience clearly loved this unexpected ballroom dance interlude.

In other kinds of incidental numbers, the sole purpose of the dance was to display the talents of the starring female performer. The ingenious choreographer Ned Wayburn, for instance, devised a specific type of exhibition number expressly for this purpose. Glides, as they were called, were actually combinations of contemporary social dance steps (such as one-steps and two-steps) and were so named because of the distinct gliding effect produced by the positioning of the female dancer in front of her partner (similar to a skating position). One noteworthy example was the Gertrude Hoffmann Glide, performed by the popular dancer and imitator in the Shubert musical *Broadway to Paris* (1912). Unlike the exhibition number in *The Kiss Waltz*, which essentially occurred unannounced, the Gertrude Hoffmann Glide was incorporated into the scene through some prefatory dialogue.

The rather improbable plot unfolded as follows: a young upstanding man, Stuyvesant, has developed a rather inappropriate infatuation for the infamous actress Anna Trelawney (played by Hoffmann). Stuyvesant's father hires two detectives (played by vaudevillians George Moore and Ralph Austin) to discourage her from accepting the young man's advances. Trelawney agrees and aids the father's plans by proposing that no man claim her affections unless he offer her one million francs. The interpolation technique used to insert Hoffmann's dance was relatively uncomplicated, if not downright obvious. Knowing full well that her persistent suitor will never be able to meet her terms, Trelawney says to her detective friends, "Then we win, don't we?" In unison the men reply "In a glide." Anna proposes, "Then let's win it in the newest one," the cue for their dance—The Gertrude Hoffmann Glide.[17]

Although glides were frequently performed as duos, the Gertrude Hoffmann Glide functioned as a trio in which the two male partners, Austin and Moore, flanked her on either side. In trios of this sort the dancers generally executed the footwork on a diagonal line toward the audience. The lyrics of the musical accompaniment for the Gertrude Hoffmann Glide offer some clues as to what the dance may have actually looked like. The song describes a selection from one of Hoffmann's vaudeville imitation acts, *The Borrowed Art of Gertrude Hoffmann*, which parodied the Salome and Spring Song dances (popular vaudeville dances), and the master showman George M. Cohan and vaudeville comedienne Eva Tanguay. It also refers to several of the most popular social dances of the day and to the Gaby Glide, another exhibition dance created by Wayburn for the French singer-dancer Gaby Deslys:

> Come, take the raggy motion of the Gaby Glide
> Try a little dash here of Salome
> Keep a-sliding and gliding on the Spring Song
> To the trots gone home (turkey trots, turkey trots, turkey trots)
> Oh take the speedy go you find in Georgie Cohan
> Use the grace with which the Russians slide
> Then to Eva Tanguay shout: Oh, gee, I don't care!
> Give us the Gertrude Hoffmann Glide.[18]

No doubt the dance, described by one reviewer as "snappy," incorporated the steps and rhythms of these ragtime numbers.[19] The structure of the dance was a variation on the standard musical comedy routine of a ballad sung by the male, followed by the dance, and concluding with a repeat by all performers of the refrain. After a seven-measure instrumental introduction, Austin and Moore sang the first two verses of the song. Although not explicitly stated in the music or in the program for the show, it is conceivable that Hoffmann sang the first verse alone and Moore and Austin followed with the second verse. All three performers sang the refrain, in any case, and then presented the glide.

As was typical for ballroom dances in musical theatre, the glide was fashioned into a relatively large production number by the use of a twenty-four-member "pony" chorus, which backed up the principals for the finale.[20]

CABARET SCENES

One of the most frequent ways of incorporating exhibition ballroom teams into shows was to present them in any setting in which social dancing might actually occur. Hotel ballrooms, roof-garden scenes, or cabarets were the most frequent staging devices. The integration of the teams into these scenes was relatively simple: usually they were featured as the star or "guest" performers and they danced three or four numbers as they would in an actual cabaret setting. No elaborate introduction or dialogue was necessary, since audiences were accustomed to seeing ballroom dancers perform in such settings. Generally the teams had no spoken lines and, if a renowned team was featured, the pair was usually billed simply as themselves. The settings replicated the oval floor pattern of an actual cabaret. Several chorus members, functioning as an onstage "audience," sat at tables or stood in groups to round out the corners of the proscenium stage. To make themselves visible to this onstage audience, as well as to the actual audience, the teams usually performed in a more circular fashion than was usual for ballroom numbers in other types of scenes.

An early instance of this type of staging was the plotted musical, *The Queen of the Moulin Rouge* (1907). Although the Parisian cabaret was being depicted in this production (the American cabaret did not materialize in this country until around 1910–1911), the staging is typical of shows that would follow. The cabaret scenes were easily and realistically integrated since the show's main action centered on the protagonist's relationship with a cabaret singer. Briefly, a young Balkan prince decides to sow his wild oats in Paris before marrying his Balkan princess. When the princess learns of her fiancé's whereabouts, however, she disguises herself as a dancer-chanteuse known as the "queen of the Moulin Rouge" and eventually lures back her lover.[21]

To help create an authentic cabaret atmosphere, the production featured dances that would actually have been seen at the genuine Moulin Rouge and other Paris cabarets. Act Two, scene three, for example, opened at the "Café Rat Mort," where the princess first practices her disguise. As an interlude, the featured entertainers, Joseph C. Smith and Louise Alexander, presented their "Dance of the Underworld"— an Apache that might have been seen regularly at Parisian clubs from about 1905 to 1910. Smith and Alexander's performance of the Apache, in fact, did much to popularize the dance in this country.[22] Directly following their number the French dancers, Mlle. Auber and M. De Veuille, performed a "Kicking Polka," considered by many reviewers to be even more sensational than the provocative Apache.[23]

Cabaret scenes were a staple in most revues, since they were a convenient way to feature several specialty acts in succession. In these scenes, often presented as "shows within shows," exhibition ballroom dancers might appear as part of a series of three to ten variety acts. This sort of interpolation occurred in the Shuberts' *The Passing Show of 1912,* a revue whose "theme" was the satirization of political and artistic personalities characterized in shows of the past season. The major social dance scene took place in a roof garden, in Act Two, scene three. However, the scene served primarily to highlight the talents of the principal performers and to feature the ballroom dancing of the star team of Adelaide and Hughes. The Shuberts lost no time, however, in helping make exhibition ballroom dance the rage it would become in musical theatre. More than half of the six acts in this cabaret scene contained some form of exhibition dance, clearly revealing the popularity of the form.[24]

No "rationale" was necessary to introduce this cabaret scene, since in revues audiences expected to see a loosely strung-together group of acts. The scene bore some connection to the show's overall theme, however, in that some of the connecting dialogue between acts contained satire. The roof-garden scene opened on a set containing small tables set upstage, with a painted backdrop depicting a cabaret. Sitting at the tables were the chorus members who introduced the scene with the refrain of the romantic ballad, 'When Was There Ever a Night Like This,' which had been sung earlier in the show by Ernest Hare. At the conclusion of the song, the chorus rose from the tables, preparing for the entrance of the first specialty—a dance by the English male tandem team of George Moon and Daniel Morris. The audience had already seen the team perform a comic eccentric pantomime in which they depicted two bumbling baggage handlers. Here they presented a classic tandem dance to the song 'Always Together.' As previously suggested, tandem work traditionally employed steps and poses from exhibition dance. Moon and Morris typically performed in the glide position; Morris, who was at least a full head taller than Moon, stood behind and to the side of his partner and did most of the stepping.[25]

These numbers were the prelude for the next featured specialty act, the ballroom team of Adelaide and Hughes. Billed as "The Guests of Honor," they presented an original creation known as the Hoop Dance (or Hoop Whirl), performed with a satin-covered aluminum hoop.[26] Ned Wayburn, the show's choreographer, frequently used props to lend variety and theatricality to social dance-based numbers. Props were typically used for dances known as "innovations," in which couples did not touch or hold one another until the end of the number. Adelaide and Hughes began this slow waltz-innovation by advancing from opposite sides of the stage. At the end of the fourth bar of music they met, whereupon Hughes took the hoop from Adelaide, raising it over her head and then placing it around her waist. They continued waltzing together in this position without touching one another. After the sixteenth measure, Hughes manipulated the hoop around both his and Adelaide's waist, so that they were now both dancing within the circumference of the ring. Then, in a demonstration of technical prowess, Adelaide and Hughes simultaneously leaned against the rim of the hoop while circling the stage area. The finale consisted of a series of breathtakingly fast turns by Adelaide, who sprang up onto the rim of the hoop, which Hughes then lifted above his neck.[27] Adelaide and Hughes closed their program with a more conventional ballroom number, a Ragtime Two-Step, for which, unfortunately, no detailed description exists.[28]

The following song and dance number featured musical comedy dancer Anna Wheaton and her partner Sydney Grant, performing a highly popular, social dance-based number called the Philadelphia Drag, backed by a partial chorus.[29] The lyrics parodied the current dance craze and give some indication of the steps used:

> This Dip has come from Dallas
> But from Turkey they brought us the Trot.
> This one is done by students,
> And there's another that's not.
> If you would like to see
> Which one looks good to me
> Hark to a beautiful rag
> One that is fuller of feeling
> It's the new Philadelphia Drag.[30]

The word "drag" was actually a catchall phrase in the musical theatre used to describe a New York form of contemporary social dance performed to a ragtime rhythm.

After a brief comic interlude by comic actress Trixie Friganza (who earlier in the show burlesqued several popular dances, from the Apache to Gertrude Hoffmann's Spring Song) and Charles Ross, the dynamic acrobatic-ballroom duo, the Ceballos, offered the final punch. A brother-sister dance team from a Mexican circus family, the Ceballos' Fearless Waltz almost stopped the show. At the pinnacle of their number, each of the performers, situated at opposite ends of the stage, executed handspring cartwheels until they met each other in the center. This was capped by a whirlwind turn in which the partners alternately swung the other by the arms to a waltz rhythm.[31]

The finale of the roof-garden scene was a song and dance number called "The Metropolitan Squawktette," led by Trixie Friganza with singer Ernest Hare and the comedy duo of William and Eugene Howard. The number concluded with an elaborate march performed by the chorus, which led directly into the final scene of the show, "In 2010"—a futurist glimpse into the twenty-first century.[32]

Throughout the teens exhibition ballroom dances seen in musical theatre productions were the subject of countless newspaper and magazine articles. The press literally "sold" these dances to the public through extensive photographic layouts illustrating the dances; many of the articles were supposedly written by the teams themselves. For producers and press agents these pieces were essential in promoting the dancers and the shows. Since the run of a show could be as long as several weeks, producers needed to keep a steady stream of press materials flowing and these articles served that purpose. Of course, the pieces turned out to be an excellent source of home dance instruction. But the articles also served another function. They gave the ballroom dancers an opportunity to dispel any lingering notions that their dances were somehow improper or objectionable. The teams were careful to point out how the more flamboyant stage dances could be converted into dances one could perform at a social dance club, or in one's own living room.

During the run of The Passing Show of 1912, for instance, the producers featured a series of syndicated articles in which Adelaide promoted her Hoop Dance, describing how it could be adapted for the ballroom. In what can be viewed as her attempt to portray the dance as one associated with breeding and good taste, Adelaide suggested that the dance be performed as part of a cotillion, a popular social dance of the nineteenth century, though still performed in some rarefied circles through the early teens.[33] Since cotillions typically made use of accessories or props, Adelaide's Hoop Dance could be easily adapted for the ballroom.

Adelaide first exhorted her readers to use a lighter-weight hoop than the kind that she and Hughes exhibited, for easier manipulation (and one might guess for greater safety), and she suggested that the hoops be of different colors to match the colors of the women's gowns. In her description of the dance itself, Adelaide omitted the more complex stage steps and, instead of the whirlwind ending, recommended that social dancers hold the rim of the hoop while waltzing inside it. As she advised, "I suppose it would really be better for the ordinary ballroom dancers not to let go of the hoop until they have a good deal of practice."[34] Of course, it is impossible to determine whether or not the public actually attempted this dance on its own, although it is conceivable that dance teachers picked it up and advertised it in their schools.

ROMANTIC INTERPOLATIONS

One of the most widespread approaches to the integration of exhibition ballroom specialties into musical theatre was through romance or flirtation scenes. There were dozens of variations on this basic technique. The standard format consisted of a love song by the romantic leads (or romantic supporting leads), followed by the dance itself. The role of audience expectation can explain, in large part, how these romantic scenes functioned. During the teens exhibition ballroom dances had become synonymous with love, romance and glamour—an image fostered, certainly, by the popular press and by the teams themselves. Because of this already ingrained association, musical theatre audiences found it natural to view ballroom dances as extensions of the traditional love duet sequence.

The 1913 production of *When Dreams Come True*, subtitled "the musical comedy of youth," featured a winning romantic lead in Joseph Santley, a musical comedy juvenile and rising exhibition ballroom star.[35] The story revolved around an idealistic and somewhat spoiled scion of a wealthy family, Kean Hedges (Santley), who, despite his family's wedding plans, discovers and falls in love with another woman. There follows several complicated plot turns, including the young woman disguising herself as his cousin. They become temporarily separated, but when Santley discovers her whereabouts, he phones her at once—the cue for "The Telephone Number," as it was named.[36]

This was a standard song and dance routine with some interesting variations. Over the telephone, Santley and Moore sang two verses of the song, 'Who's the Little Girl,' each of them alternating lines. As the principals exited, a pony chorus dressed as debutantes entered for a repeat of the refrain. Santley then reappeared, this time with dance partner Ruth Randall, for the Santley Tango.[37] Randall had not appeared at all before this number. In one sense, her relative anonymity lent a sense of drama to the dance, since Randall served as a substitute for Moore and her presence seemed to imply that Santley and his true love (Beth) would one day be reunited. More practically, Randall's appearance may have been a way of introducing her as a potential partner to Santley—indeed, after the run of the show, Santley and Randall toured in vaudeville as a popular ballroom duo.[38]

Widely publicized during the run of the show was the fact that Santley choreographed his own exhibition ballroom numbers. His Santley Tango was the biggest hit. One reviewer praised the ballroom number for its distinctly unacrobatic movements, saying, "There is no grasshopper skip in the new tango. There is no swinging of the head in jerky, pert little swings, but everything about it is musical, from the low, graceful dips, to the bird-like jumps."[39] This dance stood apart from other stage tangos in its controlled and graceful leg work. In one sequence of the dance (called the tango interlude), a turning step, the man swung his left leg around his female partner's while both of them rotated. The dance concluded with a graceful curtseying step, in which the dancers genuflected with their weight on the bent outer knees. The intricate legwork of this dance was very similar to the style of the authentic Argentine Tango.[40]

As with Adelaide and Hughes' Hoop Dance, the press latched on to Santley's Tango. One article entitled "A New Refined Tango by Joseph Santley," described, with quotes by Santley, ways in which the dance could be successfully adapted to the ballroom.[41] Other articles sought to establish Santley as the latest authority on ballroom dance. In one, he is quoted as saying that he is opposed to public dancing and "Cafés Dansants" because of the bad dancing habits they foster.[42] It is possible that, in such statements, Santley was catering not only to society's moral guardians but to the matrons of high society intent on maintaining rules of decorum and propriety. (In fact, Santley himself, during the touring production of *When Dreams Come True*, made appearances at fashionable soirées hosted by leading society ladies.) Of course, these rather reactionary statements, no doubt issued by Santley's press agent, may also have been designed to attract potential audience members to a "pre-performance" tango lesson to be given by Santley and Randall.[43]

A slightly more sophisticated use of romantic interpolation of exhibition ballroom dances occurred in the 1915 production of *Nobody Home,* the first of the renowned musicals at the Princess Theatre—the small, financially ailing theatre located on Thirty-ninth street. In an age dominated by lavish musical theatre production, the Princess musicals were distinguished by their intimacy and lack of pretension. The aim of the original producers, Elizabeth Marbury and Ray Comstock, was to create musicals with authentic, identifiable characters. The casts were generally smaller than those of typical Broadway musicals of the time, and everyone, even the exhibition dancers and chorus members, had an identity.[44] *Nobody Home* boasted a host of young, exuberant talent; witty, urbane dialogue; and a lively score by Jerome Kern.

One of the features of the show was the exhibition ballroom team of Quentin Tod and Helen Clarke, whose numbers set a precedent for ballroom dance in successive Princess musicals.[45] In the market for another ballroom team (after parting company with the Castles), Marbury brought Tod and Clarke together specifically for this show. Unlike many ballroom dancers featured in musical shows, Tod and Clarke portrayed characters (even if minor ones). Quentin Tod, as Havelock Page, was a bellboy at the hotel and throughout the show wore his bellboy uniform, a choice that reviewers considered a bold integration of dance and story.[46] Helen Clarke was "Dolly Dip," a dancer: the name was a pun on that dance step and referred to a contest held by *The New York Herald* that Clarke had recently won.[47]

The plot of *Nobody Home*—still lighthearted in tone, but with a bit more subtle humor and wit than musicals of the previous season—involved the escapades of Vernon Popple, a dance instructor (no doubt an allusion to famed ballroom dancer Vernon Castle). Popple, played by Lawrence Grossmith, is in love with young Violet Brinton (Alice Dovey), the daughter of a well-bred New York City family. Popple feared, however, that Violet's conservative relatives might object to their marriage, since he had once been a stage dancer. At the end of Act One, set at the lobby of the "Hotel Blitz," Popple unexpectedly met up with his former dance partner, a Miss Tony Miller, and begged her not to reveal the details of his past.

An unexpected plot turn made Popple even more apprehensive: as Tony was leaving the hotel, Violet's Uncle Rollo entered, recognized the danseuse, and even recalled the Military Dance he once saw her perform (though fortunately he could not recall that her partner was Popple). Tony's fiancé, Kenyon, suddenly entered and whisked her offstage, this exit the cue for Tod and Clarke's Military Glide, a character dance in which they mimed galloping horses.[48] Like other glides, the female partner was positioned in front of her male partner, facing out toward the audience. In this particular version, Clarke and Tod incorporated ballroom positions and footwork with marching and hopping steps, which could have been performed to either a one-step or two-step rhythm. The expressive, animal-like gestures of their arms and upper torsos also revealed the dancers' gift for pantomime.

While the number was certainly intended to reveal the dancing prowess of the well-publicized team, it was more fully woven into the plot than were ballroom numbers in many other musicals of the time: It actually served a clear dramatic function. Although the Military Glide was not a typical romantic number (such as a slow waltz or a tango), its purpose nonetheless was to reinforce the romantic element of the plot. By dramatizing a dance which the protagonist (Popple) had already indicated he would prefer to hide, the number highlighted the potential conflict that might occur should Violet's family learn of Popple's former involvement with Tony, the "danseuse."

COMIC-ROMANTIC INTERPOLATIONS

Other types of romance-related insertions involved comedy. In the 1925 production of *Sunny,* for instance, the supporting comic-romantic team of Clifton Webb and Mary Hay nearly stole the show. Paired by Ned Wayburn, Webb and Hay were "the dancing hit of the season" with their vaudeville "rube" act.[49] In this unique act the lanky, long-legged Webb was coupled with the four-foot-ten Hay, a cherubic-looking musical comedy soloist. The team combined elements of eccentric dance steps with ballroom forms and poses, all the while representing "country hicks." *Sunny* was really a vehicle for the Ziegfeld star Marilyn Miller, but the creators of Sunny (Otto Hauerbach and Oscar Hammerstein II) cast Webb and Hay as the comic counterparts to the "serious" romantic leads.[50]

The integration of the team into the production was relatively simple and effective. To make a long, complicated plot short, Miller (as "Sunny") portrays a famous bareback rider in the British circus, thwarted in her attempt to marry her former love (Paul Frawley), an army man; her authoritarian father wants her to marry the circus owner, played by Clifton Webb. In the meanwhile, Sunny receives a proposal from her lover's friend who has supposedly already proposed to a young villager (Mary Hay), who is distraught when she learns of the impending marriage.[51]

One of Webb and Hay's most acclaimed dances was the one that highlighted their commiseration over their lost loves. In the Act II "Poppy Field" scene, Webb and Hay eavesdrop on Sunny and Peter to find out if they are truly in love. To effect their plan, they pose as "unsuspecting bystanders." In keeping with their rube personas, Hay wore a simple white suit and scarf and Webb sported a pair of baggy trousers. Their funny, odd-fitting hats accentuated their height difference, as did Hay's manipulation of her parasol. The cue for their dance was Webb's line to Hay: "Don't take off your hat. We must look as innocent as possible."[52] The pun on their innocence was obvious, of course, since both dancers could not have looked more artless. The dance itself incorporated basic ballroom steps and postures, made distinct by Hay's jaunty, clipped style combined with Webb's exaggerated and elongated eccentric movement. Overall, the number functioned as a kind of comic commentary on the foolish exploits of the romantic principals.

Sunny was not sparing on ballroom numbers. Act One, scene four opened onto a setting for the "S.S. Triumphant," where a deck full of passengers was performing the fox trot to the tunes of George Olson and his Jazz Orchestra.[53] The rising exhibition ballroom team of Moss and Fontana made an appearance in the romantic fade-out at the scene's conclusion. After the principals kissed and were happily united, Moss and Fontana entered to perform what by now had become the obligatory ballroom number, in this case, a dreamy hesitation waltz.[54]

STAR VEHICLES

Not to be overlooked were star vehicles, in which an entire show was built around the talents of a renowned exhibition ballroom team. Productions of this sort were highly lucrative ventures for their producers, who featured teams of the caliber of Maurice and Florence Walton and Irene and Vernon Castle—sure box-office draws. Sometimes the production was partially an attempt to prove that the cabaret stars could handle dialogue as well as dance—an experiment that had mixed results.

One of the most prominent of these productions was Charles Dillingham's 1914 paean to ragtime, *Watch Your Step*, featuring Irene and Vernon Castle. In the 1913 production of *The Sunshine Girl*, Irene and Vernon Castle had already introduced musical theatre audiences to the Turkey Trot. But that was only one number and not enough to secure their fame. Critics were passionate about the Castles in this production. Said *The New York Herald*, "If there were ever doubt that the tango and the fox-trot would resist becoming a musical comedy theme it was dispelled by Mr. Dillingham's stroke of genius in making the Castles his two stars."[55] *Watch Your Step* was also one of the first musicals to glorify the contemporary ballroom dance craze and to use it as a musical comedy subject. Virtually all of the scenes in the show occurred in social dance settings, such as the "Palais de Fox Trot," "A Fifth Avenue Cabaret," and "The Foyer of the Metropolitan Opera House."[56] The production also boasted a beautifully designed and color-coordinated set by fashion illustrator Robert McQuinn.

Watch Your Step would live on in musical theatre history for its music. It was the first production containing a score composed entirely by Irving Berlin. Berlin's music was different and the critics noticed. Said one, "All sorts of notes come in when one doesn't expect them, and the fact that some composition starts as a waltz is no guarantee whatever that it won't finish as a polka."[57] Berlin departed from typical musical theatre composition of the day by omitting, for example, the conventional duets sung by the hero and heroine. He combined various kinds of songs, such as ballads with fox trots, to create a unique musical sound. Berlin's "rag" version of Verdi's *Rigoletto*, for instance, was the musical high point of the second act.[58]

In form, *Watch Your Step* was actually more akin to a revue than to a scripted musical comedy. The show consisted of a continuous stream of acts designed to highlight performers such as vaudeville comedian

Frank Tinney and singers Elizabeth Brice and Sallie Fisher. To increase the believability of the dance scenes and to facilitate the insertion
of the dances, Castle was cast, not surprisingly, as a dance teacher. Irene
Castle, who partnered him in most of the ballroom numbers, was listed
in the program simply as "Mrs. Vernon Castle."

A typical form of insertion occurred in Act One, scene three, at the
"Palais de Fox Trot." The scene opened on a cabaret setting. Irene
Castle entered upstage, between two chorus boys dressed in mauve suits.
Her gown, by leading fashion designer Lucille, Lady Duff-Gordon, was
blue-gray chiffon trimmed with light gray fur to coordinate with the
men's outfits. Typically, the number began with a song; the chorus asked
her to show them how to do the fox trot and she sang in reply, "You'll
have to watch your step." Irene Castle then partnered selected chorus
boys and "taught" them the fox trot.[59]

The success of *Watch Your Step* must have worried the Shuberts, who
in 1915 came up with their own star vehicle for the rival team of Maurice and Florence Walton. Once again, Elizabeth Marbury had been
working behind the scenes. As Maurice and Walton's new press representative, Marbury promoted them as she had the Castles—as New York
City's premiere ballroom team. She even claimed that they alone were
responsible for rejuvenating the supposedly "waning" dance craze.[60]

Like *Watch Your Step, Hands Up* contained a thinly veiled plot in which
Maurice and Walton had their first speaking parts. Maurice, as the "Waltz
King," and Walton, "La Belle Claire," mistakenly become involved in a
jewelry theft, prompting such amusing scenes as the "Dansant at Sing
Sing," in which an imprisoned Maurice teaches his fellow convicts the
latest ballroom dances.[61] Said one reviewer, "Happily there wasn't too
much acting for Maurice and Walton to do—that was left for the host
of clever people that the Shuberts had banked around the dancers."[62]
Their dancing, however, was performed "entrancingly." Except for one
Polish ballet sequence staged by the well-known Russian dancer Theodore Kosloff, Maurice choreographed all of the ballroom numbers.[63]

The Dolly Sisters enjoyed enormous critical and popular success with
their 1916 star vehicle, *His Bridal Night.* Tandem dancing (which consisted of dances performed by identical male or female teams) was well-
suited to integration into musical shows, since the dances could be easily built into plots concerning twins and mistaken identity. The dances
were usually inserted to highlight difficulties in determining one partner from the other. Written by Lawrence Rising and Margaret Mayo,
this musical farce concerned two men who cannot tell the twin sisters
apart.

The high point of the show was the series of tandem ballroom numbers the team performed to help their suitors determine the true bride.[64]
One of the men suggested that both sisters perform together, side by

side, since he recalled that one had a higher kick than the other. This prompted their number, 'Love Me At Twilight,' an exhibition one-step with the sisters dressed with their characteristic verve, in draped chiffon gowns with matching turbans. The Dolly Sisters built suspense into the dance by performing each of the concluding six kicks slightly higher than the preceding one, but then foiled the plot by timing each of their kicks exactly, thus making it impossible for their suitors to determine their true identity.[65] The wild response for an encore gave the Dolly Sisters a chance to preview two more of their latest creations, a Waltz Galop and a contemporary schottische, once a popular ballroom dance of the nineteenth century.[66]

These were some of the primary ways exhibition ballroom dance presented itself on musical theatre stages, trends and patterns that would continue, though perhaps in slightly different permutations, throughout its history. By the early twenties, certainly, exhibition ballroom dance had secured its place as a legitimate form of musical theatre dance, and these staged numbers continued to be the inspiration for hundreds of dance variations tried and tested by the public in the ballroom.

NOTES

1. Undated, unidentified newspaper clipping (*Erminie* clipping file, BRTC).

2. Edward Marks, *They All Sang* (New York: Viking Press, 1935), p. 157.

3. Cecil Smith and Glenn Litton, *Musical Comedy in America*, p. 88; Gerald Bordman, *American Operetta* (New York: Oxford University Press, 1981), p. 85.

4. "Here's the Dance That Has Killed the Two-Step and Set the World Waltz-Mad Again," *The World*, 21 October 1907 (*The Merry Widow* scrapbook, series 2, vol. 253, Robinson Locke Collection, BRTC).

5. See "*The Merry Widow* at The New Amsterdam Theatre," *The Musical Courier*, 23 October 1907; "Franz Lehar's Melodious *The Merry Widow* Captivates New York," *Musical America*, 26 October 1907 (*The Merry Widow* scrapbook, ser. 2, vol. 253, BRTC); Program, *The Merry Widow* (*The Merry Widow* Program File, BRTC).

6. Gerald Bordman, p. 85.

7. Ballet dancer and pantomimist Joseph C. Smith, for instance, performed exhibition versions of the tango and maxixe in the *Ziegfeld Follies of 1907;* famed vaudeville dancer and impressionist Gertrude Hoffmann introduced a unique version of the Maxixe (or "La Mattchiche," as it was billed) with Anna Held in Ziegfeld's *The Parisian Model* in 1908. See Program, *The Parisian Model,* The Broadway Theatre, 18 February 1908 (BRTC).

8. Julian Mitchell was the primary stage director for *The Ziegfeld Follies* of 1907–1913 and the 1924 *Follies*. Edward Royce is known for his choreographing of the *Ziegfeld Midnight Frolics* in the twenties. He also worked on such shows as *Century Girl* (1916), *Very Good Eddie* (1915), and *Sally* (1920).

9. Program, The Winter Garden Theatre, Week of 15 January 1914 (BRTC).

10. Program, The New Amsterdam Theatre, Week of 21 July 1913 (BRTC); "*Ziegfeld Follies*—Sixth Annual Summer Show at the New Amsterdam," New

York Tribune, 17 June 1913 (*Ziegfeld Follies of 1913* scrapbook, Robinson Locke Collection, vol. 84, p. 43, BRTC).

11. "Foy is Afloat in Fun, Giving 'Over the River,' " unidentified newspaper, ca. 1912 (*Over the River* Clipping File, BRTC).

12. Producers imported Viennese musicals in abundance during the years 1911–1914. Alongside the true Viennese works blossomed a host of native American operettas (some composed by Ivan Caryll and Victor Herbert), which were actually more like musical comedies. These shows were linked to operettas, however, because of their highly romantic plots and lyrical music. See Gerald Bordman, *American Operetta*, pp. 88–101.

13. *The Kiss Waltz* (Manuscript Production Scores, Script Material, no. 223–6, p. 21, The Shubert Archive).

14. *The New York Press*, 19 September 1911 (Martin Brown scrapbook, no. 18,445, BRTC).

15. *The Aisle Seat*, "The Kiss Waltz at the Casino," unidentified newspaper (Martin Brown scrapbook, no. 18,445, BRTC).

16. "*The Kiss Waltz* at the Casino is Surely a Go," unidentified newspaper (Martin Brown scrapbook, no. 18,445, BRTC).

17. *Act One*, 18 September 1912 (Manuscript Production Scores, Script Material, no. 144, The Shubert Archive).

18. *Act One*, 31 May 1912 (Manuscript Production Scores, Lyrics and Scenarios, no. 144, The Shubert Archive).

19. "Hoffmann's Show is Big," *The Evening American*, 23 March 1913.

20. Program, 29 November 1912 (MWEZ, no. 17,792, BRTC). In a memorandum to choreographer Ned Wayburn, J. J. Shubert specified that this trio dance was to be backed by a twenty-four-member pony chorus only. He wanted to reserve the taller showgirls for later numbers. Letter, 16 September 1913 (Manuscript Production Scores, Correspondence, Reviews, and Scenarios, no. 144, The Shubert Archive).

21. "New Musical Comedy Depicts Life in Paris," 20 November 1908, unidentified newspaper clipping (*Queen of the Moulin Rouge* Clipping File, BRTC).

22. Smith and Alexander's vaudeville ballroom act of the early teens included their Apache number. Other teams that helped popularize the Apache in vaudeville between 1908 and 1909 were Molasso and Corio (who appeared in an act entitled *L'Amour de l'Apache*) and Gould and Surrat (*Variety*, 9 January 1909, p. 14; 10 October 1908, p. 12). These teams and others may have been influenced by Maurice Mouvet, who introduced an exhibition Apache in Paris as early as 1907. Maurice and Walton's rendition of the Apache performed between 1911 and 1912 had tremendous influence on subsequent stagings of this dance in the U.S.

23. Program, Circle Theatre, 7 December 1908 (BRTC); "*Moulin Rouge*," 20 November 1908, unidentified newspaper (*Queen of the Moulin Rouge* Clipping File, BRTC).

24. Program, Winter Garden Theatre, 22 July 1912 (BRTC); Act Two, scene three ("Café Scene"), 23 July 1912 (Manuscript Production Scores, Script Material, The Shubert Archive).

25. Program, Winter Garden Theatre, 22 July 1912; *Variety*, 26 July 1912, p. 20. For more information on Moon and Morris, see *Variety*, 20 April 1912;

"A Dance That Took Eleven Years to Learn," *The Detroit News*, 15 January 1916 (Daniel Moon and George Morris scrapbook, Robinson Locke Collection, BRTC).

26. Program, Winter Garden Theatre, 22 July 1912; "Adelaide Does Not Like to be Misrepresented," *The New York American*, 24 August 1912 (Adelaide and Hughes scrapbook, MWEZ, no. 4423, BRTC).

27. *La Petite Adelaide*, undated, unidentified newspaper article (Adelaide and Hughes scrapbook, MWEZ, no. 4423).

28. "Adelaide Does Not Like to be Misrepresented," *The New York American*.

29. Program, Winter Garden Theatre, 22 July 1912 (BRTC).

30. Act Two, scene three, 23 July 1912 (Manuscript Production Material, Lyrics, and Scenarios, The Shubert Archive).

31. Program, Winter Garden Theatre, 22 July 1912; *New York Clipper*, 3 August 1912. For a description of their typical acrobatic act see *The World*, 25 July 1912 (The Shubert Archive).

32. "Passing Show is Full of Gloom," *The Morning Telegraph*, 23 July 1912 (*The Passing Show of 1912* scrapbook, MWEZ, no. 21,052, BRTC).

33. See Chapter 1 for further discussion of cotillions.

34. La Petite Adelaide, "Third Position," unidentified newspaper (Adelaide and Hughes scrapbook, MWEZ, no. 4423, BRTC).

35. After outgrowing a successful career as a child vocalist, Santley made his musical theatre debut in a touring production of *The Queen of the Moulin Rouge* (1908) and performed as a juvenile in such shows as *A Matinee Idol* (1910). In the mid-teens he formed a highly successful ballroom partnership with Ivy Sawyer. They performed in several Princess Theatre musicals, such as *Oh Boy!* (1917) and *Oh, My Dear!* (1918).

36. Act Three, scene one (Script, BRTC), p. 10.

37. Program, Lyric Theatre, Week of 18 August 1913, BRTC.

38. *New York Dramatic Mirror*, 13 May 1914 (Joseph Santley Clipping File, BRTC).

39. "Santley Dances Tango in When Dreams Come True," *The Springfield [Mass.] Union*, 16 September 1914 (Joseph Santley Clipping File, BRTC).

40. "A New Refined Tango Invented by Joseph Santley," *San Antonio [Texas] Light*, 19 October 1913 (Joseph Santley Clipping File).

41. Ibid.

42. "Joseph Santley Opposed to Public Dance Idea," *Toledo Times*, 27 September 1914 (Joseph Santley Clipping File, BRTC).

43. Ibid.

44. David Ewen, *New Complete Book of the American Musical Theatre* (New York: Holt, Rinehart & Winston, 1970, pp. 432–436; Smith and Litton, *Musical Comedy in America*, p. 121; Reuel Keith Olin, "A History and Interpretation of the Princess Theatre Musical Plays, 1915–1919" (Ph.D. dissertation, New York University, 1979), p. 60.

45. Olin, "A History and Interpretation of the Princess Theatre Musical Plays," p. 63. Marbury created other exhibition ballroom teams for the Princess Theatre shows, including Joseph Santley and Ivy Sawyer.

46. Olin, "A History and Interpretation of the Princess Theatre Musical Plays," p. 65.

47. "Is the Castle Reign Over," unidentified newspaper article (Quentin Tod Clipping File, BRTC).

48. Act One, scene five (Script, BRTC); "Musical Comedy is 'Nobody Home,'" unidentified newspaper article (*Nobody Home* scrapbook, MWEZ, nc, no. 23,034, BRTC).

49. "Famous Dancing Pair Soon to Return to Keith-Albee Circuit," *The Telegraph*, 21 June 1925 (Clifton Webb, C&L Brown Collection, BRTC).

50. Smith and Litton, *Musical Comedy in America*, p. 139.

51. Script (no. 5173, 1926, BRTC).

52. Ibid., Act Two, scene four, p. 19.

53. Ibid., Act One, scene five, "The Ship." Also see "An Afternoon with Sunny," *Stage and Screen*, 25 November 1925.

54. Garrick, "*Sunny*," unidentified newspaper clipping (Esther Howard scrapbook, MWEZ, no. 20,575, BRTC); "Mr. Hornblow Goes to the Play," *Theatre Magazine*, 25 December 1925, p. 16.

55. "*Watch Your Step* is a Castles' Night," undated (*Watch Your Step* scrapbook, NAFR + 495, BRTC).

56. Program, 10 February 1914 (MCNY).

57. "*Watch Your Step*," unidentified newspaper clipping (*Watch Your Step* Clipping File, MCNY).

58. Ibid.; Olin, p. 10; "*Watch Your Step* a Fine Production," *Billboard*, 19 December 1914.

59. Act One, scene three (Script, MCNY).

60. "Dance Craze Gets Stimulus in Hands Up," *The World*, 25 July 1915 (The Newspaper Annex, NYPL).

61. Script, *Hands Up* (MCNY).

62. "*Hands Up*," undated, unidentified newspaper clipping (*Hands Up* Clipping File, MCNY).

63. Program, 44th Street Theatre, 22 July 1915 (BRTC).

64. Program, Republic Theatre, Week of 11 September 1916; Script, 1916 (Samuel French, Inc.); *New York Evening Sun*, 17 August 1916 (*His Bridal Night* file, MCNY).

65. Act Two, scene five, script.

66. Program, Week of 11 September 1916; unidentified newspaper clippings (*His Bridal Night* Clipping File, BRTC).

————————————————— *Chapter 6* —————————————————

Decline and Rebirth

The early exhibition ballroom dance teams were clearly a prominent
and influential part of the popular dance and theatre of their time.
They were innovators in theatrical dance style and helped to popularize a pattern of social dancing still practiced today. By the mid-twenties,
however, exhibition ballroom dance began to wane as a major performance specialty. The form itself did not die but several causes led to a
decline, among them the breakup of teams due to the World War I
draft; the popularity of a new array of solo-oriented ballroom dances,
such as the Charleston and the Black Bottom; and the waning of cabaret entertainment due to Prohibition. The changing nature of vaudeville entertainment, too, was no longer as conducive to exhibition ballroom teams, and the trend in musical theatre veered toward solo rather
than team specialties.

TEAMS DISBAND

A significant reason for the decline in popularity of exhibition ballroom dance by the early twenties was the dissolution of some of the
most prominent teams. Many were broken up when the men were
drafted for World War I. For those who returned, attempts to revive
their careers were often futile; either they could no longer find suitable
partners or they could not recapture their following. Without the influence of these leading teams, many of whom were responsible for guid-

ing social dance practice, the public seemed to lose much of its former enthusiasm for ballroom dancing.

Perhaps the greatest blow to the public was the loss of Vernon Castle. During the run of *Watch Your Step* in 1915, Castle, an Englishman, enlisted in the British Royal Flying Corps. In 1917 he returned to the United States as a flight instructor at Fort Worth, Texas, where he was killed during a routine flight lesson.[1] Irene Castle continued to perform (on Broadway in *Miss 1917*) before making her film debut in *Patria*, a seventeen-part movie serial, in which she played a glamorous spy.[2] From 1922 through 1924 Irene Castle partnered William Reardon in a vaudeville act called *Let's Dance*, choreographed by Fred and Adele Astaire.[3] She still performed the specialty fox trots and waltzes that won her fame, but with Reardon she was never able to reignite the excitement produced by her partnership with Vernon Castle.

The public witnessed the breakup of another extremely popular team, Maurice Mouvet and Florence Walton. The war also had strained their professional and marital relationship. From 1917 to 1919 Maurice worked in the army medical corps in France while Walton performed with temporary partners; periodically she would reunite with Maurice while he was on duty for a special performance.[4] But after a brief run in the *Ziegfeld Follies of 1919*, at the war's end, Maurice and Walton were divorced, bringing their professional partnership to an end.[5]

Neither Maurice nor Walton gave up their dancing careers, however. Maurice had a string of successful partnerships during the twenties, with such dancers as Leonora Hughes and Barbara Bennett. Maurice still cropped up as a popular item in magazine and newspaper articles, offering his informed opinions about the latest dance styles. But the dancing climate was changing, and Maurice now found himself in the curious position of defending the more "traditional" ballroom dances, such as the fox trot and the waltz, from the so-called jazz dances that had recently become popular.[6]

Florence Walton went on to perform briefly with Parisian cabaret dancer Alexandre Vlad, mostly in dramatic tango numbers; then in 1922 she formed a partnership with Leon Leitrim, who was to become her husband. Walton and Leitrim established themselves in Paris before returning to the United States where they performed in supper clubs and on the Keith vaudeville circuit.[7] During an engagement at the Marigny Theatre in 1923, Walton and Leitrim set up a publicity "war" with Mouvet and Leonora Hughes, who were performing in a rival revue.[8] But while the attention helped bring Mouvet and Walton back into the spotlight, it certainly could not provide the public with the same excitement they had felt when Maurice and Walton were a team. Maurice went on to perform with his final partner and second wife, Eleonora Hughes, until his untimely death from tuberculosis in 1927.

By the late teens and early twenties many exhibition ballroom dancers disbanded in order to pursue careers in film, a rapidly growing and alluring medium. Like other performers, the teams were attracted by the lavish Hollywood salaries perpetuated by the star system. Some remained dancers, although many discovered new careers as actors and actresses. Mae Murray, for example, signed a two-year movie contract with the Lasky Company in 1917, for whom she was to perform light comedy roles.[9] She worked with several other studios throughout the twenties and achieved her greatest fame in the 1925 production of *The Merry Widow*, which created new interest in the Merry Widow Waltz. Ballroom dancers also found lucrative careers as dance directors for motion pictures. After performing in several Fox films in 1917, Joan Sawyer, for example, signed with the company in the early twenties as a choreographer.[10]

THE INFLUX OF SOLO DANCES

Another reason for the apparent decline in exhibition work during the twenties was the proliferation of newer, solo dances that were becoming popular in the ballroom and on stage, including the Charleston, the Black Bottom, and the Shimmy. Most of these dances were inspired by the craze for jazz music during the early twenties. Essentially, jazz combined syncopated rhythms with a steady, rhythmic bass, similar to ragtime, but it slurred rhythms even more than in the usual ragtime syncopation in order to create a wild cacophony of sound. The typical jazz band consisted of piano, cornet, trombone, clarinet, and trap drums, with decided emphasis on the brass instruments.[11]

One such jazz dance was the Shimmy, made popular by speakeasy queen Gilda Gray. A solo dance characterized by the isolation of alternating shoulders with a swaying of the body to one-step music, the Shimmy had actually been around as early as 1916. It became a national craze, though, once Gilda Gray performed it in the *Ziegfeld Follies of 1922*.[12] Popular lyricists and composers virtually created a genre of Shimmy songs (one of the most popular was 'I Wish I Could Shimmy Like My Sister Kate'), and the public was fascinated with the abandoned, shaking movements of the dance.[13]

The Charleston, too, became a highly popular stage dance and, more than the other solo dances of the time, it took quick root in the ballroom. The dance first appeared in the black musical *Runnin' Wild* (1923), produced by George White. James P. Johnson composed the score for the Charleston, and a male chorus of "Dancing Redcaps" brought the house down with their hand-clapping and foot-stomping to the intricate rhythms of the music.[14] Other theatre producers soon picked up the dance; it appeared in the *Ziegfeld Follies* and *Greenwich Village Follies of 1923,* and dance teachers eventually adapted it for the ballroom. Performed to a steady, syncopated rhythm, the Charleston epitomized the free-form solo jazz dances of the twenties.

Another widely popular social and theatrical dance was the Black Bottom, which first won notoriety as a result of Ann Pennington's performance in the *George White Scandals of 1926.*[15] As with the Charleston and the Shimmy, the Black Bottom owed its existence to black composers and performers. As early as 1919, Perry Bradford had composed 'The Original Black Bottom Dance,' with dance instructions that described a stomping and shuffling step and a knee sway based on a Charleston rhythm.[16] One reviewer described Pennington's staged version (performed with Tom Patricola) as "a slapping of the feet, a wriggling of the hips, a balancing of arms and a scooping movement of heel and toe."[17] The dance went through a series of "refining" stages before it was acceptable for the white ballroom.

As far as the social dance scene was concerned, the public continued to perform the basic one-steps, tangos, and fox trots introduced in the early teens. Clearly the early ragtime dances had made a lasting impression (and have remained a part of the social dance repertoire to this day). But by the mid-twenties something of the original enthusiasm engendered by these dances had begun to wear off. As veteran exhibition dancer Clifton Webb explained about the twenties in a 1933 article in *Vogue* magazine, "The public had—or thought they had—learned all they wanted to; they had conquered the art of the fox trot, waltz, one step, and tango, and they no longer sought the guiding hand of the professional educator."[18] Now it was the newer solo-type dances, such as the Charleston, Black Bottom, and Varsity Drag, that offered the public its greatest challenge.

THE DECLINE OF THE CABARET

Prohibition also inhibited the further growth of exhibition ballroom dance around the country. One of Prohibition's most visible targets, of course, was the cabaret. Some exhibition dancing continued in the speakeasy, which had sprouted to fill the vacuum produced by the declining cabaret. In these inconspicuous-looking cellars and back rooms, owners improvised simple dance floors and presented an occasional exhibition ballroom team.[19] But club owners were naturally wary of investing money in establishments that could be raided and closed within an evening.[20]

Around 1924, supper clubs and nightclubs—more respectable forms of nightlife—began cropping up along with the speakeasies. To compensate for the absence of liquor, the owners of these clubs tried to create an enticing, plush atmosphere, featuring name entertainers, big bands, and revue-format shows. The supper clubs, which catered to the before-and-after theatre crowds, were more likely to offer smaller-scale, intimate kinds of entertainment, including exhibition ballroom teams.[21] Some of the teams included Moss and Fontana and Cortez and Peggy, who specialized in Argentine-style numbers, and the De Marcos, who had begun their career in vaudeville in 1921.[22] As a profession, however, straight exhibition ballroom dance was not in the same demand as it had been earlier, and there was no single team, at this point, that could capture the public imagination. It was not until the mid-to-late-thirties that exhibition teams would again dominate the nightclub scene.[23]

THE EFFECTS ON VAUDEVILLE
AND MUSICAL THEATRE

Vaudeville producers, like nightclub managers, sought out larger and flashier acts, though for different reasons. By 1925, vaudeville had begun experiencing major changes in its structure, due largely to the encroaching presence of film. During the early development of the movies, vaudeville producers had actually encouraged the presentation of silent shorts in order to remain in competition with the growing movie industry. As early as the teens, in fact, managers frequently presented newsreels as chasers at the end of a bill or short films as featured fifteen-minute acts.[24] But the growth of the film business ultimately threatened both vaudeville's traditional performers and its exhibition ballroom dance teams.

Vaudeville owners tried to stay abreast of developments in the movie industry, but they faced keen competition from the powerful movie czars with their grand, enticing movie palaces. The new theatres were lavishly decorated, with huge seating capacities, featuring continuous shows at low cost.[25] This fact alone, however, was not enough to wreak permanent damage on the vaudeville industry, which continued to compete with the movie industry by building even larger vaudeville houses with greater numbers of films on their bills. In the mid-twenties, though, when the movie industry began presenting what were known as "super specials"—feature-length films—vaudeville managers began to worry. In order to stay abreast of their competitors, managers rented these longer films and featured them in their own houses. But because the films were costly the vaudeville part of the show had to be trimmed—a fact that hurt many performers, including ballroom teams.[26] Vaudeville managers were now increasingly likely to feature cheaper variety acts, and thus they could not afford the salaries of the top ballroom teams. While the Keith and Orpheum circuits were hit the hardest, this decline was true for all of the smaller black and ethnic circuits.

Perhaps one of the biggest blows to vaudeville (and to exhibition ballroom teams) was the unit show packaged by the major film and theatre conglomerates, such as Paramount Publix and RKO, around 1926. Also known as "Prologs," "Presentations," and "Ideas," the unit shows consisted of a series of live variety acts designed to precede a feature film. The shows generally lasted about thirty minutes and often featured forty or more performers.[27] By the late twenties, and into the thirties, Prolog entertainment virtually eclipsed traditional vaudeville in popularity. The unit shows were able to lure performers from standard vaudeville because they paid more and offered their clients extra weeks of playing time.

Exhibition ballroom teams were virtually lost in this shuffle from vaudeville to Prolog entertainment. The large stages in the grandest film houses (The Capitol Theatre at Fifty-first Street and Broadway had a stage measuring 110 feet by 75 feet) lent themselves more readily to choruses and full-size orchestras rather than to intimate ballroom numbers.[28] Also, because the Prologs functioned as a kind of preview of the film, their dance acts tended to be larger and showier—ballet troupes, choruses, and adagio teams known for their spectacular acrobatic displays.[29]

A popular act at the gigantic Roxy Theatre in 1927, for instance, featured the simultaneous performance of five adagio teams. This style of dance was particularly popular in the late twenties and was conducive to the new, ever-expanding vaudeville and movie theatre stages. Unlike ballroom-adagio dance, in which ballroom dance was the basis of the act, "straight" adagio work was predominantly acrobatic and was often performed by a team or line of dancers. Each team, spaced at fairly wide intervals, all performed the same fast-paced routine. In the typically breathtaking finale the men exited in single file, carrying their female partners on the upraised palms of their hands.[30] The typical closing acts of Prologs were precision choruses, often consisting of up to forty-eight dancers, whose final poses dissolved into the screen credits.[31] Ballroom forms were still seen in Prolog entertainment; some adagio routines, in fact, were based on adaptations of the tango and Apache dances. But the presentation of single exhibition teams performing a straight series of three or four ballroom numbers was an increasing rarity.

By the late twenties exhibition ballroom teams no longer enjoyed the same featured status in the musical theatre either. Producers spent millions of dollars advertising jazz numbers, and in many of the lavish postwar revues, single exhibition ballroom numbers simply could not compete with these larger, showier acts.[32] The most prominent dance numbers of the twenties typically featured a solo female performer, facing the audience, framed by a chorus. Some of the most sought-after female soloists included Marilyn Miller, Ann Pennington, and Gilda Gray.[33] While social dance instructors tried to adapt the Charleston, Black Bottom, and Shimmy as couple dances, for performance specialties they were almost always choreographed as solos.

Some exhibition ballroom dancers, such as Clifton Webb, made successful transitions from team dancing to solo work. In *The Little Show* (1929) he proved to audiences and reviewers alike that he was a good light comedian and solo-eccentric dancer, as well as a graceful ballroom performer. One widely acclaimed solo number was the "Moanin' Low" sequence performed with Libby Holman, in which Webb combined movements from the rugged Apache dance with the slithering Snake Hips routine originated by Earl Tucker at the Cotton Club.[34] The scene dramatized an exchange between a prostitute and her angry pimp who comes to collect money from her. As the dejected Holman sang 'Moanin' Low,' Webb launched into his dance, becoming a "one man Laocoön, writhing in rhythm and tossing his pelvis about in figure-eights like a cowboy's lasso."[35] The number proved Webb's ability to compete with solo performers, enabling him to continue his musical career.

THE ALLURE OF THE MOVIES

Although the film industry continued to lure dancers away from live theatre, there was a limited amount of actual exhibition ballroom dance *specialties*, featured in silent films or talkies, that required the skills of trained ballroom dancers. In the transition-era films, ballroom dance sequences tended to be used to create mood and establish milieu, as in depicting cabaret and club scenes or fashionable hotel ballrooms. In the domestic comedies and melodramas of the period, ballroom dance was often used as a device to integrate plot and further the story line, accentuating themes of love and romance.[36]

The Four Horsemen of the Apocalypse, in fact, is a good example of the thematic method in which ballroom numbers were used in 1920s' film. The film's' star, Rudolph Valentino, was of course an exemplar of the Argentine Tango, and his talents are amply demonstrated in early scenes of the film. But one of the best-remembered images from the film is that of Alice Terry and Valentino in his living room before the Victrola, in which he attempts to teach her the tango. The focus is less on the specifics of the dance, certainly, than on the wooing by the free-spirited artist, Julio (played by Valentino) of the young, married Madame Laurier (Terry). The dance steps, the suggestive tango poses, and the flirtatious glances to one another across the Victrola became a classic symbol of temptation and romantic seduction.[37]

Exhibition ballroom dance specialties fared little better in the transfer to sound in 1927. The kinds of dances featured in early sound movie musicals were usually large production numbers; the settings of these films essentially mimicked the proscenium, movie-going experience itself, and the numbers typically began and ended with a proscenium effect. The dance specialties that *were* featured were more likely to contain Charleston or adagio numbers, or other popular jazz dances of the period, than the classic ballroom dances.[38] It was not until the mid-to-late-thirties when the movie musical came of age that exhibition ballroom dances became featured specialties.

THE REBIRTH

In 1932, *American Dancer* reporter Sam Bernard lamented the absence of exhibition ballroom dance specialties in musicals or the movies. He claimed that neither medium had "fostered new ballroom ideas" or invested enough money in advertising these dances.[39] But by 1933, there were growing signs that this state of affairs might be changing. For one thing, the country gradually began to recover from the Depression, which had put a lid on the growth of most entertainment forms. In 1933 Franklin Delano Roosevelt became President and his New Deal programs inspired progress both in business and the arts. People began to feel a renewed interest in recreational activities, and ballroom dancing took on a new life.[40]

The repeal of Prohibition in 1933 helped open up many more hotels and public ballrooms. During the nightclubs' transitional years (from about 1932 to 1937), the radio had come to advance dancing at home, and weekly broadcasts of ballroom dance instruction had become popular.[41] By the mid-thirties, owners who had closed down their clubs during Prohibition were reopening. Many of them, no doubt, hoped to capture business from the Broadway theatre trade, which had picked up after the Depression. This turn of events heartened many unemployed ballroom dancers who, in the words of one commentator, "sadly, still clutter up the agency offices."[42] Ballroom dancing also received a renewed sense of professionalism through the efforts of noted choreographer and dance teacher Fred Le Quorne, who began organizing dancers into unions. (One of his proposals was that dancers be paid routinely for any "audition engagements" given at clubs or hotels.[43])

New types of ballroom dances were also emerging to capture the public's imagination, such as the rumba. Originally a Cuban dance, combining African and Caribbean rhythms, the rumba, with its suggestive hip movements, soon become one of the most popular couple dances in the ballroom. Later in the 1930s, the Brazilian samba caught on, distinguished by its subtle undulations of the chest and lilting rising and falling motion of the body. The big bands associated with these dances were led by such conductor/composers as Benny Goodman, Glenn Miller, Artie Shaw, Count Basie, and Xavier Cougat.[44] Their unmistakable swing style, with its pulsating rhythm, and distinctive combination of brass and reeds harmony, inspired a new generation of social and professional dancers. Vying with the Latin American dances in popularity were the energetic dances born of swing music (a form of jazz), such as the Lindy Hop, the Shag, and the Suzy-Q.[45]

The Lindy Hop (or Jitterbug as it was called in white society) was the most popular of the swing dances, originating in Harlem's Savoy Ballroom around 1936. The basic movement of the lindy step was a syncopated two-step, or box-step, which stressed the offbeat.[46] Its distinguishing feature was a breakaway section, in which partners separated to improvise acrobatic jumps and lifts. Alongside the lindy, a crop of so-called fad dances sprung up in ballrooms around the country, such as the Big Apple. In this group dance, described as "a square dance in swing time,"[47] each couple came forward, in the center of a large circle, to perform some spirited swing steps, such as the quick, hopping steps of the Shag, or those from the Lindy Hop. The lindy and some of its offshoot dances, however, were optimally performed as a group dance, and did not lend themselves to the exhibition ballroom format.

NIGHTCLUBS

By 1937 a visible nightclub community was in full swing, making it possible for ballroom teams to flourish once again. Since the early thirties the supper clubs had gradually enlarged their space from some 200 to 1,200 diners, and without the heavy cover charge enforced by the speakeasies the clubs attracted greater numbers and classes of patrons. As Bosley Crowther of *The New York Times* noted, "The nightclubs have stood forth as witnesses to the return of liberal spending and good times. The dollar is rolling freely again not only in New York's resorts but in the familiar gathering places of nightlife from Boston to Hollywood."[48] Around 1936 the Broadway area theatre-restaurants experienced their greatest boom in years, and soon after other clubs and restaurants around the city followed suit.

There were several types of nightclubs during the late thirties and early forties, each of them providing dining, drinking, and dancing. The Broadway nightclubs that catered to out-of-towners were among the largest, accommodating upwards of 1,200 guests; they were moderately priced and featured nonstop entertainment. These theatre-restaurants with large stages, such as the highly publicized International

Casino at Forty-fifth Street and Broadway, featured two shows nightly, consisting of large dance bands and huge, splashy production numbers. Essentially the shows functioned like mini-revues, with a variety of specialty acts, dancers, and choral groups. Harlem was also home to many well-known clubs, such as Connie's Inn and the Cotton Club, which featured spectacular entertainment catering primarily to white audiences.[49]

The most fashionable clubs, generally more expensive and with a definite cosmopolitan air, were those hotels and restaurants around Fifth Avenue in the Fifties, an area that came to be designated as The "Montmartre of New York." The Persian Room at the Plaza Hotel, the Coconut Grove at the Park Central Hotel, and the Rainbow Room at Rockefeller Center were some of the more popular and best-known nightspots. Then, dotted all across New york City, from Greenwich Village to Harlem, were the smaller, unrestricted clubs or so-called "swing dens" featuring "hot" swing or Cuban music, open until the small hours of the morning.[50]

In most nightclubs the major form of entertainment was the floor show, consisting of renditions from a name band (the tango-rumba combinations were the most popular) followed by a series of specialty acts, including singers, solo musicians, and exhibition ballroom teams. There were generally two shows, one at 9 p.m. and the other at midnight. In large part, nightclub acts had come to replace vaudeville, which had been on a steady decline since the late twenties. As commentator Maurice Zolotow noted in *American Mercury* magazine, "After vaudeville was killed off by the sound movies, the night clubs became one of the few exhibitors of 'flesh' entertainment."[51] Many former vaudeville professionals turned their sights to nightclub work as the vaudeville market dwindled. As a result, the quality of the shows improved greatly.[52]

The floor show from the 1938 season at the Rainbow Room possessed all the winning ingredients. The entertainment opened with solo pianist Evalyn Tyner, followed by the well-known bandleader Nano Rodrigo and his tango-rumba combo, who "do the standard Latin tempos with occasional interludes of Johann Strauss and other Viennese waltzes."[53] Eva Ortega, "a personality songstress" followed next in a number with the orchestra, followed by Lester Cole and his orchestral octet the Musical Midshipmen, who performed "spirited medleys of pops in unusual arrangements." Next to last on the program was the exhibition ballroom team of Maurice and Cordoba, a popular Latin dance duo who performed "distinguished and distinctive arrangements of the maxixe, tango, and other terps." Vocalist Kathleen Barrie closed the show.

TEAMS OF THE THIRTIES AND FORTIES

This combination of new musical compositions, new dances, and expanded venues all helped spawn a new generation of exhibition ballroom teams. The Latin vogue, in particular, gave rise to a host of new, smoldering duos, including the renowned teams of Gomez and Winona, Rosita and Ramon, Mary Raye and Naldi, and Georges and Jalna. No longer billed as "modern" or "society" dancers, the teams of this period came to be designated as "dancers" "dance impressionists," or "dance stylists." One reason for this change in usage was that exhibition ballroom dances were no longer viewed as revolutionary in form and had become an established part of American dance and culture.

American popular entertainment provided few venues for black ballroom teams performing in the prevailing romantic-adagio mode. Some, however, still managed to make a name for themselves. One of the best-known was Margot Webb and Harold Norton (Norton and Margot) who performed between 1933 and 1946 on the black entertainment circuits. They appeared as the featured dance team with the Earl "Fatha" Hines Band in vaudeville and in revue shows at major black nightclubs in New York and other major cities. But unfortunately, as historian Brenda Dixon-Stowell notes, "a romantic ballroom team performing a white repertory of waltz, tango, rumba and bolero numbers was ahead of its time. Western art forms were reserved for whites only."[54] Because Norton and Webb were denied access to the major white vaudeville and club circuits, they never achieved the full measure of acclaim due to them.

For the exhibition teams of the late thirties and early forties, the standard repertory consisted of rumbas, tangos, fox trots, waltzes, and perhaps a specialty jazz number of some sort. The host of Latin teams, of course, specialized in the rumbas and tangos. By and large, the dancing of the late thirties and early forties veered more toward the spectacular and dramatic than had the ballroom work of earlier decades; the predominant style was ballroom-adagio dance, in which the teams wore elegant evening clothes and executed breathtaking lifts, spins, and whirls.

Unlike teams from the 1910s, ballroom dancers of the late thirties and forties regularly employed choreographers. Lola Andre, an adagio-ballroom dancer who performed as part of the team known as Lola and Andre, worked with Alberto Galo, one of the most prominent dance teachers and choreographers of the thirties. Galo would choreograph while listening to the music the team had selected for their dances. Once the dances had been set, the team brought their piano sheet to their arranger, who then made up twenty-five scores for each of the band members.[55]

Some highly celebrated dance teams of the late thirties and early forties were Veloz and Yolanda and Tony De Marco and his two partners,
Renée, from the thirties, and Sally, of the forties. Veloz and Yolanda
and each of the De Marco teams had remarkably long-lasting careers,
and were able to sustain themselves in all of the theatrical venues open
to them during this time, including nightclubs, vaudeville, and the
movies. Each of them epitomized contemporary styles of ballroom dance
and furthered the appeal of this dance form.

A classic waltz-rumba team, Veloz and Yolanda (Frank Veloz and
Yolanda Casazza) started out on the amateur circuit in the late twenties,
winning a major competition that brought them appearances at dance
palaces and supper clubs around the city. At one club, the Everglades,
an agent for the Shubert Brothers spotted them as youthful and re-
freshing talent, and placed the team in a 1927 operetta *The Love Call.*
Here Veloz and Yolanda won accolades for their whirling Latin-tinged
"Fiesta" dance. By their second Shubert show, the musical revue *Pleasure Bound* (1929), Veloz and Yolanda had graduated to featured dance
team in the Act II cabaret scene, performing "one of those centrifugal
dances that spin the feminine heels in the air." [56]

Coveted nightclub engagements followed, such as their thirty-two week
stint at the revered St. Regis Roof, which ensured Veloz and Yolanda's
fame. The mainstays of their act were their waltzes and rumbas, performed in a typically "suave and svelte" manner. [57] The team helped
introduce an elegant, adagio style of breathtaking spins, and small but
perfectly executed dramatic lifts. Yolanda also made dramatic, imagi-
native use of her clothing, swirling the folds of her dress around her
as she spun to reinforce the team's line of movement. It was also the
sense of personal communication, of unquestioned romance between
each of the partners, that endeared them to audiences.

Veloz and Yolanda are responsible for helping elevate exhibition
ballroom dance to the status of concert dance. In 1938 they appeared
at Carnegie Hall in a recital devoted exclusively to their ballroom specialties. What was originally designed as a prepublicity boost to kick off
their nationwide tour turned out to be an enormously successful venture. Although Carnegie Hall had been the site for recitals of other
types of dance and even for the Benny Goodman Orchestra, it was the
first time the revered concert hall had presented an evening exclusively
devoted to ballroom dance. [58]

Veloz and Yolanda's varied program at Carnegie Hall attested to the
diversity of their range. Accompanied by Pancho and His Orchestra
from the Plaza Hotel's Persian Room and accordionist Jerry Shelton,
Veloz and Yolanda performed a novel maxixe done as a dancing lesson, two fast jazz numbers to 'Darktown Strutters Ball' and 'Alexander's
Ragtime Band,' as well as their signature tangos, rumbas, and waltzes.

The show would not have been complete without their popular Veo-landa, in which Veloz performed any basic ballroom steps while Yolanda followed with quick sliding steps in double time. Veloz and Yolanda continued to appear as concert performers; in 1942 they appeared at the American Theatre in New York City in a show billed as "Veloz and Yolanda in an evening of Dansation."[59]

Rivals to Veloz and Yolanda during the thirties were Tony and Re-née De Marco. Tony De Marco performed with several dance partners during his career, each of them named "De Marco" and taught the trademark De Marco style. After performing with Nina (born Helen Kroner) in the twenties, Tony De Marco recruited Renée LeBlanc; she was a chorus girl in a production of Harry Carroll's 1929 *Music Box Revue*, who had studied ballet with Ernest Belcher and Theodore Kos-loff. The dancers married, and as Tony and Renée De Marco they won acclaim at the Persian Room in 1934 just as the nightclub scene was being revived.

Their style was distinct: they specialized in a brisk, sharply executed quick-step (almost in double-time) punctuated with fast turns and pirouettes performed with "machine-gun precision."[60] Their routines typically included a bit of playful competition, where they tried to outdo one another in solo breaks during the numbers. They also joked and talked with one another during their dances, a technique new to ball-room dance acts at that time.

In addition to the standard rumbas, tangos, and waltzes of the day, the De Marcos fashioned ballroom routines to classical music, such as Debussy's 'Clair de Lune' and Chopin's 'Waltz in C Sharp Minor.' One of their most popular routines was an exhibition waltz performed to the Jerome Kern ballad, 'The Way You Look Tonight.' The dance was a romantic-pantomimic number. Renée, while peeking into her hand mirror and fixing her hair, attracted the attention of Tony De Marco, who entered and danced around her in awe. The team eventually fash-ioned the impromptu routine into an exhibition waltz performed to Noel Coward's composition 'I'll Follow My Secret Heart.'[61] The couple were divorced in 1941, but Tony carried on the De Marco tradition with yet another mate, Sally (formerly Sally Craven). Their act was per-haps the most acrobatic of all the partnerships, but contained many of the same types of routines. Tony and Sally De Marco appeared to-gether for nearly thirteen years, in nightclubs, films, and on tele-vision.[62]

LATE VAUDEVILLE AND MUSICAL THEATRE

In addition to working in hotels and restaurants, exhibition ballroom teams also toured vaudeville theatres around the country. Of course, by the mid-to-late thirties, vaudeville entertainment was a much less structured enterprise than it had been in earlier decades. Instead of organized circuits employing teams, talent agencies, such as the Music Corporation of America (MCA), might organize several of their acts and send them out on the road for six weeks in theatres large enough to make a profit. Variety shows usually consisted of half the number of acts featured in traditional vaudeville, with less emphasis on comedy. Ballroom teams were most often booked along with one or two featured orchestras, a vocalist, and perhaps another dance offering.[63]

Typically, the shows were featured before or after a motion picture, as at the popular Roxy Theatre and Radio City Music Hall in New York City. Ten years earlier exhibition ballroom teams had fared poorly in these unit shows, largely because the intimacy of the numbers was generally lost in the hugeness of the stages. But modes of ballroom dance had changed once again. Not only were the newer ballroom dances more likely to be more spectacular, with aerial lifts and spins, the numbers themselves were generally placed before a large chorus, or one of the large bands headlining the show.

Exhibition ballroom teams also reappeared in greater numbers in the musical theatre, particularly in revues. With the popularity of Latin song numbers it had become relatively simple for choreographers to insert an accompanying dance team. As early as 1930, even before the nightclub boom, several productions featured exhibition ballroom dance, signaling a revival of the form as a musical theatre specialty. *Three's A Crowd*, Max Gordon's stylish 1930 revue, featured Clifton Webb and Amy Revere in a romantic waltz sequence. Revere was a ballet-trained specialty dancer who had performed in several editions of the *Earl Carroll Vanities* and in George Gershwin's *Tip-Toes* (1925). Their riveting waltz, "The Moment I Saw You," occurring at the close of Act I, was "practically the dance to end dances."[64] It was, perhaps, the number's quiet intimacy and understated elegance, in contrast to the flashy production numbers of the era, that caught audiences' attention. Webb's charm combined with Revere's ethereal grace prompted one reviewer to note, "The days of the Castles and the other kings and queens of ballroom dances were recalled and most pleasantly."[65]

By the mid-thirties (and into the early forties) most of the popular nightclub teams made appearances in the musical theatre. They were seen in some of the most popular shows and revue series of the decade, such as Roy and Grace Macdonald in Rodgers and Hart's *Babes in Arms* (1937), Veloz and Yolanda in *The Ziegfeld Follies of 1937*, and Jeanne Tyler and Gower Champion in *The Streets of Paris* (1939). The comedic duo of Paul and Grace Hartmann enjoyed particular staying power. In the 1936 production of *Red, Hot and Blue*, starring Jimmy Durante and Ethel Merman, they scored a hit with their hilarious ballroom antics.

The plot, as such, was a vague satire of the New York social set, but for the most part it was an unabashedly glorified vaudeville affair featuring a variety of featured turns. The Hartmanns provided the evening's memorable dance moments. After a waltz-song, sung by Dorothy Vernon and Thurston Crane, the action segued into the Hartmann's "devastating takeoffs" on contemporary dance styles, including their noted "hoke Bolero."[66]

By the forties, ballroom numbers had become an expected part of musical theatre production. Ballroom dance was one of several musical comedy dance techniques that existed alongside jazz, tap, and ballet. In fact, choreographers often staged ballroom-based routines for the principals in the show, thereby obviating the need for a featured team. Perhaps one of the greatest differences between the insertion of ballroom dancers into musicals of the teens and of this later period was that, during the teens, there was often a more self-conscious use of exhibition numbers. Because of the newness of the form, plots and scenes were often built around ballroom dancers, and conscious references were made to their dances in the dialogue. By the forties, ballroom dances did not need a rationale, since audiences had become accustomed to their use as a musical theatre convention.

THE MOVIE MUSICAL

The forum in which exhibition teams of the thirties and forties ultimately achieved their greatest exposure was in the movies. By the late thirties the movie musical had finally come of age, technologically and artistically. Because of film's increased technical capabilities and the new vogue for ballroom teams, the dancers began appearing with greater frequency. Latin love scenes, featuring star performers, such as Delores del Rio, had become particularly popular, so it seemed only natural to feature the latest Latin dance teams.[67] For the most part, however, the ballroom dancers were not promoted as stars; the 1936 film *Born to Dance,* for instance, spotlighted the team of Georges and Jalna, but the star was Eleanor Powell. Instead, the team tended to be featured as specialty dancers in nightclub or ballroom scenes, or in some kind of festive or holiday setting. Typically the exhibition ballroom routines were framed by huge production numbers, with large choruses and lavish settings.

One stunning instance of this type of staging was the 1936 movie *Champagne Waltz,* featuring the renowned dance team Veloz and Yolanda with dance direction by Busby Berkeley. The movie starred Metropolitan Opera soprano Gladys Swarthout as the daughter of Franz Strauss, a composer and proprietor of a waltz establishment, and Fred MacMurray as Buzzy Bellew, leader of the swing band at the neighboring jazz club. Despite the protestations of the elder Strauss, the couple fall in love and their union is sealed in one of the film's most celebrated scenes at the Blue Danube Roof. Here the modern sounds of brassy swing music met the melodious harmonies of the Viennese Waltz. Said Frank S. Nugent of *The New York Times,* "This 'production number,' probably the one in which Paramount invested its $40,000, appears to be staffed by the combined orchestras of the Metropolitan, the Philharmonic, Paul Whiteman and Fred Waring, staged anywhere but on the hotel roof it is supposed to represent."[68] The scene featured several dance numbers, including a huge group waltz followed by Veloz and Yolanda's show-stopping Champagne Waltz itself.[69]

Of course, the team that helped increase the vogue for ballroom dancing on film was that of Fred Astaire and Ginger Rogers, who were to star in a series of movie musicals throughout the thirties, beginning with *Flying Down to Rio* (1933). Their dances inspired several popular dance crazes, such as the Carioca, with its bouncy two-quarter time rhythm reminiscent of the maxixe. Supported by a lavish production number of Carioca-dancing couples, Astaire and Rogers' novel dance, with its slight swaying motion to and fro and tilted head movement, became an overnight sensation in the ballroom.[70] In the 1934 production of *The Gay Divorcée,* Astaire and Rogers delighted audiences with yet another number destined to become a hit. "Last season it was the Carioca which persuaded the foolhardy to bash their heads together," mused one reviewer. "Now the athletic RKO-Radio strategists have created the Continental, an equally strenuous routine in which you confide your secret dreams to your partner under the protective camouflage of the music."[71] Performed to the strains of Cole Porter, Astaire and Rogers' Continental epitomized the sense of joyous romance capable between couples.

Certainly Astaire and Rogers did much to promote ballroom dance as a popular art, but they were to a large degree in a class by themselves. Astaire was more than a ballroom dancer—he was a virtuosic performer who fused tap, ballet, and ballroom to create a highly personal style. He and Rogers were also actors, which set them apart from other teams of their day and which helped to develop their enormous popular and critical success. Although it has been claimed that Astaire and Rogers were as dominant as the Castles in their time, Astaire and Rogers' function within the culture was actually quite different. A unique facet of the Castles' dancing (and, in fact, of most of their contemporaries) was its instructional capacity. The Castles were as much teachers and role models as they were performers, and actively promulgated their dances to the public (by way of their dance school and their dance publications).

For the most part, Astaire and Rogers (and other well-known ballroom dancers of the day) did not themselves become actively involved with the social dance scene in this way.[72] Of course, it was Fred Astaire himself, along with business associate Charles L. Casanave, who founded the first Fred Astaire Dance Studio in 1947. But it was really the dance teachers of the day who were responsible for adapting the ballroom novelty dances of Astaire and Rogers, and other professional teams, for the ballroom. Although the thirties public certainly admired the dancing of Astaire and Rogers (and may even have fantasized dancing like them) it did not have the same sense of identification with them, since their dancing ability was well beyond what the public would realistically expect from itself. As one reviewer noted wryly of Astaire and Rogers' rendition of the Continental, while the dance "provides Mr. Astaire with a musical theme to match his nimble feet . . . when executed domestically it probably will lack something of his polish."[73]

THE TRADITION CONTINUED

While exhibition ballroom teams of the thirties and forties developed their own unique patterns and styles of dance, they were inheritors of pre–World War I traditions. Ballroom dancers of the teens were clearly an inspiration to later teams, who emulated them in choice of repertoires. The team of Woods and Bray, for instance, performed their acrobatic version of the once highly popular Apache dance. Veloz and Yolanda regularly included the maxixe and Argentine tango in their concert ballroom tours of the late thirties and early forties. In their dance manual, *Tango and Rumba: The Dances of Today,* Veloz and Yolanda describe the history of the dances they perform and pay a debt to the work of such teams as Irene and Vernon Castle and Maurice and Florence Walton. And, of course, Fred Astaire and Ginger Rogers starred in the movie tribute to the Castles—*The Story of Vernon and Irene Castle* (1939). Other teams, too, either acknowledged the contribution of earlier teams or used their knowledge of earlier dance styles to enhance their own technique.

Irene Castle, in fact, sponsored several teams during the thirties, of whose ballroom style she approved. Among these were Veloz and Yolanda and Tony and Sally De Marco. On one occasion she held a "Gold and Black Pooch Ball" at the Congress Hotel (for the benefit of Orphans of the Storm, her animal welfare society) and featured Veloz and Yolanda among other performers.[74] Irene also gave her stamp of approval to the young team of Jeanne Tyler and Gower Champion, who in 1936 had won the "Waltz to Fame" concert cosponsored by Veloz and Yolanda. Generally the teams she admired were those that exuded a simple elegance and gracefulness, characteristics that had exemplified her own dancing with Vernon.[75]

All of these preeminent teams of the late thirties enjoyed success through the early forties. With the start of World War II in 1941 there was actually a boom in ballroom dance, both as an exhibition specialty and as a popular national pastime. Nightclubs expanded their entertainments to serve as an escape from wartime anxieties,[76] and the musical theatre presented an increasing number of new shows with wartime experiences as themes. The government also sponsored hundreds of wartime movie reels, usually clips of various popular singers and dancers, including exhibition ballroom teams.

There was a sense, too, that performers had an important role to play in serving the national welfare. In 1942, *Dance Magazine* commented that two popular exhibition ballroom teams—Tony and Sally De Marco, in the musical *Banjo Eyes*, and Grace and Paul Hartmann, appearing at the Waldorf—"are doing more than their share in bolstering public morale through sheer artistry. And, let no one belittle the importance of dancing in these troubled times!"[77] Exhibition ballroom teams, as well as other entertainers, donated their talents for numerous benefit dances to raise money for the war.

Certainly the public continued to dance. The range of dances included the waltz, fox trot, rumba, lindy, and samba, as well as one of the newest rages, the conga. A dance of African-Cuban origins, the conga was performed by couples or as a line dance, and characterized by three steps followed by a quick kick on the syncopated fourth beat. Some commentators noted that dancing was a perfect vehicle for wartime factory workers to keep "physically and mentally fit" after hours of painstaking labor.[78] The U.S.O. dances were popular around the country and did much to stimulate social dancing. Roseland, too, Louis Brecker's great ballroom at Fifty-second Street and Broadway, was at its peak during the war years, holding up to 3,800 avid dance patrons every weekend.[79] For soldiers the dances were their last gasp of fun and relaxation before being shipped overseas. In fact, ballroom dancing during the war years intensified romantic, intimate feelings, as couples understood that at any moment they might become separated. Ballroom dancing eased the sense of impending doom: as professional dancer Lola Andre reflected on nightclub dancing of the era, "everybody tried to be happy for an hour or two during dinner."[80]

The effects of the continued war, however, began to grind down the country. For one, the nightclubs suffered a major blow beginning in 1944 when federal government imposed a 30 percent tax as part of a wartime austerity measure. Some clubs got around the tax by getting rid of their dance floors and simply offering food and drink and perhaps a string orchestra; others partitioned off the bar area, isolating it from the dance area, and also escaped the surcharge. In either case, both the nightclub-going public and professional performers suffered.

The higher entrance fees (an unfortunate result of the surcharge) discouraged attendance, and many clubs could not afford the salaries of the best teams. The entire concept of nightclub life was being eroded, and many clubs were eventually forced to close.[81]

By 1945 it was clear that the war had permanently altered the course of professional ballroom dance in this country. Hundreds of couples had separated when the male partners were drafted for World War II. When those partners returned from the war, efforts to revive former partnerships were usually not successful; too much time had passed and teams found it difficult to regain their former popularity. The audience for ballroom dancing certainly waned in the years immediately after the war, since the uppermost concerns for those returning home were of reestablishing family ties and securing jobs. The failure of exhibition ballroom dance to stage a full comeback was tied up with the country's adjustment from a wartime to peacetime economy, when people found less time and inclination for entertainment.

INTO THE FIFTIES

While exhibition ballroom dance had lost much of its former momentum in the traditional venues, the nightclubs and musical theatre, it would reemerge in the late 1940s primarily in the newly expanding medium of television. The popular variety shows with their live audiences, guest hosts, and star-studded line-ups had come to replace vaudeville, and were a primary vehicle for dance teams. Many were amateurs from the competition circuit breaking into show business; others were veteran ballroom dancers trying to sustain their careers. Although ballet and Broadway dances were popular, ballroom team dancing was always a part of the show. Television was able to capture the intimacy and sense of romance of ballroom dance, and the dancers themselves liked performing for live audiences.

One of the earliest teams to acquire acclaim through television was Marge and Gower Champion. Through the thirties both dancers had been part of exhibition partnerships—Gower with the youthful and ebullient Jeanne Tyler, and Marge with dark and handsome Louis Hightower. After Gower returned from the Coast Guard in 1945, Jeanne had remarried, and Gower was searching for a way to revive his professional career. Drawing on their training in ballet and folk forms as well as ballroom dance, Marge and Gower evolved a sophisticated choreographic style by building dance steps around dramatic situations.[82]

Although they got their start in major nightclubs of the period, it was in television that they were able to capture a huge, popular following. Their debut was on the *Admiral Broadway Revue*, NBC-television's ninety-minute variety special sponsored by the Admiral Television

Company. Starring Sid Caesar and Imogene Coca, the *Admiral Broadway Revue* was the first television variety show to feature renowned Broadway talent. In their nightclub work, Marge and Gower had already developed a compelling style of romantic dance-dramas. In one of their best-known numbers, "Marseille," Gower portrayed an American sailor and Marge a young Frenchwoman, each of them pining for their lost loves. Gower set the action by reminiscing about his lover as Marge danced in front of him in free-form movement in rhythm with Gower's monologue.[83] For their first appearance on the *Admiral Broadway Revue,* in January 1949, the team performed a balletic interpretation of 'The Night Has a Thousand Eyes,' sung by the Broadway ingenue and juvenile Estelle Loring and Loren Welch, and "Dance With Me," a number from their nightclub act.[84]

Other television appearances followed throughout the 1950s. On June 7, 1953 Ed Sullivan's variety show, then called *Toast of the Town*, featured a single show devoted to Marge and Gower performing numbers from their nightclub act as well as clips from two of their films, *Lovely to Look At* and *Show Boat*.[85] The team also made guest appearances on variety shows hosted by celebrities Perry Como, Dinah Shore, and Steve Allen. They often choreographed numbers with their guest host, such as a riotous Latin ballroom dance spoof with Jack Benny on his 1956 series *Shower of Stars*. Other popular routines were their flirtation numbers, such as "I'm in a Dancing Mood," performed for an April 1958 Perry Como program. The number was a kind of choreographed "hide and seek" in which Gower sings to Marge, enticing her into dancing with him by naming different ballroom dances, from the polka to the samba.[86]

Marge and Gower Champion's longevity through the 1950s, at a time when exhibition ballroom teams were no longer being booked as headliners, was something of a phenomenon. What was the fascination? In large part, they were the first of their kind. Marge Champion is the first to insist that she and Gower were not really a *ballroom* team, that they were a "show dancing team," incorporating Broadway-styled choreography with singing and dialogue.[87] Their brand of dramatic story dance was new to exhibition couple dancing, and provided an immediate, emotionally engaging experience for audiences. Marge and Gower Champion, in fact, came to symbolize the values of the 1950s; their cover story in *Life* magazine in 1949 established them early as one of America's brightest dance teams. The couple's romantic dancing, rooted in the expression of the connectedness between men and women, was a compelling image for audiences that extolled the virtues of marriage, family, and relationships.

Although Marge and Gower Champion were in large part in a class of their own, other television teams followed in a similar mold. The successor to the *Admiral Broadway Revue,* Max Liebman's *Your Show of*

Shows, continued to feature an array of Broadway talent, including ballroom teams; in the 1953 season the team of Bambi Linn and Rod Alexander took the limelight. Linn herself was a ballet-trained dancer whose stage roles included acclaimed portrayals of Aggie in the 1943 production of *Oklahoma!* and Louise in *Carousel* (1945). Alexander, who had performed in the company of famous movie musical choreographer Jack Cole, had already made a name for himself in the Broadway revues *Lend An Ear* and *It's Great to Be Alive,* opposite Linn. After their success in that show, the dancers decided to form a team-act which they brought to nightclubs around the country. Their trademark was their interpretive ballet numbers, along with exhibition variations on the waltz and contemporary mambo.[88]

Hailed as "TV's answer to Irene and Vernon Castle," Linn and Alexander (now married) exuded an engaging exuberance with a "gentle grace and unaffected manner."[89] Like Marge and Gower Champion, they were of the new breed of actor-dancer whose numbers were really mini dance-dramas. Their rendition of "Younger Than Springtime" revolved around a young man and woman parting as he goes to war. As John Martin of *The New York Times* said of Linn and Alexander, "We are constantly aware of them as people and not just as clever automatons."[90] The team found success in television for several years. In 1955 they performed in a series of NBC television specials, or "spectaculars," such as *A Connecticut Yankee,* for which Alexander was the principal choreographer.

Comedy, of course, was popular on television variety shows, and satiric-comic dance teams successfully fit the bill. The Swiss-born duo Mata and Hari, for instance, had been on the nightclub circuit for many years and found a welcome audience on *Your Show of Shows.* In a style that incorporated ballet, acrobatic, and ballroom dance, the team satirized most contemporary ballroom and theatrical dance styles. One of their most popular numbers, "Chichumba," was a spoof on the Latin musical numbers featured in Carmen Miranda films; in another, "Carnegie Hall," they parodied the solemnity of concert recitals in a hilarious "impressionistic dance-portrait of a symphony orchestra at work."[91]

The dance team of Nelle Fisher and Jerry Ross also contributed a comedic touch. Fisher was a well-rounded dancer; she had previously trained in ballet and modern dance (she studied with Martha Graham's company for two years). Fisher had been a former chorus dancer at Radio City Music Hall and a featured dancer in several Broadway musicals. For *Your Show of Shows,* she and Ross pioneered a characterizational dance act in which Fisher, for instance, depicts a French maid who launches into a variation on the maxixe; in other versions, she portrays a scrubwoman who joins her janitor-partner (Ross) in a comic version of a classic waltz. In 1954 Fisher went on to become the principal choreographer for the ABC television variety show *Melody Tour*, in which each week the cast "visited" a different European country.[92]

A prominent promoter of ballroom teams was the renowned television host Ed Sullivan. On *The Ed Sullivan Show* he featured well-known teams, such as Marge and Gower Champion, as well as rising professionals—the winners of the yearly Harvest Moon Ballroom Dance Championships. Sponsored by the *Daily News* Welfare Association since 1934, these competitions had become highly publicized annual events at New York City's Madison Square Garden. (As a young *Daily News* columnist, Ed Sullivan had been host for the competitions.[93]) Other variety shows of the fifties, too, featured the Harvest Moon champs, including *The Jackie Gleason Show* and Gleason's summer replacement show hosted by Tommy and Jimmy Dorsey.[94]

One of the most popular all-dance television programs, which helped revive an interest in social dancing, was *The Arthur Murray Dance Party*. Produced by the well-known dance teacher Arthur Murray and hosted by his wife, Katherine, the *Dance Party* aired on NBC for approximately thirteen years from 1950 through the early 1960s. As with other variety-styled television programming, *Dance Party* featured well-known theatrical personalities. The January 1, 1958 program boasted an impressive talent roster including Paul Winchell, Tallulah Bankhead, Sarah Vaughan, and Hedy Lamarr. Current and former ballroom stars frequently made guest appearances, such as the famous team of Mary Raye and Naldi from the forties.[95]

Part of the reason for *Dance Party's* mass appeal was that it featured dances currently being performed by the public. The standard fox trots and waltzes were still popular, while the rumba and samba were being overtaken by the mambo and cha-cha. A combination of swing and Afro-Cuban rhythms, the sensual mambo required continuous body undulations; the cha-cha, an outgrowth of the mambo, also quickly took hold with its energetic triple-shuffle step. The highlight of the show was the "lesson" segment, featuring demonstrations of the latest dances by a corps of dancer-teachers from the Arthur Murray Studios and sometimes by Arthur Murray himself. Audience participation was a vital part of the program. A so-called "Mystery Dance" concluded each segment, in which viewers were asked to identify the title of the song; in return, the winners earned two free lessons at the Arthur Murray Studio.

The long-term success of *Dance Party* can be attributed to the fact that it brought ballroom dancing into living rooms of people across the country. Murray himself noted that, "With television, people in the smallest towns see every brand-new dance."[96] The program, of course, brought people in droves to Murray's schools of dance located all over the country. By the late fifties, Arthur Murray operated approximately

300 studios in the United States and abroad with profits near $25 million per year.[97]

When asked by a reporter if there was room in television for more dancing Murray said he thought there was, noting that, "It pains me to admit it, but straight dance numbers do not sustain general public interest for over two or three minutes."[98] What Murray knew, of course, was what had made teams such as Marge and Gower Champion the popular success that they were: a sure sense of theatre and showmanship, and an ability to create interest through numbers evincing drama and emotion.

As long as there were such teams around, exhibition ballroom dance could maintain a place on television and continue to exert its influence on viewers. By 1960, however, Marge and Gower Champion, Linn and Alexander, and others had either retired from the stage or disbanded as teams. Then, too, the sixties brought along massive cultural changes including new styles of music, namely rock and roll, which would drastically change the look of social dance. It would be another twenty years or so before exhibition ballroom dance would take on a new life.

NOTES

1. Irene Castle, as told to Bob and Wanda Duncan, *Castles in the Air* (New York: Doubleday & Co., 1958), pp. 172–173.

2. Ibid., pp. 144–145, 159–160.

3. Unidentified newspaper clipping, ca. 1923 (Irene Castle File, Theatre Collection, The Philadelphia Free Library).

4. "An Ambulance Worker in France: Two Famous Dancers," *The Sketch*, 20 June 1917 (Maurice and Walton Folder, MCNY); *The Graphic*, 5 January 1925 (Florence Walton scrapbook, C&L Brown Collection, BRTC).

5. "Maurice Mouvet, Dancer, Is Dead in Switzerland," *The Herald Tribune*, 19 May 1927 (Maurice and Walton Folder, MCNY).

6. Karl L. Kitchen, "Blame Jazz," unidentified magazine article (Maurice and Walton Folder, Theatre Collection, MCNY).

7. One of their acts was a plotted piece called *Montmartre*, which featured nine cast members and dealt with life in the Latin Quarter since the war. See miscellaneous newspaper clippings in Florence Walton scrapbook, C&L Brown Collection, BRTC. For further information on Walton's partnership with Vlad see *Dancing Times*, August 1914, and miscellaneous newspaper clippings (Florence Walton scrapbook, C&L Brown Collection, BRTC).

8. Alfred A. Cohn, "Maurice and Walton Stage Dance War in Paris," *Zit's Weekly Newspaper*, 6 July 1923.

9. "The Girl with the Bee-Stung Lips," *Photoplay*, 17 November 1922. Some of Murray's other early films included *On With the Dance* (1920) for Paramount, and a series of "picture plays" based on contemporary novels for Cosmopolitan Productions, also in 1920. See *Shadowland*, February 1920 (Mae Murray scrapbook, Rob. Locke Col., vol. 281, BRTC); *Cosmopolitan*, April 1920.

10. "Joan Sawyer Joins Fox," *The Toledo Blade*, 22 August 1916 (Joan Sawyer, Rob. Locke clippings, BRTC).

11. Sigmund Spaeth, *A History of Popular Music in America* (New York: Random House, 1948), p. 415; Marks, Edward B. *They All Sang* (New York: Viking Press, 1935), p. 174.

12. For further descriptions of the Shimmy, see Albert and Josephine Butler, *Encyclopedia of Social Dance*, 1976 ed., unpaginated entry for the Shimmy (DC-NYPL); "Shimmy Shake," trans. from the German, *Jazz und Shimmy*, Koebner, Berlin, 1921 (Shimmy File, DC-NYPL). Marshall and Jean Stearns point out that Perry Bradford composed 'The Bullfrog Hop,' whose lyrics include directions for performing a Shimmy. They also have evidence that a dance bearing the name Shimmy appeared in a Southern honkytonk as early as 1901. Marshall and Jean Stearns, *Jazz Dance*. (New York: Shirmer Books, 1968), pp. 104–105.

13. Don McDonagh, *Dance Fever* (New York: Random House, 1979), p. 144.

14. Stearns and Stearns, *Jazz Dance*, p. 111.

15. Program, Apollo Theater, 9 August 1926 (BRTC).

16. Stearns and Stearns, *Jazz Dance*, p. 110; Albert and Josephine Butler, *Encyclopedia of Social Dance*, unpaginated entry for Black Bottom.

17. Joseph Mulvaney, "Beauty, Melody and Comedy Rule at Apollo," unidentified newspaper clipping (*George White Scandals of 1926* scrapbook, MWEZ, 17, 881, BRTC). George White choreographed Pennington's dance to the musical composition 'The Black Bottom,' composed by Ray Henderson, with words by Bud De Sylva and Lew Brown.

18. Clifton Webb, "Where Do We Dance From Here?" *Vogue*, 15 September 1933, pp. 86, 90.

19. Lloyd Morris, *Incredible New York* (New York: Random House, 1951), pp. 322, 324.

20. Erenberg, *Steppin' Out: New York Nightlife and the Transformation of American Culture* (Westport, CT: Greenwood Press, 1981), p. 238; Billy Rose, for example, devised innovative Broadway-styled entertainment at his Fifth Avenue cabaret. *Billboard*, 6 February 1926.

21. Ibid., pp. 241–243. Interview with Doris Vinton (former Ziegfeld Follies dancer), New York City, 14 June 1985.

22. Webb, "Where Do We Dance From Here?" p. 90; "Ballroom Acts Taking First Place as Popular Offering," *Billboard*, 11 April 1925.

23. In May 1929 the editor of *Dance Magazine* lamented that, "There is no such couple of international repute sufficient to make every ballroom dancer follow in its footsteps."

24. Robert C. Toll, *On With the Show* (New York: Oxford University Press, 1976), p. 293. Shirley Staples, *Male-Female Comedy Teams in American Vaudeville: 1865–1930* (Ann Arbor: UMI Press, 1984), p. 202. Staples points out that in 1925 the Riverside, a big-time vaudeville house, had as many as five films on its bill.

25. Marcus Loew, "The Motion Picture and Vaudeville," in Joseph P. Kennedy, ed., *The Story of the Films* (Chicago and New York: A. W. Snow Company, 1927), pp. 287–89; 293–96; W. A. S. Douglas, "The Passing of Vaudeville," *American Mercury*, October 1927, pp. 188–194.

26. Staples, *Male-Female Comedy Teams in American Vaudeville,* pp. 202, 301.

27. For further information on Prolog entertainment see Edward Reed, "Vaudeville Again," *Theatre Arts Monthly,* 17 October 1933, pp. 803–806; Charles W. Stein, *American Vaudeville As Seen By Its Contemporaries* (New York: Alfred A. Knopf, 1984), pp. 335–336; Barbara Naomi Cohen, "Chain Prologs: Dance at the Picture Palaces," *Dance Scope* (Spring, 1978): 12–23; "Vaudeville Hit by Film Presentations," *Billboard,* 16 January 1926.

28. Cohen, "Chain Prologs," p. 18.

29. See "The Dancers of Variety" section n *Dance Magazine,* 1927–1929.

30. *Dance Magazine,* May 1929, p. 34.

31. Cohen, "Chain Prologs," p. 18.

32. Sam Bernard, "Elevating Ballroom Dancing," *American Dancer,* October 1932, p. 17.

33. One prominent example is Gilda Gray surrounded by a chorus for her South Sea Hula dance from the *Ziegfeld Follies of 1922.* See White Studio Photographs, BRTC.

34. Stearns and Stearns, *Jazz Dance,* pp. 160–161; Program, The Music Box Theatre, Week of September 30, 1930.

35. Stearns and Stearns, p. 160.

36. For descriptions of some of the plot summaries of these films see Larry May, *Screening Out the Past: The Birth of Mass Culture and the Motion Picture Industry* (New York: Oxford University Press, 1980); pp. 209, 216. Barbara Cohen-Stratyner, Curator of Exhibitions at The New York Public Library for the Performing Arts, offered critical insights and information about transition-era films.

37. *The Four Horsemen of the Apocalypse* (Photo File B, BRTC).

38. One notable example is Joan Crawford in *Our Dancing Daughters* (1928), in which she displayed her talent for Charlestoning.

39. Bernard, "Elevating Ballroom Dancing," p. 17.

40. Frederick Lewis Allen, *The Big Change: America Transforms Itself, 1900–1950* (New York: Harper & Row Publishers, 1952), pp. 151–157.

41. "Educating the Trade, Chi[cago] Ballrooms Giving Hoofing Instructions Over WGN," *Variety,* 24 October 1933. Radio broadcasts of ballroom dance music were common during the late twenties and early thirties and enabled people to dance in their own homes.

42. *The American Dancer,* February 1933, pp. 12, 13. For the beneficial effects of Repeal on nightlife see "Nightclub Reviews," *Variety* 24 October 1933; "Paradise and Hollywood Restaurants Set Pace in Night Life Struggle," *Variety,* 17 October 1933; "Straight Hoofing Not Enough," *Variety,* 21 April 1937.

43. *The American Dancer,* March 1933, pp. 5, 23.

44. The trend toward large bands actually began in the late 1920s with the Paul Whiteman and Vincent Lopez orchestras and reached its peak of popularity in the late 1930s. For more on the big band era and early swing see Albert McCarthy, *The Dance Band Era: The Dancing Decades From Ragtime to Swing, 1910–1950* (Radnor, PA: Chilton Book Company, 1971); Stanley Dance, *The World of Swing* (New York: Charles Scribner's & Sons, 1974); Gunther Schuller, *The Swing Era: The Development of Jazz, 1930–1945* (New York: Oxford University Press, 1989).

45. For further information on these dances see Butler, *Encyclopedia of Social*

Dance. For discussion of these and some of the shorter-lived fad dances of the period see Brenda Dixon-Stowell, "Dancing in the Dark: The Life and Times of Margot Webb in Aframerican Vaudeville of the Swing Era" (Ph.D. dissertation, New York University, 1981), pp. 360–361.

46. Stearns and Stearns, p. 323.

47. "After the Theatre," *The Playbill*, 25 October 1937.

48. "Hi-De-Ho! The Night Clubs Turn 'Em Away," *The New York Times*, 21 March 1937.

49. "Night Clubs Reviews: Connie's Inn," *Variety*, 1 May 1935; Frank X. Lynch, "The Supper Clubs," *The New York Evening Post*, 17 March 1934; Gilbert Seldes, "From Chicken Shack to Casino," *Esquire Magazine*, March 1938.

50. Bosley Crowthers, "Hi-De-Ho," *Nightlife, Directory of Approved Entertainment* (pamphlet in Clubs: Night: NY: 1937, BRTC). For a wonderful collection of materials on New York City's nightlife in the 1930s and 1940s see clipping files in the Billy Rose Theatre Collection under Clubs: Night: US: NY.

51. "The Night-Club Business," *American Mercury*, October 1942.

52. Seldes, "From Chicken Shack to Casino."

53. "Night Clubs Review," *Variety*, June 1936.

54. Brenda Dixon-Stowell, "Between Two Eras: 'Norton and Margot' in the Afro-American Entertainment World," *Dance Research Journal* 15, 2 (Spring 1983): 11. For more on Norton and Webb, see Dixon-Stowell's dissertation, "Dancing in the Dark: The Life and Times of Margot Webb in Aframerican Vaudeville of the Swing Era."

55. Lola Andre, interview with author, New York City, March 28, 1985.

56. Brooks Atkinson, "The Play," *New York City Times*, 19 February 1929; *Pleasure Bound*, Program, The Majestic Theatre (Programme File, BRTC): E. W. Osborn, *"Pleasure Bound," New York City Eve World*, 19 February 1929; Gilbert Brown, "Franz Lehar's *'Love Call'* Has Gorgeous Premier," *The Los Angeles Times*, 20 January 1926. For more biographical information on Veloz and Yolanda see Veloz and Yolanda, *Tango and Rumba: The Dances of Today and Tomorrow* (New York: Harper & Brothers, 1930), pp. 15–18.

57. "Veloz and Yolanda Draw Capacity in New York Ballroom Concert Debut," *Variety*, 27 April 1938.

58. Ibid.

59. Program, "Veloz and Yolanda in an Evening of Dansation," American Theatre, Week of 29 November 1942 (Veloz and Yolanda clipping file, MWEZ, nc 18,331, BRTC).

60. Gus Leonard, (title obscured), *The Boston Herald*, ca. 1935 (De Marcos clipping file, *MGZR, BRTC).

61. Margaret Case Harriman, "Profiles," *The New Yorker*, 6 January 1940.

62. For more on Tony and Sally De Marco see Robert W. Dana, "De Marcos Dance Home to the Pierre," unidentified newspaper, 17 October 1951 (De Marcos Clipping File, *MGZR, BRTC); Thomas Riley, "Reflections," *Dance Magazine*, May 1942, p. 18.

63. Lola Andre, interview; David Payne-Carter, "Gower Champion and The American Musical Theatre," Ph.D. dissertation (New York University, 1987), pp. 29–30.

64. *"Three's A Crowd," Town Topics*, 23 October 1930.

65. J. B. C., " 'Three's A Crowd' Is an Unusual Revue," *The Springfield [Mass] News*, ca. 1930 (Amy Revere, private collection).

66. "Red, White and Blue," *Variety*, 4 November 1938.

67. Brenda Dixon-Stowell, "Dancing in the Dark," p. 360.

68. "The Screen," *The New York Times*, 4 February 1937.

69. Kate Cameron, " 'Champagne Waltz' Exhilarating Movie," *The New York Daily News*, 4 February 1937.

70. Regina Crewe, " 'Flying Down to Rio' Is Gay Musical Romance on Screen," *The New York American*, 22 (month obscured) 1933; Philip K. Scheur, "Musical Film Pretentious," *The Los Angeles Times*, 4 January 1934; Rose Pelswick, *"Flying Down to Rio," The New York Journal*, 22 December 1933 (*Flying Down to Rio* Clipping File, BRTC).

71. Andre Sennwald, "The Screen," *The New York Times*, 16 November 1934 (*The Gay Divorcée* File, MFL + , BRTC).

72. Even from his early days with his sister, Adele, Fred Astaire shunned the nightclub scene (where one has more direct contact with audiences). Marshall and Jean Stearns quote Astaire regarding his nightclub performances from the twenties: "Adele and I were not ballroom dancers particularly. . . . A night club was an atmosphere we had never worked in before, and we didn't like it. . . . We were really out of our element. . . ." (*Jazz Dance*, p. 225). Astaire did not perform in nightclubs or involve himself in the social dance scene much in the thirties, either.

73. Sennwald, "The Screen."

74. Program for the Pooch Ball, Gold Room, Congress Hotel (Irene Castle Folder, Theatre Collection, MCNY).

75. Correspondence from Barbara Kreutz (Irene Castle's daughter), 18 February 1985. Says Kreutz, "Yolanda was lovely to look at, very graceful, and dressed simply but elegantly, all of which counted for a lot with my mother." Kreutz claims that Irene Castle liked the De Marcos for much the same reasons.

76. "Night Clubs: In Wartime They Are More Lavish," *Life Magazine*, 9 February 1942.

77. Thomas Riley, "Reflections," *Dance Magazine*.

78. Joy Richards, "Dance and War," *Dance Magazine*, September 1942.

79. "Profiles," *The New Yorker*, 27 June 1942.

80. Lola Andre, interview.

81. "Night Club Trade Reported 50% Off," *The New York Times*, ca. 1944 (Clubs: Night: US: NY: 1945, BRTC); Theodore Laymon, "Taverns to Shut Dance Floors As Too Costly," *The New York Times*, 29 March 1944; Jack Gaver, "Running Night Club Is Just One Big Headache," *The Morning Telegraph*, 20 March 1944; "Harlem Niteries Tune Swan Song; No Ofay Business," *Variety*, 29 June 1949.

82. David Payne-Carter, "Gower Champion and The American Musical Theatre," p. 97.

83. Ibid., pp. 92–94.

84. *"Admiral Broadway Revue"* (television review), *Variety*, ca. 1949; " 'Admiral Revue' To Get Two-Web, 38-Station Spread," unidentified newspaper, (*Admiral Broadway Revue* Clipping File, BRTC).

85. David Payne-Carter, "Gower Champion and The American Musical Theatre," pp. 171–72.

86. *The Perry Como Show,* television performance, NBC, April 1958 (private videotape collection, Marge Champion Sagal).

87. Marge Champion, interview by author and David Payne-Carter, 1 June 1990.

88. "Dancers Bambi Linn and Rod Alexander to Entertain Knights and Ladies at Camelot," Press Department, NBC, 3 March 1955; "Bambi and Rod," [Dance section] *Newsweek,* 15 June 1953.

89. L. B., "Bambi's A Dear," unidentified magazine, ca. 1952 (Bambi Linn Clipping File, BRTC).

90. John Martin, "The Dance: Debut," *The New York Times,* 1 June 1952.

91. Edmund Leamy, "Mata-Hari Flair Is Satiric Dance," unidentified newspaper, ca. 1952; "Pixies of the Dance," unidentified magazine, ca. 1952 (Mata and Hari Clipping File, BRTC); "TV Dancers," This Week in Chicago, 12 January 1952.

92. Judith Crist, "Petite Dance Expert Plans Big Things for TV 'Tour,' " *The New York Herald Tribune,* 11 July 1954.

93. Wood, "State, N.Y.," *Variety,* 13 September 1944; "The Winners!" *Dance Magazine,* October 1945. Appearances by the Harvest Moon Dancers became a staple of *The Ed Sullivan Show:* in 1968, during Sullivan's twenty-first season, the competition winners shared the show with Steve Lawrence and Eydie Gorme and The Jefferson Airplane; see *Variety,* 2 October 1968.

94. Jack Smith, "Last Week for Harvest Ball Entries," *The [Sunday] News,* 8 August 1954.

95. Art., "The Arthur Murray Party," *Variety,* 1 January 1958. Also see Bril, "Arthur Murray Party Time," *Variety,* 2 August 1950.

96. Marie Torre, "Murray's Dilemma: 'My Heart and My Pocketbook,' " *The New York Herald Tribune,* 1957.

97. Eric Pace, "Arthur Murray, Dance Teacher, Dies at 95," *The New York Times,* 4 March 1991.

98. Marie Torre, "Murray's Dilemma."

Chapter 7

The Contemporary Renaissance

From the early 1960s through the late 1970s, exhibition ballroom dance suffered a sharp decline in popularity. One of the main reasons was the continued popularity of rock and roll music. Social dancing, which typically inspires exhibition forms, had changed radically in structure, beginning in the sixties with the Twist and followed by such popular fad dances as the Mashed Potato and the Frug. What was different about these dances is that they were solo-oriented; although couples might face each other as they performed them, there was little or no body contact. Couples improvised their own movements to the basic rhythm of the dance, using little movement around the floor. This is in direct contrast, of course, to classic ballroom dances, such as waltzes and fox trots, which require dancers to move gracefully across large areas of dance floor.

Disco dancing of the 1970s was part of this solo-dance trend, although when the Hustle arrived on the scene it reintroduced the idea of dance *partners*, who touch hands and coordinate their movements with one another. In the Hustle, a smooth Latin dance with quick footwork, couples maneuver together around the floor, instead of dancing in just one spot. The Hustle reintroduced a feeling of intimacy to disco dancing, which contributed to the success of the 1977 film *Saturday Night Fever*.[1]

The popularity of the film certainly helped revive interest in couple dancing, but the fad took hold mostly in the social dance world. The reemergence of exhibition ballroom dance—professional couples per-

forming theatrical renditions of social-based dances—did not really occur again until the 1980s. Several well-known choreographers began
integrating ballroom forms into their repertory, and various ballroom
dance productions surfaced in Broadway and Off-Broadway theatre
venues. The large and enthusiastic audiences for these shows indicated
newfound appreciation for the form.

THE RETURN OF PROFESSIONAL
BALLROOM DANCERS

Professional ballroom dance in recent years has reappeared in various forms. In the early 1980s, established dance companies began
making forays into ballroom choreography. Modern dance choreographer Twyla Tharp, for instance, in 1982 introduced "Nine Sinatra Songs"
into her repertoire, consisting of a medley of ballroom-based numbers.
George Balanchine's "La Valse" and "Vienna Waltzes" have been particularly popular dances at the New York City Ballet in recent years.[2]
Ballet Hispanico, a professional dance company, has incorporated tango-
based numbers into its regular program, such as the well-received "Cada
Noche . . . Tango," choreographed by Graciela Daniele, which evokes
the world of 1930s Argentinian dance halls.[3]

One company in particular that has singlehandedly demonstrated the
new capacities for ballroom dance as theatrical art is American Ballroom Dance Theatre (ABRT). Formed in 1984 by dancers Yvonne
Marceau and Pierre Dulaine, American Ballroom Theatre features an
evening of dramatically linked ballroom numbers performed by four
professional couples. Not since Veloz and Yolanda in the forties has
ballroom dance been so eloquently celebrated on the concert stage. Although conscious of the social dance ancestry of exhibition ballroom
dance, American Ballroom Theatre takes these dances and exploits their
potential for theatricality.

Marceau, a ballet-trained dancer, and Dulaine, a successful competitive dancer based for many years in England, met in 1974 at a Fred
Astaire Dance Studio in New York and have been a team since. Decid-
ing they had a compatible style, Marceau and Dulaine formed an adagio-ballroom team, and went on to win the prestigious British Exhibition Competition four times. For several years they performed in Europe
and then in the United States before forming their company.[4] The establishment of ABRT afforded the artistic directors and their company
members the opportunity to exercise creativity outside of the regula-
tion styles characterizing the professional competitions.

In American Ballroom Theatre, numbers are set typically in obvious social dance settings, such as "The Rainbow Room," where the dancers move elegantly through a medley of ten different songs and dances from the thirties and forties. In others, the numbers contain a trace of a story line, as in "Summer in Havana," choreographed by company member Willie Rosario. This spirited number features several Latin dances woven around the activities at a popular nightclub; in a 1987 production, Dulaine and Marceau portray naive American tourists who wander into the club as the ensemble is engaged in a steaming samba.[5] In a 1991 number, "Posin'," choreographed by Patricia Birch, the dancers evoke the emotions of couples separated during World War II, affording the ensemble the opportunity to perform popular dances from the period, such as the Jitterbug.[6]

Rather than simply preserving ballroom styles of yesteryear, the company experiments with the notion of a modern ballroom dance style. While several guest choreographers are responsible for at least one number in each program (such as the late John Roudis of the thirties dance team Roudis and Renell, and Graciela Daniele), Marceau and Dulaine, and other members of the company, serve as principal choreographers. Adding variety to the company, each of the teams specializes in a particular technique—smooth-adagio, lyrical-waltz, and Latin-styled dance.[7]

Since 1988 Yvonne Marceau and Pierre Dulaine have been featured dancers in the Broadway musical *Grand Hotel*, choreographed by Tommy Tune. An engaging instance of contemporary ballroom dance interpolation, *Grand Hotel* represents the potential for a revival of exhibition ballroom dance as an extension of dramatic narrative. Marceau as a countess, in her elegant, swirling gown, and Dulaine, her dapper-looking gigolo, perform brief, lyrical sequences of tango and waltz steps, slipping gracefully through the onstage action of the characters.[8] Their ballroom dancing is woven into the production, serving as a leitmotif reflecting the dreams, fears, and dashed hopes of the hotel guests. Their one extended solo number is a tour de force, an impassioned Bolero in which the couple express the emotion and pathos of the main characters. In one riveting adagio sequence, Marceau alights on Dulaine's shoulder, then winds down his body, her black dress a cascade of satin.[9]

During the past few years, the Broadway stage has offered other vehicles for exhibition ballroom dance, most notably the highly popular *Tango Argentino* (1985). Conceived and directed by Hector Orezzoli and Claudio Segovia, this music and dance revue created something of a tango fever in New York City when it previewed at City Center (the show later moved to Broadway's Mark Hellinger Theatre). The production brought together some of Argentina's best-known tango dancers, singers, and musicians for an evening's tribute to this enduring dance form. Seven dance couples of different ages performed various Argentine tango styles from periods of the country's history.[10]

Much of the appeal of *Tango Argentino* was its presentation of dances vital to the life of people in their communities, rather than purely stylized exhibitions. From the rugged tango of the late nineteenth century characterized in "El Apache Argentino" to the more refined, middleclass version performed by two sisters in "La Morocha," the show demonstrated the tango's rich vocabulary of expression.[11] Dramatic dance vignettes were interspersed with plaintive, lyrical song numbers and instrumentals to create, in producer Orezzoli's words, "a tango landscape" filled with the passion of this vibrant dance.[12]

Since the appearance of *Tango Argentino*, other professional tango-inspired productions have become popular, including Graciela Daniele's 1987 dance/theatre work *Tango Apasionado*, presented at New York City's Westbeth Theatre, as well as her 1989 Broadway production of *Dangerous Games*, two tango pieces set to the music of Astor Piazzolla. Other smaller productions, too, have cropped up, such as *Samba Rio*, the 1988 piece choreographed by artistic director Rosamaria Moraes, exploring the rich varieties of the samba. Moraes' company, also named Samba Rio, strives to introduce American audiences to authentic versions of the samba, that "go beyond the usual cliches of showgirls and carnival in Rio."[13]

THE COMPETITIVE BALLROOM WORLD

A major venue for professional ballroom dance in recent years are the hundreds of ballroom dance competitions held annually across the country. Such contests are hardly new; the Harvest Moon Ball established in the 1930s was one of the most renowned in New York City, and at its height in the 1940s became the "dance classic" event of the year. But with the renewed enthusiasm for ballroom dance in the past decade, dancers have been entering contests in record numbers.[14] Some of the major national competitions include the United States Ballroom Championships held yearly in Florida and the Imperial Championships sponsored by the Imperial Society of Teachers of Dance, as well as the hundreds of regional competitions occurring at different times of the year.

Competitive dancing is a tough world, guided by demanding rules and regulations. In the major divisions up to fifty couples or more are selected from successive rounds generally lasting less than two minutes. The final choice is made among six finalists. Exacting competition judges look for several qualities: timing and rhythm, hip movement and head control, accuracy of footwork, and the level of difficulty of routines. The two main categories of dance are the Latin division, including the rumba, samba, cha-cha, paso doble, and jive, and the Modern Division, consisting of the waltz, tango, fox trot, quickstep, and Viennese waltz.[15] For both categories couples compete for amateur, professional, or pro/ am status. Although most couples specialize in just one style of dance, some compete in all ten dances, such as the team of Jennifer Ford and Stanley McCalla, members of American Ballroom Theatre, who have won the Amateur Ten Dance Championship title several times.

Ice-dancing, too, has become an arena for the display of exhibition ballroom forms. In the Olympic ice-dancing competitions ballroom steps and poses are regularly part of the teams' routines, as well as in the *Ice Capades* and other theatrical ice-skating extravaganzas. The 1984 British Olympic skating winners Jayne Torvill and Christopher Dean have emerged as innovators, performing ballroom-based numbers such as "Bolero" and "Gershwin Suite." To the ballroom rhythms and poses characteristic of these routines, Torvill and Dean lend a dramatic intensity and a cool, understated sensual allure, underscoring ballroom dance's alliance with romance.[16]

Television has played an enormous part in increasing public awareness of exhibition ballroom dance. Not only is Olympic ice-dancing a nationally televised event, but since 1981 WGBH, Boston's public television station, has been broadcasting one of the largest ballroom dance competitions, the Ohio Star Ball. This telecast, also shown on hundreds of affiliate stations, brings exhibition ballroom dancing into homes across the country.[17] The competitions are exciting television spectacles, combining theatrical performance with the aura of a sports event. Spirited audience members, many of whom are dancers themselves, cheer on their favorite dancers, the tension building as successive teams are eliminated from the make-or-break ninety-second rounds. The women dancers are typically outfitted in sequined, satin gowns adorned with feathery plumage and beads; their male counterparts look sleek and suave in their tuxedos and tails. Together the partners cut a fascinating image as they alternately leap, lift, and soar across the dance floor.

Other television programs also have cultivated audiences for ballroom dance, namely the syndicated variety shows *Dance Fever* and *Star Search*. Both are essentially talent competitions in which a panel of celebrity judges determines the winners. Created in 1978 and lasting through 1988, *Dance Fever* took hold just as the disco-dance phenomenon hit. Each half-hour weekly show featured four dance teams competing for $1,000 prizes; $5,000 if they reached the semi-finals. Much of the partner dancing in the early years of the show was of the disco-ballroom variety—often heavily jazzy routines, incorporating adagio lifts and spins and acrobatics. By the mid-1980s an increasing number of more traditional ballroom teams wound their way into the finals, from fox trotters and waltzers to tangoers.[18]

The syndicated talent show *Star Search,* created in 1982 and still running, features several categories of competitors including singers, comics, dramatic actors, and dance teams. A panel of producers and talent agents chooses the winner, while the audience has the role of breaking ties. Winners receive $2,000 (runners-up $1,000), and return to subsequent shows where they continue to compete. After twenty-four weeks, the three longest-standing contestants in each category compete against one other for a grand prize of $100,000.[19] Several ballroom dance teams have appeared on *Star Search;* the most successful are those in the flashy Latin mode, among them Ricky Quintana, a former U.S. and World Ballroom Dance champion, and top competitive Latin champion Elizabeth Curtis.[20] The exposure brings not only financial rewards but the kind of exposure ballroom dancers crave as they seek future professional engagements.

MAINTAINING CAREERS

For all professional ballroom dancers, careers are typically pieced together through a combination of performing and teaching. Many dancers own and operate social dance studios or offer private lessons. Competitive team dancers can earn money by winning competitions, but these prizes are typically reserved for only the top six championship winners. Other sources of income are derived from serving as judges at regional and national competitions, and through coaching other competitive teams rising up through the ranks. Since Europe has become a mecca for competitive ballroom dancing—England, Holland, West Germany, and Japan are popular centers—the top winners are frequently invited to perform at contests as special guest dancers (for which they are compensated). An ever-increasing source of employment for these elite teams consists of guest appearances at a range of events sponsored by civic and community groups and businesses, including retirement dinners and charity balls.[21]

Another group of professional exhibition ballroom dancers are those who have evolved independently of the competition world, and make their living performing at resort venues, from major cruise lines to nightclubs located in the Catskills and Pocono Mountains. The adagio-ballroom team of Judie and Stan Martin, for instance, has appeared as featured dancers in productions starring Carol Channing, Rodney Dangerfield, and Pearl Bailey. Their aerial-acrobatic brand of dance is particularly suited to the large stages found at Radio City Music Hall and the Las Vegas Hilton and can be easily accommodated to large revue-entertainment and spectacles. Like other ballroom teams, Judie and Stan Martin supplement their professional engagements by teaching, as well as by performing at private parties and weddings.[22]

THE SOCIAL DANCE SCENE

The increased visibility of professional ballroom teams, particularly on Broadway stages, has in turn awakened audiences to the pleasures of social dancing. Since the early 1980s people have enrolled in ballroom dance classes in steadily increasing numbers. At present there are over 580 Fred Astaire schools across the country, as well as classes taught at private dance studios, colleges, high schools, and YWCAs, and by individuals. Major health clubs and gymnasiums have also discovered eager audiences for their aerobic workouts set to cha-cha and jitterbug rhythms.[23] Many social dancers, proud of their adeptness, have been entering competitions themselves. The United States Amateur Ballroom Dance Association (which sponsors its own network of contests) reports a dramatic rise in membership, blossoming from fifteen to forty member organizations during the last two years.[24]

Avid social dancers can hone their ballroom skills at the increasing numbers of clubs and discotheques opening their doors across the country. In New York City during the past several years, a variety of clubs have sprung up to help create simultaneous revivals of several ballroom dance styles; many of them also offer weekly dance classes. Some places, like Roseland, with its huge dance floor holding up to 2,000 people, and the newly renovated Rainbow Room, cater solely to ballroom aficionados; both feature two alternating bands—one for Latin-based numbers, another to accompany fox trots and waltzes.[25]

Some clubs, primarily discotheques catering to the rock and roll crowd, have begun featuring special ballroom dance evenings. The downtown disco Cat Club and uptown's Baja Club now have designated evenings each week (Sunday and Tuesday, respectively) devoted to swing music, where forms of the lindy and jitterbug are surfacing. Red Blazer Too, a theatre-district restaurant, features live big-band music every Tuesday through Friday. The Club El Morocco, on East Fifty-fourth Street, open Mondays through Saturdays, features two kinds of bands— "American" pop-disco on the second floor and Latin on the fourth floor. Riding on the wave of the current Latin music and dance vogue, Club El Morocco has built an audience for the cha-cha, rumba, and mambo, in particular.[26]

Awareness of ballroom dance has been spurred by recent civic events, such as "Ballroom Week," sponsored by New York City's Mayor's Office. In the spring of 1990 this week-long celebration of social dance began with an official opening ceremony at the famous Rainbow Room, hosted by celebrities Tommy Tune, Ann Reinking, and members of the cast of *Grand Hotel* and other Broadway musicals. Noted former dancer Marge Champion served as honorary chair.[27] The publicized events included free lindy lessons at local studios, dance contests, performances by former Savoy ballroom dancers Frankie Manning and Norma Miller, a variety of Salsa bands at the Palladium club, and dancing parties on the Staten Island ferry. There is even a movement afoot to establish "National Ballroom Dance Week." Local Alabama dance enthusiasts have convinced their U.S. Senator, Howell Hefflin, that ballroom dance has garnered nationwide appeal. He has introduced a resolution to the Senate to designate a weeklong, countrywide salute to this dance form.[28]

The potential for the continued growth of ballroom dance is reflected most vividly in its popularity among young, college-aged students across the country. Brigham Young University has the nation's largest ballroom dance program and sponsors a student performance group that has toured internationally. The Universities of Wisconsin and Texas and University of California-Berkeley also are active centers.[29] New York University offers several outlets—ballroom dance classes and the NYU Social Dance Club, which features special dance parties at local clubs. For the more competitive-minded, there is the NYU Ballroom Dancing Team, cosponsored by the Department of Athletics, Recreation, and Intramurals. Columbia University, too, has jumped on the bandwagon; in preparation for a recent annual Winter Ball at Barnard College, over ninety students enrolled in an on-campus dance session in which they learned the waltz, fox trot, and lindy.[30]

People of all ages seem to be attracted to ballroom dancing. A large part of the fascination has to do with its romantic appeal. It is an outlet that enables people to indulge in healthy fantasies of love. For young adults the appeal may have much to do with the fact that the classic fox trots, waltzes, and tangos allow contact and intimacy, in contrast with the more distant but provocative rock and roll dances of the last twenty years. For baby-boomers now in their late thirties and early forties, previously reared on rock and roll, learning ballroom dance can provide a sense of self-assurance and "savoir-faire," and can be a source of social advancement. Larry Shulz, co-owner of the popular Sandra Cameron Dance Center in New York City, has noted that many of this generation are "now at an age where they find themselves in professional situations—company functions, galas, balls—that require a certain sophistication."[31] Today's increasingly older population experiences nostalgia for current ballroom dance vogue. They grew up with this type of dance, and now welcome and contribute to its present revival.

THE FUTURE OUTLOOK

Exhibition ballroom dance has definitely seen a comeback in recent years, although its popularity does not match the boom years of the 1910s and early 1920s. Why not? One reason is the insufficiency of appropriate music to accompany ballroom numbers. Although the melodies of George Gershwin and Cole Porter are some of America's most beloved music, their use tends to perpetuate the notion of ballroom dance as merely a nostalgic enterprise.[32] There are very few contemporary composers writing music for ballroom dance, as was the case in the 1910s. At that time the music industry experienced one of its greatest booms, as composers churned out numbers that were distributed as sheet music. Without this kind of prominence and accessibility of the music, it becomes harder for the form to take hold.

Another reason forestalling a major revival is the lack of appropriate spaces for dance and performance. For serious social dancers there exists a core circuit of dance clubs and ballrooms, such as Roseland, Café Society, the Rainbow Room, and others. In general, though, not enough clubs in New York and other major cities have remodeled their floors and restructured their layouts to accommodate the emergent interest in social dancing. Likewise, clubs (and talent agents) are not booking exhibition ballroom dancers as featured entertainers in large enough numbers to secure them guaranteed work. Club owners may be waiting for the ballroom dance revival to become a clear trend before they commit financial resources.

There is good reason to believe that exhibition ballroom dance will again prosper in the theatre. The work of professional companies such as the nationally renowned American Ballroom Theatre is helping promote a contemporary, late-twentieth-century concept of exhibition ballroom dance. This concept may inspire more, similarly creative expressions. Furthermore, the public's current romance with ballroom dance augurs well for its continuation as a *theatrical* dance form. In the best scenario, ballroom dance's popularity with the public will induce theatrical choreographers, composers, producers, and writers to expand the use of ballroom dance on stage.

NOTES

1. For discussions about the Hustle as a renewed form of couple dancing, see Agnes de Mille, "Do I Hear Violins," *The New York Times*, 11 May 1975 and Denis O'Neill, "Having A Ball," *The [Boston] Sunday Globe*, 20 January 1985; Don McDonagh, *Dance Fever* (New York: Random House, 1979), pp. 109–110.

2. Laura Shapiro, "The Art of Ballroom Dancing," *Newsweek,* 19 November 1984.

3. Ballet Hispanico in "Cada Noche . . . Tango," New York City, Joyce Theatre, 21 October 1988.

4. Yvonne Marceau, interview by author, 30 January 1991.

5. American Ballroom Theatre in *Sheer Romance,* Dance Theatre Workshop, New York City, 28 October 1984; American Ballroom Theatre in *Rendezvous with Romance,* The Joyce Theatre, New York City, 5 May 1989; Jennifer Dunning, "They Do Dance All Night. Isn't It Romantic?" *The New York Times,* 27 April 1989. For other reviews of American Ballroom Theatre, see Arlene Croce, *The New Yorker,* 19 November 1984; Deborah Jowitt, *The Village Voice,* 20 November 1984; Marilyn Hunt, *Dance Magazine,* February 1985.

6. Anna Kisselgoff, "Waltzing and Jitterbugging From Ballrooms of Yore," *The New York Times,* 11 April 1991.

7. Another company, similar in form to American Ballroom Theatre and also formed during the mid-1980s, was Peter Maxwell's Ballroom Dance Theatre. They toured the show "Ballroom to Broadway" around the country and abroad. Some other notable companies attempting to recreate historical social dance styles on stage are Elizabeth Aldrich's Court Dance Company and Carol Teten's Dance Through Time, based in California.

8. See Barbara Gilford, "Ballroom Style Glides Onto Concert Stage," *The New York Times,* 1 July 1990.

9. *Grand Hotel,* The Martin Beck Theatre (New York City), 30 January 1991.

10. *Tango Argentino,* City Center Theatre (New York City), 30 June 1985.

11. For interesting discussions of *Tango Argentino* see Perry A. Bialor, *Ballet News,* vol. 7, no. 7 (January, 1986): 11–15; *"Tango Argentino," Attitude,* vol. 3, no. 9, 10 (Fall/Winter, 1985–86): 19–20; Sally R. Sommer, "Tango Argentino" [review], *Dance Magazine,* November 1985, pp. 35–36; Lois Draegin, "Tango Traces a Society," *The New York Times,* 23 June 1985.

12. Bialor, *Ballet News,* p. 13.

13. "Samba Rio," Fact Sheet, Samba Rio, Inc., private collection, undated.

14. The first Harvest Moon Ballroom Competition was held on the Mall in Central Park where it drew close to 75,000 spectators. Because of the unexpectedly large crowds, the event was postponed until Madison Square Garden became available, "Harvest Moon Ball," *Dance Magazine,* September 1945. For more information on ballroom dance contests from the 1930s and 1940s, see "Harvest Moon Ball Comes Back to Town," *Dance Magazine,* October 1942; "Harvest Moon Ball," *Dance Magazine,* September 1945, p. 30; William Murtha, "Harvest Ball Sponsors Define Pros," *The [New York] Daily News,* 27 July 1946; W. G. Raffe, "Blackpool Ballroom Dance Competition," *Dance Magazine,* April 1948.

15. For some interesting and varied sources on contemporary ballroom dance competitions see: Denis O'Neill, "Having a Ball," *The [Boston] Sunday Globe;* Melanie Menagh, "The Return of Ballroom Dancing," *Family Weekly,* 19 May 1985; Jerry Carroll, "Slow Dancing Comes Back Hot and Flashy," *The San Francisco Chronicle,* 8 March 1985; Ken Graves and Eva Lipman, photographs, Sally Sommer, text, *Ballroom* (Minneapolis, MN: Milkweed Editions, 1989); Nan Robertson, "Ballroom Champs Twirl at the Garden," *The New York Times,* 5

October 1984; Jennifer Dunning, "Reality and the Light Fantastic," *The New York Times*, 27 November 1987.

16. See John Hennessy, "Ice Dancing Pair Excites Britain," *The New York Times*, 30 January 1984; Anna Kisselgoff, "New Ice Partnership: Soviet Skating Stars Join Torvill and Dean," *The New York Times*, 12 October 1989. Several ballroom dance teachers and officials have petitioned the International Olympic Committee to include ballroom dance as an Olympic event. See Janet Romaker, "Romance is back, and so is Ballroom Dancing," *The [Toledo, Ohio] Blade*, reprinted in *Dancing U.S.A.*, vol. 5, no. 3, August/October, 1987.

17. Aida Moreno, Executive Producer, interview by author, New York City, 7 May 1991.

18. Norma Mclain Stoop, "dancevision," *Dance Magazine*, February 1980, p. 119; Robert MacKenzie, *"Dance Fever"* [review], *TV Guide*, 16 October 1982; Andy Meisler, "Calling All Amateurs: The Right Steps Will Win You $50,000," *TV Guide*, 1 March 1986.

19. Robert MacKenzie, *"Star Search"* [review], *TV Guide*, 19 May 1984; Andy Meisler, *"Star Search* Auditions: It's Like Panning for Gold with a Soup Strainer," *TV Guide*, 23 February 1985; Janice Berman, *"Star Search* winners strut their stuff," *New York Newsday*, 20 March 1986.

20. See O'Neill, "Having a Ball," for more on competitive champion Liz Curtis. On Ricky Quintana see program, Pathmark Hispanic Arts Festival, RM Marketing, Inc., 1991.

21. Jennifer Ford, interview by author, 25 May 1991.

22. See *Eye on Dance*, #283, television program, Julie Malnig, Judie and Stan Martin, WNYC-TV, 3 April 1989. Julie Malnig, moderator, "Dancing Till Dawn: Exhibition Ballroom Dance in America," for "Ballroom Week 1989," featuring ballroom dancers Judie and Stan Martin and Tony and Anne Brienza, The New York Public Library, April 1989.

23. Arlene Schulman, 'Waltzing and Jitterbugging to Fitness," *The New York Times*, 24 June 1990. Dance instructors Phil Martin and Betty Rose Griffith have produced a ballroom dance-workout home video; see Romaker, "Romance is back, and so is Ballroom Dancing."

24. Connie Townsend, National Secretary of the United States Amateur Ballroom Dance Association, interview by author, New York City, 5 May 1991.

25. For information on Roseland see "Profiles: Home of Refined Dancing," *The New Yorker*, 27 June 1942; Robert W. Dana, "Roseland Huge But Intimate," *The World Telegram and Sun*, 22 January 1957; Sal Gerage, "This Joint is Still Jumpin," *After Dark*, June 1980; Gregory Jaynes, "In New York: Celebrating an Eternal Prom," *Time Magazine*, 17 August 1987.

26. For information on ballroom dance at contemporary clubs see Lisa Wolf, "Dancing Up A Storm in the Clubs," *The New York Times*, 5 April 1985; Michael Gross, "Night Life: The Latest Clubs," *The New York Times*, 22 August 1986; Andrew L. Yarrow, "Where to Glide Across Ballrooms To Big-Band Hits," *The New York Times*, 9 September 1988; Evelyn Nieves, "The Mambo is Back, Forty Years Later," *The New York Times*, 12 May 1991; Kelvin, p. 84.

27. To date, "Ballroom Week" has occurred in spring of 1989 and 1990 in New York City.

28. Senator Hefflin introduced a resolution to the Senate Judiciary Commit-

tee that should be voted on in September 1991. Leah Garchik, "Personals," *San Francisco Chronicle*, 3 April 1991.

29. For information on Brigham Young University see Connie Townsend, interview; "This is the Place: Salt Lake City—Heart of the Mormon Faith," *Dance Scene*, May/June 1991, p. 25; Robertson, "Ballroom Champs Twirl at the Garden." For other news on college interest see "Ballroom Dancing is Hit on College Campus," *Associated Press*, 2 June 1985; Alice J. Kelvin, "Cheek to cheek is doubly chic, the second time around," *Smithsonian*, March 1989.

30. Nadine Brozan, "Box Step Follows A Big Band to Barnard," *The New York Times*, 6 February 1987.

31. Larry Schultz quoted in Kelvin, p. 86.

32. Yvonne Marceau, interview by author, New York City, 1 April 1985.

Social Dances, 1908–1919

During the teens the repertoires of the teams consisted of variations on five or six of the most popular social dances of the day, including the one-step, the walk, the fox trot, the hesitation waltz, the tango, and the maxixe.[1] These were the basic dances from which exhibition ballroom dancers adapted and theatricalized their numbers for presentations in theatres.

Exhibition ballroom technique modeled itself after twentieth-century social dance form. This so-called "modern" ballroom style emphasized the use of the upper chest and torso (more so than in the nineteenth-century form), and physical stress was evenly distributed over the entire body.[2] The physical ideal was that of an upright, balanced carriage in which the spine functioned as a central axis from which the arms, hips, and legs moved relatively parallel to the dance floor. This emphasis on balance, of course, promoted the smooth and coordinated functioning of two bodies moving as one.

One-step: Consisting of a series of smooth walking steps taken to each beat of the music, one-steps were usually accompanied by musical compositions in brisk, two-four time. In the opening position of the dance, couples faced one another with the man moving forward on his left foot and the woman stepping backward with her right. The entire dance consisted of a variety of step patterns, such as the eight-step and the spin, all of which were performed to the same upbeat tempo.[3]

The Walk: Like the one-step the walk required the dancer to execute a step to each rhythmic beat. Its characteristic strutting motion was produced by maintaining straightened knees and raising up slightly on the balls of the feet. The distinguishing factor of the walk was its circular floor pattern. The line of direction consisted of a clockwise motion around the perimeter of the ballroom floor. At the beginning of each new revolution partners decreased the scope of the circle until they were practically dancing in one spot. After the smallest possible rotation had been maneuvered, the couple started on a larger circle.[4]

Fox Trot: Introduced in ballrooms around 1915, it added new vigor to the social dance scene. The fox trot combined one-steps and two-steps (marchlike movements) performed to a moderate four-four tempo. The basic pattern consisted of two slow steps followed by three quick ones, then a hold. The identifying feature of the dance was its box (or angled) floor pattern, produced by a combination of forward travel and lateral steps. By the late teens the fox trot had superseded the one-step in popularity, largely because it contained more rhythmic variety.[5]

Hesitation Waltz: One of the most frequently performed social dances, it first became popular during the 1912–1913 season. It developed from the slower-tempoed waltzes (such as the Boston) of the late nineteenth century. It was a basic three-step waltz performed to a syncopated melody. The effect of the syncopation was a slurring of the second and third (and fifth and sixth) beats in a two-measure musical grouping. This slurring, or "hesitation," sequence, enabled dancers to improvise by adding extra steps or sways. For instance, couples might execute a dip step (a genuflection by both partners on alternate knees) on the second and third beats, and then come into an upright position on the fourth beat.

Tango: Catching on quickly in American ballrooms during the teens, the dance, throughout its long history (dating back to the mid-nineteenth century), underwent several transformations. A combination of the habanera and milonga dance rhythms, the tango filtered into Argentinian ballrooms around 1899 as a sinuous couple dance. By 1909 it reached Paris where, after further modifications, it became a widely performed ballroom dance in the United States. The defining characteristic of the tango was its rhythmic pattern, consisting of alternating rests and action. The basic movement sequence was the cortez, which was made up of five steps taken in alternating tempo (slow-slow-quick-quick-slow). Most social dance versions of the tango included other sequences in addition to the cortez, among them the media luna, the scissors, the promenade, and the eight-step or grapevine.[6]

Maxixe: Another dance of South American origin that was widely performed in American ballrooms, it is also known as the Brazilian tango. The maxixe combined steps from the tango and the two-step. The distinguishing feature of the dance was its heel step. In the characteristic *les-a-Cote* (or single step) position, couples, facing each other, performed a sideways sliding step done on the heel of one foot and the flat of the other. From this position partners moved into the skate step, in which the male partner placed himself behind and slightly to the side of the woman, and both performed a two-step. The maxixe tended to be too difficult a dance for the public, largely because of its swiftly executed step changes.[7]

NOTES

1. For descriptions of these dances, see Mr. and Mrs. Vernon Castle, *Modern Dancing* (New York: The World Syndicate Co., 1914); Maurice Mouvet, *The*

Tango and the New Dances for Ballroom and Home (Chicago: Laird and Lee, 1914); Troy and Margaret West Kinney, *Social Dancing of Today* (New York: Frederick A. Stokes and Co., 1914).

2. For further discussion of movement theory from this period, see "The Modern Dance and Physical Culture," *The Modern Dance Magazine*, February 1914, pp. 16–17; March 1914, p. 13.

3. Irene and Vernon Castle promoted the one-step as a "refined" version of the Turkey Trot and rid it of its excessive swaying and rocking motions. Their exhibition version itself eventually caught on as a social dance. See Castle, *Modern Dancing*, p. 20.

4. Irene and Vernon Castle originally introduced this dance in around 1912 as the Castle Walk, although other exhibition ballroom teams soon devised their own versions. Mrs. Vernon Castle, *My Husband* (New York: Da Capo Press, 1979), p. 54.

5. The exact origins of the fox trot are unclear. Several sources contend that the dance was introduced at Florenz Ziegeld's Danse de Follies cabaret in 1914 by professional dancer Harry Fox, who performed a trotting-type dance. Ziegfeld supposedly asked Oscar Duryea, a prominent dance teacher, to present a number at intermission to rouse the cabaret audiences. Duryea and a student from his school performed a dance similar to Fox's number, but in half-time. It then caught on with the public as Fox's Trot—or the fox trot. The Castles, as well, claim responsibility for introducing the fox trot. They contend that James Reese Europe introduced them to the dance with William Handy's musical composition, 'The Memphis Blues.' See Oscar Duryea Clipping File, BRTC, and *Steppin' on the Gas, Rags to Jazz 1913–1927* (New World Records). Liner notes by Lawrence Gushee.

6. Most historians agree that the tango originated as a combination of the tangano—a dance of African-Latin origin—and the habanera, a Cuban rhythm. Migrating blacks took this combination to Argentina where it mingled with the milonga, a popular folk dance of Buenos Aires. The first ballroom tangos were published in Buenos Aires in 1899 and were usually a combination of milonga and habanera rhythms. See Peter Buckman, *Let's Dance* (New York: Paddington Press, 1978), p. 171; Albert and Josephine Butler, "The Tango Story," *Dance Magazine*, February 1951, p. 24; A. H. Franks, *Social Dance* (London: Routledge & Kegan Paul, 1963), pp. 178–179.

7. The maxixe supposedly originated as a Brazilian folk dance that combined syncopation with the Cuban habanera rhythm. Its movements were similar to that of the European polka, although it is unclear how exactly the maxixe was altered for ballroom use. This social dance version was exported to Paris around 1910 and was then brought to the United States, where it became popular around 1912. One can assume that the dance went through several transformations by the time it became part of the American ballroom dance repertoire. The dance was alternately spelled as maxixe and mattchiche.

Appendix B

Exhibition Ballroom Dance Technique, 1908–1919

Appendix B explains the major ways in which social dances were theatricalized and describes the styles of exhibition ballroom dancing established during the years 1908 through approximately 1919. The available pool of dances from which professional teams could choose was actually quite large. In many instances dancers or choreographers built exhibition numbers around one element of a basic waltz, one-step, or tango; these dances in turn became perceived as entirely new dances. Some of these "second generation" dances included the innovation, the glide, and the whirlwind, each of which spawned individual variations.

METHODS OF BALLROOM DANCE THEATRICALIZATION

Innovation: A sequence from the tango or waltz in which partners performed without holding hands,[1] it became the basis of a very popular stage specialty. Because there was minimal physical contact, partners often performed with props of some sort. In Adelaide and Hughes' Hoop Whirl dance in *The Passing Show of 1912* (discussed in Chapter 5), the dancers manipulated a silk-covered hoop. In an innovation performed by Jose Collins and Martin Brown in *The Whirl of Society* (1912), called the Cinderella Waltz, the dancers performed the primary steps of the dance by manipulating Brown's long red silk sash.[2] Innovations actually served several functions. They lent a sense of drama and suspense since often the couples did not touch one another until the conclusion. Also, because dancers performed the innovation apart from one another and used greater stage space, the dance could be used to create a sense of spectacle.

Glide: An embellished one-step or two-step that was characterized by the positioning of the female dancer in front and slightly to the side of her male partner, producing a distinct gliding effect. In the musical theatre, these dances usually served to feature a starring (usually female) performer and were named after her, such as the Gaby Glide, created for dancer Gaby Deslys in *Vera Violetta* (1911), and the Gertrude Hoffmann Glide, from *Broadway to Paris* (1912).

Whirlwind: Actually a one-step or waltz that ended in what was called a "whirlwind turn." The turn consisted of three spinning movements beginning in the standard waltz position. As the couple spun, they straightened and extended their arms until they were leaning away from each other. Finally, the woman lifted her feet and was whirled by the man. There were many variations on this dance, and a variety of striking ending poses. In some versions the woman landed on the shoulders of her male partner, while in others, particularly as performed by acrobatic teams, the man clasped his female partner by the waist as she leaned back into a deep bend. Whirlwinds were frequently seen in vaudeville where they served as particularly flashy act-closers.

STYLES OF EXHIBITION BALLROOM DANCE PERFORMANCE

Since exhibition ballroom dancers were all drawing from the same basic repertoire of ballroom dances, it became necessary for teams to differentiate themselves from one another. This could be done by varying rhythm, changing tempo and speed or directional patterns, improvising steps, exaggerating poses, or pairing partners of a different size to create an unusual movement style. Another possibility for change and differentiation lay in the incorporation of movement from other dance genres, such as ballet or acrobatics.

Basically the exhibition teams may be placed in one of six broad categories of movement style. These included the standard, eccentric, tandem, adagio, ballet, and acrobatic modes. Of course, many of these modes overlapped— adagio ballroom dancers, for instance, might (and usually did) incorporate elements of ballet into their dance numbers. But these six categories include most of the predominant styles displayed during the teens and early twenties. As a rule, exhibition ballroom dance from the teens and twenties was more grounded and less acrobatic than ballroom dance of later decades.

Standard or "normal": The majority of teams (particularly cabaret teams) performed in this mode. Their dances basically conformed to ballroom work as taught in social dance schools although, of course, they might theatricalize their numbers by adding new step variations, changing basic floor patterns, or varying rhythm. Their style of dancing, however, incorporated little or none of the exaggerated movements or body dislocations characteristic of certain other modes such as eccentric or whirlwind dancing. Irene and Vernon Castle were among the most popular standard teams.[3] In fact, many people considered them to be the quintessential exhibition ballroom team because they perfected basic ballroom form of upright carriage, poise, grace, and unity of movement. Maurice Mouvet and Florence Walton were also among standard exhibition ballroom teams. Unlike the Castles, however, their style depended on exaggeration of steps and poses. By extending the scale of dips and bends, or by lengthening particular steps, they achieved a dramatic, sinuous look.[4]

Eccentric: Depending on the degree to which exhibition ballroom teams exaggerated their movements, they might be considered eccentric-exhibition ballroom dancers. The primary characteristic of eccentric work was its distinctive displacement of the hips and pelvis, often combined with acrobatic movements. Dancers Leon Errol and Stella Chatelaine frequently performed in this mode; one of the clearest examples of this sort of work was their comic ballroom number, "Turkish Trottishness," from the *Ziegfeld Follies of 1913.* They performed the steps in dizzyingly rapid succession, prompting one reviewer to describe the dance as "convulsive."[5] The technical skill required for this dance involved the appearance of a loss of control while they maintained a steady, fast tempo.

In another type of eccentric-exhibition ballroom alliance unevenly matched dancers were paired for comic effect, as in the case of Clifton Webb and Mary Hay (discussed in Chapter 5). Often they wore "rube" or country-hick costumes, such as Webb's top hat and his oversized trousers clearly designed to accentuate his and Hay's height difference. A characteristic comedy step was the hitch kick, also known as the Pendulum, in which the dancer swung the leg from back to front at a vertical angle without shifting weight. In eccentric-exhibition work this was usually performed by the man over the woman's head.[6]

Tandem: A ballroom style created largely through symmetry of movement, the tandem always featured dancers of the same gender. These dance acts incorporated several steps and poses characteristic of ballroom work, such as the *les-a-Cote* and glide positions. It was most frequently performed as an innovation with performers not holding hands.

The principal techniques employed in tandem dance were mirror and shadow work. In the mirroring position the two dancers generally stood directly next to or facing one another while moving opposite arms, legs, or shoulders. For shadowing work, the team frequently assumed the glide position and performed evenly paced, identical leg and arm movements. Tandem dance, characteristic of exhibition ballroom teams such as the Dolly Sisters, required precision timing and a finely tuned sense of balance and rhythm.

Adagio: Slow, sustained, flowing movements characterized this style of ballroom dance. Joan Sawyer epitomized a type of adagio-ballroom work seen frequently in the teens. In describing Sawyer's work, dance teacher Troy Kinney remarked that "she flows her steps together like a finely rendered legato passage on a cello with never a suspicion of slurring of detail of the forms the movements should describe."[7] Sawyer's Aeroplane Waltz best exemplified this style of dance. She and her partner performed what was basically a hesitation waltz to an unusually slow (6/8) tempo, adorning it with gentle glides, pivots, and attenuated holds.

Other types of adagio-ballroom dancers during the twenties included those employing acrobatic lifts and leaps (usually performed to slow, lyrical music), in which the female partner typically alighted on her male partner's arms or shoulders. The exhibition ballroom team of Tony and Nina De Marco popularized an adagio-ballroom style in the early twenties with their graceful and perfectly balanced, synchronized movements.

Acrobatic: There were several ways in which this style was manifested. In some cases the dancers were acrobats who added ballroom steps and postures to their standard acrobatic routine as in the case of the brother-sister team Hilarion and Rosalia Ceballos, of the Mexican circus family. Their unique one-steps and waltzes typically contained a series of double somersaults and breath-taking turns.[8] Because Hilarion was taller than Rosalie, he could spin her to his shoulders for dramatic effect.

Other teams, who were not necessarily from an acrobatic tradition, nonetheless incorporated acrobatic movements into a standard ballroom act. Jack Clifford, for example, added exciting acrobatic movement to his whirlwind waltz, which he performed in vaudeville with Evelyn Nesbit. There appear to have been two different conclusions to this dance. In one, Nesbit is positioned upside down, with Clifford holding her by the waist. In the other—which seemed to defy the laws of gravity—Clifford swung Nesbit around him while she clasped her hands around his neck.[9]

Ballet: Frequently dancers combined ballet and ballroom work to create a unique style. Many vaudeville dancers proficient in ballet and toe work began adding these forms to their repertoire to diversify their acts. Adelaide and Hughes were forerunners in this balletic-ballroom mode. Typically the team's numbers began and ended with a traditional ballet pose. The light and ethereal qualities associated with their work can be attributed largely to Adelaide's use of pointed, lifted toes (instead of the flat-footed stance characteristic of most ballroom work), and the gestural, undulating use of her arms.

NOTES

1. See Mr. and Mrs. Vernon Castle, *Modern Dancing* (New York: World Syndicate Co., 1914), p. 88, for illustrations of innovation steps in the tango.

2. Brown and Collins's dance was also promoted as the "No Clasp Dance." *The Louisville Herald,* 14 April 1912 (Jose Collins scrapbook, Robinson Locke Collection, ser. 2, vol. 316, BRTC).

3. A rendition of the Castle Walk and other exhibition numbers of the Castles has been preserved in the film, *Social and Theatrical Dancing 1909–1936* (Film Studies Center, The Museum of Modern Art).

4. See photographs in Maurice Mouvet, *The Tango and Other New Dances for the Ballroom and Home* (Chicago: Laird & Lee, 1914).

5. "Follies of 1913," *New York Dramatic Mirror,* 15 June 1913 (Leon Errol scrapbook, Robinson Locke Collection, ser. 2, vol. 49, BRTC).

6. Barbara Namoi Cohen, "The Dance Direction of Ned Wayburn" (Ph.D. dissertation, New York University, 1980), p. 111.

7. Troy Kinney, "The New Dances: A Study of Art and Good Taste as Expressed in Modern Ballroom Dancing," *Woman's Home Companion,* October 1914, pp. 14, 64.

8. The Ceballos were, in fact, the first known team for whom Ned Wayburn staged a whirlwind dance in 1907. Cohen, "The Dance Direction of Ned Wayburn," p. 117.

9. See Clifford and Nesbit photograph file, MWEZ, 9982 and 9986, BRTC.

Selected Bibliography

BOOKS

Allen, Frederick Lewis. *The Big Change: America Transforms Itself, 1900–1950.* New York: Harper & Row, 1954.

Anderson, Hugh Abercrombie. *Out Without My Rubbers: The Memoirs of John Murray Anderson.* New York: Library Publishers, 1954.

Ardmore, Jane. *The Self-Enchanted, Mae Murray: Image of An Era.* New York: McGraw-Hill Co., 1959.

Berlin, Edward A. *Ragtime: A Musical and Cultural History.* Berkeley: University of California Press, 1980.

Blesh, Rudi, and Harriet Janis. *They All Played Ragtime.* New York: Oak Publications, 1950.

Bordman, Gerald. *American Operetta: From H.M.S. Pinafore to Sweeney Todd.* New York: Oxford University Press, 1981.

Buckman, Peter. *Let's Dance.* New York: Paddington Press, 1978.

Butler, Albert, and Josephine Butler. *Twenty Five Years of American Dance.* New York: Rudolf Orthwine, 1954.

———. *The Encyclopedia of Social Dance.* New York: Albert and Josephine Butler, 1975.

Castle, Irene. *Castles in the Air.* New York: Doubleday & Co., 1958.

———. *My Husband.* New York: Charles Scribner's & Sons, 1919; reprint ed., New York: Da Capo Press, 1979.

Cohen-Stratyner, Barbara Naomi. *The Biographical Dictionary of Dance.* New York: Macmillan & Co., 1982.

Dance, Stanley. *The World of Swing.* New York: Charles Scribner's & Sons, 1974.

DeMille, Agnes. *America Dances.* New York: Macmillan Pub. Co., 1980.

DiMiglio, John E. *Vaudeville U.S.A.* Bowling Green, OH: Bowling Green University Popular Press, 1973.

Dorr, Rheta Childe. *What Eight Million Women Want.* Boston: Small, Maynard & Co., 1910; reprint ed., New York: Kraus Co., 1971.

Dulles, Foster Rhea. *A History of Recreation: America Learns to Play.* New York: Appleton-Century-Crofts, 1965.

Emery, Lynne Fauley. *Black Dance In the United States: From 1619 to 1970.* New York: Arno Press, 1980.

Erenberg, Lewis A. *Steppin' Out: New York Nightlife and the Transformation of American Culture.* Westport, CT: Greenwood Press, 1981.

Evans, Sara M. *Born for Liberty: A History of Women in America.* New York: Free Press, 1989.

Ewen, David. *The Complete Book of the American Musical Theatre.* New York: Holt, Rinehart and Winston, 1958.

———. Great Men of American Popular Song. Englewood Cliffs, NJ: Prentice-Hall, Inc., 1972.

Franks, A. H. *Social Dance: A Short History.* London: Routledge, Paul & Kegan, 1963.

Gilbert, Douglas. *American Vaudeville: Its Life and Times.* New York: Dover Publications, Inc., 1940.

Goldberg, Isaac. *Tin Pan Alley.* New York: Frederick Ungar Pub. Co., Inc., 1961.

Grau, Robert. *The Business Man in the Amusement World.* New York: Broadway Pub. Co., 1910.

Graves, Ken, and Eva Lipman, photographs, Sally Sommer, text. *Ballroom.* Minneapolis, MN: Milkweed Editions, 1989.

Henderson, Mary C. *The City and the Theatre.* New York: James T. White & Co., 1973.

Jasen, David A. *Recorded Ragtime: 1897–1958.* Hamden, CT: Archon Books, 1973.

Johnson, James Weldon. *Black Manhattan.* New York: Alfred A. Knopf, 1930.

Johnson, Stephen Burge. *The Roof Gardens of Broadway Theatre: 1883–1942.* Ann Arbor, MI: UMI Research Press, 1985.

Jones, Howard Mumford. *The Age of Energy: Varieties of American Experience, 1865–1915.* New York: The Viking Press, 1975.

Keller, Julius. *Inns and Outs.* New York: G. P. Putnam's Sons, 1939.

Kendall, Elizabeth. *Where She Danced.* New York: Alfred A. Knopf, 1979.

McCabe, James D., Jr., *The Lights and Shadows of New York Life.* Philadelphia, PA: National Publishing Co., 1872; reprint ed., Farrar, Straus and Giroux, 1970.

McCarthy, Albert. *The Dance Band Era: The Dancing Decades from Ragtime to Swing, 1910–1950.* Philadelphia, PA: Chilton Books, 1971.

McCarthy, James Remington. *Peacock Alley: The Romance of the Waldorf-Astoria.* New York: Harper & Bros., 1931.

Marbury, Elizabeth. *My Crystal Ball.* New York: Boni & Liveright Pub., 1923.

Marks, Edward. *They All Sang.* New York: Viking Press, 1935.

Martin, John. *Introduction to the Dance.* New York: W. W. Norton & Co., Inc., 1939.

May, Lary. *Screening Out the Past: The Birth of Mass Culture and the Motion Picture Industry*. New York: Oxford University Press, 1980.

Morris, Lloyd. *Incredible New York: High Life and Low Life of the Last Hundred Years*. New York: Random House, 1957.

Ostrander, Gilman M. *American Civilization in the First Machine Age: 1890–1940*. New York: Harper & Row., 1970.

Poggi, Emil John. *Theatre in America: The Impact of Economic Forces, 1870–1967*. Ithaca, NY: Cornell University Press, 1966.

Pulitzer, Ralph. *New York Society on Parade*. New York: Harper & Bros. Pub., 1910.

Rector, George. *The Girl from Rector's*. New York: Doubleday, Page & Co., 1927.

Richardson, Philip J. S. *Social Dances of the Nineteenth Century*. London: Charles Birchall & Sons, Ltd., 1960.

Riley, Glenda. *Inventing the American Woman: A Perspective on Women's History 1865 to the Present*. Arlington Heights, IL: Harlan Davison, Inc., 1986.

Roberts, John Storm. *The Latin Tinge: The Impact of Latin American Music on the United States*. New York: Oxford University Press, 1979.

Rust, Frances. *Dance in Society*. London: Routledge & Kegan Paul, 1969.

Ryan, Mary P. *Womanhood in America: From Colonial Times to the Present*. New York: Franklin Watts Pub., 1979.

Schlesinger, Arthur Meier. *The Rise of Modern America: 1865–1951*. New York: The Macmillan Co., 1951.

———. *The Rise of the City*. New York: The Macmillan Co., 1933.

Schuller, Gunther. *The Swing Era: The Development of Jazz, 1930–1945*. New York: Oxford University Press, 1989.

Silvester, Victor. *Modern Ballroom Dancing: History and Practice*. London: Barrie & Jenkins, 1977.

Smith, Bill. *The Vaudevillians*. New York: Macmillan Pub. Co., 1976.

Smith, Cecil, and Glenn Litton. *Musical Comedy in America*. New York: Theatre Arts Books, 1981.

Smith, Harry B. *First Nights and First Editions*. Boston: Little, Brown & Co., 1931.

Snyder, Robert. *The Voice of the City: Vaudeville and Popular Culture in New York*. New York: Oxford Univesity Press, 1989.

Southern, Eileen. *The Music of Black Americans: A History*. New York: W. W. Norton & Co., Inc., 1971.

Spaeth, Sigmund. *A History of Popular Music in America*. New York: Random House, 1948.

Staples, Shirley. *Male-Female Comedy Teams in American Vaudeville: 1865–1932*. Ann Arbor, MI: UMI Research Press, 1984.

Stearns, Marshall, and Jean Stearns. *Jazz Dance: The Story of American Vernacular Dance*. New York: Schirmer Books, 1968.

Stein, Charles W., ed. *American Vaudeville As Seen By Its Contemporaries*. New York: Alfred A. Knopf, 1984.

Sullivan, Mark. *Our Times: The United States, 1900–1925*. 4 vols. New York: Charles Scribner's & Sons, 1932.

Toll, Robert C. *On With the Show*. New York: Oxford University Press, 1976.

Walker, Stanley, *The Night Club Era*. New York: Frederick A. Stokes Co., 1953.

Wiebe, Robert H. *The Search for Order: 1877–1920*. New York: Hill & Wang, 1967.

Wayburn, Ned. *The Art of Stage Dancing*. New York: The Ned Wayburn Studios of Stage Dancing, Inc., 1925.

DANCE INSTRUCTION MANUALS

Baron, Samuel. *Professor Baron's Complete Instructor in All the Society Dances of America*. New York: M. Young, Publisher, 1881.

Butler, Albert, and Josephine Butler. "Encyclopedia of Social Dance." New York: By the Authors, 1975. Typescript housed in the Dance Collection, The New York Public Library.

Carpenter, Lucien O. *J. W. Pepper's Universal Dancing Master, Prompters Call Book, and Violinists Guide*. Philadelphia, PA: J. W. Pepper, 1882.

Castle, Mr. and Mrs. Vernon. *Modern Dancing*. New York: Harper & Bros., 1914.

Chalif, Louis H. *The Chalif Text Books of Dancing*, 5 vols. New York: The Chalif Normal School of Dancing, 1918–1925.

Clendenen, Leslie F. *The Art of Dancing*. St. Louis, MO: By the Author, 1919.

———. *Dance Mad, or The Dances of the Day*. St. Louis, MO: Arcade Print Co., 1914.

Coll, Charles J., and Gabrielle Rosiere. *Dancing Made Easy*. New York: Edward J. Clode, 1919.

Crozier, Gladys Beattie. *The Tango & How to do it*. London: Andrew Melrose, Ltd., 1913.

Cruz, Carlos. *The Modern Ballroom Tango*. New York: By the Author, 1925.

DeGarmo, William B. *The Dance of Society: A Critical Analysis of all the Standard Quadrilles, Round Dances, 102 Figures of Le Cotillion*. New York: By the Author, 1879.

Dodworth, Allen. *Dancing and Its Relation to Education and Social Life*. New York: Harper & Bros., 1885.

Ferraro, Edward. *The Art of Dancing*. New York: By the Author, 1859.

Gilbert, Melvin Ballou, ed. *The Director, Dancing, Deportment, Etiquette, Aesthetics, Physical Training*. Portland, ME: By the Author, 1898.

Hopkins, J. S. *The Tango and Other Up-to-date Dances*. Chicago: The Saalfield Pub. Co., 1914.

Hostetler, Lawrence A. *The Art of Social Dancing*. New York: A. S. Barnes & Co., Inc., 1930.

Kinney, Troy, and Margaret West. *Social Dancing of Today*. New York: Frederick A. Stokes Co., 1914. Dances demonstrated by Mr. John Murray Anderson.

———. *The Dance*. New York: Frederick A. Stokes Co., 1914.

Lee, Betty. *Dancing*. New York; Pioneer Publications, Inc., 1945.

Mouvet, Maurice. *Maurice's Art of Dancing*. New York: G. Schirmer, 1915.

———. *The Tango and the New Dances for Ballroom and Home*. Chicago: Laird & Lee, Inc., 1914.

Murray, Arthur. *The Modern Dances*, 2 vols. New York: By the Author, 1923.

Veloz and Yolanda. *Tango and Rumba: Dances of Today and Tomorrow.* New York: Harper & Bros., 1938.

Walker, Caroline. *The Modern Dances.* Chicago: Saul Bros., 1914.

Walker, H. Layton. *Twentieth Century Cotillion Figures.* Buffalo, NY: Two-Step Publishing Co., 1912.

Zorn, Frederich Albert. *The Grammar of the Art of Dancing.* (1887 unpublished.) New York: Burt Franklyn, 1970.

DANCE INSTRUCTIONS PRINTED IN NEWSPAPERS AND SHEET MUSIC

(Several of these sources appeared in the Robinson Locke scrapbooks at the Billy Rose Theatre Collection, The New York Public Library, abbreviated here as Rob. Locke Col., BRTC).

Brian, Donald. "How to Dance the Futurist Twirl." *San Francisco Call,* 24 October 1913 (Carol McComas scrapbook, Rob. Locke Col., ser. 2, vol. 277, BRTC), p. 64.

Castle, Irene, and Vernon Castle. "New Dances for this Winter." *Ladies Home Journal,* ca. 1914 (Irene and Vernon Castle scrapbook, folder no. 1, Museum of the City of New York).

Dolly, Roszika, and Martin Brown. "How to Dance the Tango-Classique." *New York Evening Journal,* 22 July 1913, p. 2.

The Dolly Sisters, "Cuba Contributes to the Rumba." *Newark Star Eagle,* 25 October 1915 (Newark Public Library, microfilm).

"The Dolly Waltz and How to Dance It." Undated newspaper clipping in the *Buffalo Enquirer* (Dolly Sisters scrapbook, Rob. Locke Col., ser. 2, vol. 127, BRTC).

Errol, Leon. "The Brighter Side of Turkey Trotting." *Cleveland Leader,* 5 August 1913 (Leon Errol scrapbook, Rob. Locke Col., ser. 3, vol. 454).

"Extra! Dancing Masters Convention Indorses [sic] Comet Schottische and Boston Glide!" *New York World,* Sunday, 19 June 1910, sec. E, p. 9.

"How to Dance the Jazz," illustrated by Frances White. *Los Angeles Examiner,* 25 November 1917 (Frances White scrapbook, Rob. Locke Col., ser. 2, BRTC).

"The Latest Dances and How to Dance Them." *Louisville Herald,* April 1912 (Jose Collins scrapbook, Rob. Locke Col., ser. 2, vol. 316, BRTC).

"Latest Society Dances for the Parlor or Ballroom." Sheet music for 'The Cadet Valse.' Music by L. W. Vizay. Pub. 1914.

INSTRUCTIONS FOR DANCES AND INDIVIDUAL STEPS PUBLISHED IN THE FOLLOWING PERIODICALS:

The American Dancer, The Dance, Dance Culture Magazine, Dance Lovers Magazine, The Dance Magazine, Dance Review, The Dancing Times, The Director, The Modern Dance Magazine, The Two-Step.

UNPUBLISHED THESES

Bandy, Linda S. "Dance as a Dramatic Device in Nineteenth Century English Melodrama." M.F.A. thesis, York University, Toronto, Ontario, 1980.

Carter, David Payne. "Gower Champion and The American Musical Theatre," Ph.D. dissertation, New York University, 1987.

Cohen, Barbara Naomi. "The Dance Direction of Ned Wayburn: Selected Topics in Musical Theatre Staging." Ph.D. dissertation, New York University, 1980.

Dixon-Stowell, Brenda. "Dancing in the Dark: The Life and Times of Margot Webb in Aframerican Vaudeville of the Swing Era." Ph.D. dissertation, New York University, 1981.

Johnson, Stephen Burge. "The Roof Gardens of Broadway Theatres, 1883–1941." Ph.D. dissertation, New York University, 1983.

Olin, Reuel Keith. "A History and Interpretation of the Princess Theatre-Musical Plays, 1915–1919." Ph.D. dissertation, New York University, 1979.

ARTICLES

Allen, Frederick Lewis. "When America Learned to Dance." *Scribner's Magazine,* September 1937, pp. 11–17, 92.

Anderson, Jack. "When Ballroom Dance Takes to the Stage." *The New York Times,* Sunday, 7 July 1985.

Bialor, Perry A. "Tango Argentino." *Attitude,* vol. 3, no. 9, 10 Fall/Winter, 1985–86, pp. 19–20.

Butler, Albert, and Josephine Butler. "The Tango Story." *Dance Magazine,* February 1951, pp. 24–25, 38–40.

Cohen, Barbara Naomi. "Chain Prologs: Dance at the Picture Palaces." *Dance Scope,* Spring 1978, pp. 12–23.

Cooper, H. E. "A Cycle of Dance Crazes." *The Dance,* February 1927, pp. 28–29, 50.

———. "Rag on the Barbary Coast." *Dance Magazine,* December 1927, pp. 31, 60.

Dana, Robert W. "Roseland Huge But Intimate." *The World Telegram and Sun,* 22 January 1957.

Davy, Kate. "An Interview with George Burns." *Educational Theatre Journal,* October 1975, pp. 345–355.

De Mille, "Do I Hear Violins," *The New York Times,* 11 May 1975, pp. 35–46.

Dixon-Stowell, Brenda. "Between Two Eras: 'Norton and Margot' in the Afro-American Entertainment World." *Dance Research Journal,* 15/2 (Spring 1983).

Douglas, W. A. S. "The Passing of Vaudeville." *American Mercury,* October 1927, pp. 188–194.

Draegin, Lois. "Tango Traces a Society." *The New York Times,* 23 June 1985.

Dunning, Jennifer. "Reality and The Light Fantastic." *The New York Times,* Thursday, 26 November 1987.

Erenberg, Lewis A. "Everybody's Doin' It: The Pre–World War I Dance Craze, the Castles, and the Modern American Girl." *Feminist Studies*, Fall 1975, pp. 155–170.

Hallmark, Harrydele. "If You Dance You Must Pay the Piper." *Vogue*, 15 January 1914, pp. 24–25.

Inglis, William. "Is Modern Dancing Indecent?" *Harper's Weekly*, 17 May 1913, pp. 11–12.

Kelvin, Alice. "Cheek to cheek is double chic, the second time around." *Smithsonian*, March 1989, pp. 84–95.

Lambert, Pam. "The Enduring Romance of Ballroom Dance." *The Wall Street Journal*, 24 September 1987, p. 24.

Lorenz, John. "The First Turkey Trot." *Variety*, 23 December 1911, p. 19.

Loxley, Ellis. "The Turkey Trot and Tango, America 1900–1920." *Educational Dance*, December 1939, pp. 7–9 (Turkey Trot clipping file, Dance Collection, The New York Public Library).

McGovern, James R. "The American Woman's Pre–World War I Freedom in Manners and Morals." *The Journal of American History*, September 1968, pp. 312–333.

Moore, Lillian. "George Washington Smith." *Dance Index*, Spring 1945, pp. 88–135.

Nye, Russel B. "Saturday Night at the Paradise Ballroom, or Dance Halls in the Twenties." *Journal of Popular Culture*, Summer 1973, pp. 14–15.

O'Neill, Rosetta. "The Dodworth Family and Ballroom Dancing in New York." *Dance Index*, April 1943, pp. 44–56.

Pulaski, I. B. "The Origin of the Cabaret." *Variety*, 20 December 1912, p. 51.

Scott, Edward. "Modern Dance Music and Its Influence on Ballroom Dancing." *The Dancing Times*, November 1911, pp. 28–29.

Seldes, Gilbert. "From Chicken Shack to Casino." *Esquire Magazine*, March 1938.

Shapiro, Laura. "The Art of Ballroom Dancing." *Newsweek*, 19 November 1984.

Sommer, Sally R. "Capturing the Ritual of Ballroom Dance." *Dance Magazine*, February 1990.

Spitzer, Marian. "The Business of Vaudeville." *Saturday Evening Post*, 24 May 1924, pp. 125ff.

"The Turkey Trot, Grizzly Bear and Other Naughty Diversions." *New Bedford Sunday Standard*, 4 February 1912.

Watts Mumford, Ethel. "Where Is Your Daughter This Afternoon?" *Harper's Weekly*, 17 January 1914.

Wayburn, Ned. "The Dance and the Stage." *The Modern Dance Magazine*, June/July 1917.

Webb, Clifton. "Where Do We Dance From Here?" *Vogue*, 15 September 1933, pp. 51, 84–86, 90.

White, George, and Nanette Kutner. "The Song and Dance Game." *The Dance*, February 1927, pp. 31–32, 62–63.

Williams, Arthur. "Two Feminists and Dance Managers." *Vanity Fair*, August 1914, pp. 45, 70.

Wilson, Edmund. "Nightclubs." *New Republic*, 9 September 1925, pp. 44, 71.

Wilson, G. Hepburn. "Dance as a Factor in Social Evolution." *The Modern Dance Magazine*, April/May 1917, pp. 9–10, 34.

———. "Modern Dances Are Not Vulgar." *The Modern Dance Magazine,* December/January 1917, pp. 25–26.

SCRAPBOOKS

Clipping files and scrapbooks housed in the Billy Rose Theatre Collection, The New York Public Library (Note: Robinson Locke scrapbooks are denoted by the abbreviation Rob. Locke Col.).

Adelaide and Hughes (MWEZ n.c. 2221, no. 2)

Alexander, Rod

Astaire, Fred and Adele

Atteridge, Harold (MWEZ n.c. 705)

Brice, Elizabeth (Rob. Locke Col., ser. 2, vol. 84)

Brown, Martin (MWEZ n.c. 4423)

Cansino, Eduardo and Elisa (MWEZ n.c. 18,661)

Castle, Irene and Vernon (MWEZ n.c. 21,499)

Ceballos, Hilarion and Rosalia

Champion, Marge and Gower

Clark, Helen (Rob. Locke Col., ser. 2, vol. 312)

Clifford, Jack (Rob. Locke Col., ser. 3, vol. 334)

Clifford, Jack, and Evelyn Nesbit

Collins, Jose (Rob. Locke Col., ser. 2, vol. 316)

Cohan, George (Rob. Locke Col., ser. 2, v. 80)

Crane, Mrs. and Mrs. Douglas (Rob. Locke Col., ser. 3, vol. 443)

Cross, Wellington, and Lois Josephine (MWEZ n.c. 22,522)

Cross, Wellington, and Lois Josephine (Rob. Locke Col., ser. 3, vol. 387)

De Haven, Carter and Flora Parker (Rob. Locke Col., ser.3, vol. 363)

De Marco, Tony and Renée De Marco

Dickson, Dorothy (Rob. Locke Col., ser. 3, vol. 127)

Dolly, Yancsi, and Harry Fox (Rob. Locke Col., ser. 3, vol. 495)

Dolly Sisters, Roszika and Yancsi (Rob. Locke Col., ser. 2, vol. 127; ser. 3, vol. 371)

Dressler, Marie (Rob. Locke Col., ser. 2, vol. 164)

Errol, Leon (Rob. Locke Col., ser. 2, vol. 161)

Fairbanks Twins, Madeleine and Marion

Fisher, Nelle, and Jerry Ross

Folies Bergere (MWEZ n.c. 19,590)

Glass, Bonnie (Rob. Locke Col., ser. 2, vol. 204)

Hay, Mary

Held, Anna (Rob. Locke Col., ser. 2, vol. 265)

Hoffmann, Gertrude (Rob. Locke Col., ser. 2, vol. 274)

Jackson, Ethel (ser. 2, vol. 253)

Jarrott, John

Kalem Company (MFL + n.c. 249)

Linn, Bambi

McCutcheon, Wallace

Mata and Hari

Maxwell, Vera

Moon, George, and Daniel Morris

Moss and Fontana

Mouvet, Maurice (Rob. Locke Col., ser. 2, vol. 276)

Murray, Mae (Locke Col., ser. 2, vol. 281)

Natalie and Ferrari

Nesbit, Evelyn (MWEZ + + + 24,271)

Nice, Fred, Jr.

Pennington, Anne (MWEZ 17,881)

Pilcer, Harry

Programs of Performances Given in New York City (MWEZ + 706)

Rock, William, and Maude Fulton (Rob. Locke Col., ser. 3, vol. 506)

Rooney, Pat (MWEZ n.c. 22,959)

Rooney, Pat, and Marion Bent

Sanderson, Julia (MWEZ n.c. 9191)

Santley, Joseph (Rob. Locke Col., ser. 2, vol. 292)

Santley, Joseph (MWEZ n.c. 22,032)

Sawyer, Joan (Rob. Locke Col., ser 2, vol. 290)

Schwartz, Oscar (MWEZ n.c. 22,984)

Sebastian, Carlos

Smith, Joseph C. (Rob. Locke Col., ser. 2, vol. 147)

Walton, Florence (C & L Brown Col.)

Walton, Florence (Rob. Locke Col., ser. 2, vol. 304)

Wayburn, Ned (MWEZ 21,053–21,063)

Webb, Clifton (MWEZ n.c. 23,406)

Webb, Clifton (MWEZ n.c. 11,388)

White, Francis (Rob. Locke Col., ser. 2, vol. 306)

White, George (MWEZ n.c. 22,852)

Valentino, Rudolph (MFL + n.c. 2207)

Vanderbilt, Gertrude (MWEZ n.c. 23,226)

Veloz and Yolanda

Weeks, Ada Mae (MWEZ n.c. 23,400)

Other personality and production clipping files used were from the Dance Collection, The New York Public Library; the Theatre Collection, The Museum of the City of New York; and the Theatre Collection, The Philadelphia Free Library.

MISCELLANEOUS EPHEMERA

Bray, Billy. *The Wonder Dancers Woods and Bray, the Autobiography of Billy Bray* (pamphlet). Wisconsin: By the Author, 1974.

Castle House, Invitation to subscription dance (Irene and Vernon Castle folder, no. 1, folio 2, Theatre Collection, the Museum of the City of New York).

Columbia double-disc records, Complete Catalogue (*LC-C6, the Rodgers and Hammerstein Archives of Recorded Sound, the New York Public Library).

New Victor Records, Victor Records monthly catalogue (*LC-V6, Rodgers and Hammerstein Archives of Recorded Sound, the New York Public Library).

FILMS

Bally Hoo Cakewalk (*MGZHB2-194, Dance Collection, The New York Public Library).

Bowery Waltz (1905), *Cozy Corner Dance* (1903), *Coney Island Cakewalk* (1904), from the collection of Ernest Smith, New York City.

Charity Ball (*MGZHB2-181, Dance Collection, The New York Public Library).

Theatrical and Social Dancing, 1909–1936 (*MGZHB2-1029, the Dance Collection, The New York Public Library).

The Whirl of Life (Pathe, 1915), starring Irene and Vernon Castle (Film Studies Center, The Museum of Modern Art).

SONG LISTING AND RECORDINGS

All songs have been listed in alphabetical order. Please note the following abbreviations for collection sources:

BLC—The Bella Landauer Collection, The New York Historical Society.

MCNY—Theatre and Music Collection, The Museum of the City of New York; organized by show title.

MD—Special Collections, Music Division, The New York Public Library; organized by show title.

PC—Private Collection.

SA—The Shubert Archive, New York City.

"The Aeroplane Dip," "Hesitation Waltz," "Valse Boston." Music by Arthur Pryor. Carl Fischer Co., 1914. BLC

"The Aeroplane Waltz." Music by Mamie R. Apple. Alice Martin, 1911. BLC

"The Argentine Tango." Music by Paul A. Rubens. Chappell & Co., Ltd., 1912. *The Sunshine Girl.* MD

"Buena Vista Tango." Music by Louis Hirsch. Shapiro, Berstein & Co., 1913. BLC

"Castle House Rag." Music by James Reese Europe. *Steppin on' the Gas: Rags to Jazz 1913–1927.* New World Records, Recorded anthology of American Music, Inc., NW 269, Side one, cut one.

"Castle Innovation Waltz—Esmerelda." Music by C. deMesquita. Edward B. Marks Music Corp., 1914. BLC

"Castle Walk." Music by James Reese Europe and Ford T. Dabney. Jos. W. Stern & Co., 1914. BLC

"Castle Walk." Music by James Reese Europe and Ford T. Dabney. *Steppin' on the Gas,* New World Records, Side One, cut three.

"The Chicken Walk." Music by Irving Berlin. Irving Berlin, Inc., 1916. *The Century Girl.* MCNY

"Dengozo (Parisian Maxixe)." Music by E. Nazareth. Jos. W. Stern & Co., 1914. PC

"The Gaby Glide." Lyrics by Harry Pilcer. Music by Louis A. Hirsch. Shapiro Music Pub. Co., 1911. *Vera Violetta.* SA

"The Gertrude Hoffmann Glide." Lyrics and music by Max Hoffmann. T. B. Harms & Francis, Day, Hunter, 1912. *Broadway to Paris.* MD

"How Do You Do Miss Ragtime." Music by Louis Hirsch. Shapiro Music Pub. Co., 1912. MD

"I'm Simply Crazy Over You." Music by Jerome Schwartz. Lyrics by William Jerome and Ray Goetz. Irving Berlin, Inc., 1915. *Hands Up.* MD

"Joan Sawyer's New Dance Creation, the Aeroplane Waltz." Music by Chas. Konedski-Davis. Presto Pub. Co., 1914. BLC

"The Junk Man Rag." Music by C. Luckyth (Luckey) Robert. Jos. W. Stern Co., 1913. BLC

"Just a Kiss (The Raffles Dance)." Lyrics and music by Bobby Jones. O. E. Story, 1913. *Broadway to Paris.* MD

"Lusitania Waltzes." Music by Edwin E. Goffe. Gaffe Bros., 1910. BLC

"The Maurice 5 to 7 (cinq-a-sept) Tango." Music by Jose Sentis. Edward Marks, 1914. BLC

"Maurice Lame Duck Waltz." Music by Sylvester Belmont. Jos. W Stern, 1914. BLC

"Maurice's Irresistible Tango." Music by L. Logatti. Jos. W. Stern Co., 1913. BLC

"The Maurice Syncopated Waltz." Music by D. Onivas. Edward Marks, 1914. BLC

"Maxella." Music by Charles Konedski-Davis. Presto Pub. Co., 1915. SA

"The Memphis Blues." Music by W. C. Handy and W. George Norton. *Steppin' on the Gas,* New World Records. Side One, cut three.

"My Tango Girl." Lyrics and music by George Arthur, E. Ray Goetz, and Louis A. Hirsch. Chas. K. Harris, 1915. *Ziegfeld Midnight Frolics of 1915.* MD

"The Odeon March." Music by Harry A. Montgomery. Harry A. Montgomery, 1908. SA

"Ravioli Rag," (as danced by Lorain and Burke). Music by Frank Lucanese and Charles Lucotti. Jerome Remick, Inc., 1914. BLC

"Show Us How to Do the Fox Trot." Music and lyrics by Irving Berlin. Irving Berlin, Inc., 1914. *Watch Your Step*. MCNY

"Sing-Sing Tango Tea." Music by Sigmund Romberg. Lyrics by Harold Atteridge. T. B. Harms Co., 1915. *Hands Up*. MD

"The Syncopated Walk." Lyrics and music by Irving Berlin. Irving Berlin, Inc., 1914. *Watch Your Step*. MD

"Tango d'Irene," (for Gene Hodgkins and Irene Hammond). Music by R. Firpo. Edward Marks, 1914. BLC

"Three O'Clock in the Morning." Lyrics by Dorothy Terriss. Music by Julian Robledo. Wests, Ltd., 1922. PC

"Tumble in Love" (introduced by Evelyn Nesbit and Jack Clifford). Lyrics by Wilkie White. Music by Malvin Franklin. Jos. C. Stern & Co., 1915.

"Un Appel D'Amour (Half Step or Hesitation Waltz)." Music by Chas. Konedski-Davis. Presto Pub. Co., 1914. SA

"Underneath the Stars," (as danced by the Dolly Sisters in the *Ziegfeld Midnight Frolic*). Music by Herbert Spencer. Jerome H. Remick & Co., 1915. BLC.

"The Valse Classique Hesitation, a Paraphrase on Dvorak's *Humoresque*." Arr. by Ford T. Dabney. Moffett Co., 1913. BLC

"Valse Maurice." Music by Sylvester Belmont. Jerome H. Remick & Co., 1913. BLC

"Watch Your Step." Lyrics and music by Irving Berlin. Irving Berlin, Inc., 1915. *Watch Your Step*. MD

LYRICS WITHOUT EXTANT MUSIC

Atteridge, Harold, et al. (Collection of Uncredited Song Lyrics from shows produced by the Mssrs. J. J. and Lee Shubert, ca. 1912–1919. Bound typescript, the Shubert Archive.)

The Kiss Waltz, Broadway to Paris, The Passing Show of 1912. (Manuscript Production Scores, Lyrics, and Scenarios, the Shubert Archive.)

Index